Staffing for
Foreign Affairs

WILLIAM I. BACCHUS

Staffing for Foreign Affairs:

Personnel Systems for the 1980's and 1990's

PRINCETON UNIVERSITY PRESS

Library of Congress Cataloging in Publication Data will be
found on the last printed page of this book

ISBN 0-691-07660-X

This book has been composed in Linotron Times Roman.
Clothbound editions of Princeton University Press books
are printed on acid-free paper, and binding materials are
chosen for strength and durability. Paperbacks, although satisfactory for personal collections, are not usually suitable for library rebinding.

Printed in the United States of America by Princeton University
Press, Princeton, New Jersey

FOR

Louise Heinlein Bacchus

AND

Mary Dreiling Bacchus

—for the support and encouragement
they have unfailingly provided

CONTENTS

The United States—like other modern nations—is faced with a growing crisis in finding and keeping the caliber of people needed to conduct its foreign relations. A few titles and headlines from recently published articles about the Foreign Service will help to convey the flavor of this problem:

"Foreign Service Stay-at-Homes," *Newsweek*, October 29, 1979

"Overseas and Under Fire for Uncle Sam: The Frustrations of a Foreign Service Family," *Washington Post*, December 28, 1979

"Behind Disarray in U.S. Foreign Policy: Just when the nation faces massive problems overseas, American diplomacy is being hamstrung by confusion and indecision at home," *U.S. News and World Report*, September 29, 1980

"The Rough Side of Embassy Rue," *Washington Post*, January 3, 1981

"Foreign Service Blues: Foggy Bottom Breakdown," *New Republic*, January 3 & 10, 1981

"The Siege of the Foreign Service: Diplomacy used to be fun—living in exotic foreign lands, tea parties on embassy lawns, champagne, and fanfare. Now there's terrorism, anti-Americanism, and the threats of kidnapping and death," *Boston Globe*, August 2, 1981

And from Canada, showing the problem is not ours alone:

"Foreign service: Trouble abroad? Foreign postings are losing some of their glamor due to security problems and a quiet rebellion by many wives," *Toronto Star*, August 2, 1981

The change in tone from some of the earlier critical writing about the Foreign Service in the "cookie-pusher" vein is notable, although in fact the new problems are superimposed on the older ones. Problems accrue; they do not replace one another.

The American case is presented here as one and probably the leading example of the troubles at hand, but all Western and Westernized Foreign Services are going through their own versions of the same difficulties. For example, as good a list of these issues as any was developed in 1981 by the Canadian Royal Commission on Conditions of Foreign Service,[1] as a guide to its inquiry:

I. ENVIRONMENT

    1. Security
        a) Physical (Terrorism)
        b) Political (Iron curtain)
        c) Psychological effects
    2. Monetary
        a) Pay and Allowance package
        b) Savings and Investment
        c) Housing Costs
        d) Incentive Payments
        e) Compensatory Payments
        f) Comprehension of philosophy governing compensation packages
    3. Socio-Cultural
        a) Working Spouses
        b) Cohabitation
        c) Living Styles
        d) Canadian Progress
        e) Culture Shock
        f) Isolation—Cultural and Geographical

---

[1] This commission, headed by the Honorable Pamela McDougall, was created in April 1980 and completed its report in the fall of 1981. The list was not published, but was used as an internal working document and as background material for a conference of Canadian government officials, academics, businessmen, and private citizens on the role of the Canadian Foreign Service, held in July 1981. For its report, see note 76, Chapter IV.

4. Family
   a) Separation
   b) Boredom, Isolation
   c) Divorce
   d) Constraints on Members
   e) Demands on Members
   f) Education
   g) Effects of Constant Change
5. Physical
   a) Accommodation
   b) Recreation
   c) Climate, Health
   d) Isolation
   e) Availability of Goods
6. Administrative
   a) Pre-posting Arrangements
   b) Cash Flow (Rapidity of Payments)
   c) Ottawa Rulings
   d) Post Rulings
   e) Post Support, Counselling
   f) Personnel Administration

II. FUNCTION

   1. Scope and Content of International Relations
   2. Methods of Conducting International Relations
   3. Management Systems
   4. Career
      a) Motivation
      b) Job Challenge
      c) Planning and Training
      d) Career Progression

This book is about how to contend with these issues: the problems and dilemmas inherent in doing so, and recent efforts at reform. The emphasis is primarily on the *system* needed to recruit, train, assign, evaluate, promote, reward, and separate the right kinds of people, and somewhat less on the individual members

of the Foreign Service and other career officials who spend their
working lives dealing with international matters. Thus it differs
from most studies of the Foreign Service, which tend to concentrate on the individual officer, as for example John Ensor Harr's
The Professional Diplomat,[2] which still remains a highly relevant
study of the individual Foreign Service officer, the backbone of
the system. The premise here, however, is that the personnel
systems within which these individuals and their counterparts in
Washington must serve have suffered from analytic neglect. In
the individualistic profession of modern diplomacy, this is understandable; but unless the system as a whole is sound, the people
in it will spend a substantial part of their time—as they do now—
contending with and, in many cases, fighting the personnel administrative apparatus, and correspondingly less time doing the
job they were hired to do. The systemic and individual perspectives are clearly related, but they are not the same. It is time to
give the former its due.

The fundamental problem is to devise an improved personnel
system which can simultaneously meet the needs of individual
members and their families; the needs of the foreign affairs agencies (for most purposes those using the Foreign Service personnel
system—the Department of State, the Agency for International
Development, the United States Information Agency, the Foreign
Agricultural Service, and the Foreign Commercial Service—but
sometimes including other agencies with a direct concern for foreign policy and foreign relations); the needs of the government
as a whole; and those of American society at large. It is an open
question whether all these demands can be reconciled. This study
explores the possible worst case—when something must be sacrificed, since all these needs cannot be satisfied at once.

The method of attacking this problem will be to attempt to link
the demands which are imposed on foreign affairs personnel (including those whose functions are performed in the United States
as well as overseas), the problems of system management, and
several alternative approaches, on the one hand, with compre-

[2] John Ensor Harr, *The Professional Diplomat* (Princeton, N.J.: Princeton University Press, 1969).

hensive planning for change, on the other. Unless all these elements can be linked into a coherent whole, the chances of improvement are slight, and the prospects for reform minimal. Thus the material which follows is approached from several overlapping perspectives. At the risk of repetition, it is hoped that this design clarifies the problems and sets forth what is needed to correct them.

Chapter I starts from a macro perspective, examining the environment in which foreign affairs officials will practice their trades during the 1980's and 1990's, together with the kinds of major policy issues which seem likely to dominate. The argument is that the old agenda of political and military issues is being increasingly supplemented with a newer one of global issues such as economics, science and technology, environment, and population. But foreign policy now involves more than just issues and developments abroad. What happens at home is also relevant, whether one looks at the domestic issues of the day or the process by which foreign policy is made. Chapter I concludes with a discussion of the implications that this new policy environment has for the kinds of individuals needed to develop and carry out national policy.

Obviously, if the current system were equipped to meet these new and continuing demands, there would be little reason for concern, and none for this book. This, unfortunately, is not the case. Chapter II attempts to illustrate the failures of current personnel systems to supply people with the needed types of competence, particularly with respect to the three most important areas of specialization—diplomatic work, policy development, and policy synthesis—introduced in Chapter I. The pattern of performance has been mixed, but on balance not nearly strong enough for the demands faced.

Chapter III explores the causes of these system weaknesses. It focuses on the ambiguity about what the various parts of the system and in particular the Foreign Service should be doing, on structural complexity and fragmentation, on weak and indifferent management, on the system's inflexibility and unresponsiveness, and on the debilitating effects of misplaced elitism, declining morale, and an adversarial approach to relations between management and employees.

The last part of the book moves toward prescription. Chapter IV deals with the dilemmas of personnel system design, starting from the premise that there is no perfect system and therefore that it is necessary to choose an approach which has the fewest liabilities and, ideally, the most advantages in a particular case. In the process, additional information about past and current problems is cited.

Chapter V takes up a more mundane but nevertheless critical subject: how to provide the managerial tools which are fundamental to a system that can be operated in accordance with a predetermined plan. Arguably, this is the fundamental weakness of foreign affairs personnel systems in the United States as of the early 1980's. Because solutions require that technical competence be applied over a considerable period of time, they have proved to be especially difficult in a system which appears to value highly neither deep expertise nor continuity.

Chapter VI is the story of two recent efforts, one a failure and the other at least initially successful, by the Department of State and the Congress to deal directly with a number of the problems previously identified. It discusses in some detail statutory changes, both proposed and adopted, which were designed to provide some of the needed improvements. One lesson these episodes should teach is that while it may be easy for observers to criticize existing practices and to propose reform, it is much more difficult to do something constructive and enduring. Reform is sometimes possible, but it owes a considerable debt to luck. Even serious and determined efforts to confront problems can be easily sidetracked. While there is some question about the transferability of the techniques used, Chapter VI concludes with reflections about the factors which made the Foreign Service Act of 1980 possible.

But as Chapter VII attempts to demonstrate, there is always more to be done. It compares the new Act's provisions with the weaknesses identified in earlier chapters in order to assess how well the existing needs were met. It also discusses some problems which the Foreign Service Act, being structural in nature, did not and could not address.

The problems of staffing for foreign affairs in the 1980's and 1990's, while obviously demonstrating a number of unique elements, seem nevertheless to illustrate the kinds of challenges facing the public service as a whole, both in the United States and elsewhere, during a particularly trying period of societal and environmental change. If so, then perhaps this book can be read more broadly, not only as one of many studies of the difficulties the United States faces in managing its foreign relations but also as a general prescription for change.

ACKNOWLEDGMENTS

In the British House of Commons, there is a tradition of demanding, sometimes rudely, that members speaking on a particular issue state their interests. As will become obvious, I should do the same. This book is in part analysis of problems and possible solutions, and in part recent history, due to my own involvement in personnel developments in the Department of State and the other agencies using the Foreign Service system in the period 1973-82. Writing was begun in the fall of 1977, at the end of the episode described as "Structure I" in Chapter VI, almost as a diatribe against the Department of State and its apparent unwillingness to confront mounting personnel problems. As the legislation which was to become the Foreign Service Act of 1980 (P.L. 90-465) began to be developed and shepherded through the Congress (see "Structure II" in the same chapter), my personal problem with respect to this book became one of avoiding an apologia for the reform efforts with which I was intimately involved. What appears here is an effort to step back and to analyze the current situation objectively, but it is never easy to disengage from issues about which one has felt strongly. The opinions expressed are those of the author, and do not represent official positions of the Department of State.

This book owes a major debt to many people. Without in any way sharing blame for errors, mistaken interpretations, or examples of bullheadedness which may appear, it is only fair to thank those who contributed in one way or another to its preparation.

To start with, three successive Directors General of the Foreign Service, by being willing to include a somewhat obstreperous outsider as part of their management teams, gave me an opportunity to learn from the inside about the problems, demands, and opportunities facing the Foreign Service and the foreign affairs agencies. Ambassadors Carol C. Laise, Harry G. Barnes, Jr., and

Joan M. Clark were not only bosses but patrons and friends. To this group must be added Ben H. Read, who as Under Secretary of State for Management from 1977 to 1981 was the driving force in the reform efforts which make up a major topic of this book, and a source of strong personal support.

Next, many others in government and in the academic world contributed, usually unknowingly, by teaching me about federal personnel systems, both Foreign Service and Civil Service, during the time I was on staff of the Murphy Commission, and later when I worked in the Bureau of Personnel at State. At the risk of failing to mention some, this list must include James W. Clark, Fisher Howe, and Peter Szanton of the Murphy Commission staff; many colleagues from 1975 to 1982 in State's Bureau of Personnel, including especially Phil Bourbon, Mike Durkee, Hal Fuller, Bob Gershenson, Dick Howland, Bob Hull, Tony Kern, Al Hyde, Clint Lauderdale, Bart Moon, Ron Palmer, Tom Ranson, John Rouse, Larry Russell, Dorothy Sampas, Ruth Schimel, Myra Howze Shiplett, Andy Steigman, Doug Watson, and Art Wortzel; some elsewhere in State, in particular Paul Coran, Bill Galloway, Gene Malmborg, Dick Martin, Dwight Mason, John Sprott, and Rick Weiss; and my closest associates through the years on the Bureau of Personnel's Policy and Coordination Staff, Phyllis Bucsko, Charles Hill, Kang S. Huang, Stephanie Smith Kinney, Jacques Paul Klein, Don Kursch, Larry Lesser, Shaw Smith, and Torrey Whitman. Outside State, I benefited especially from exposure to the ideas of Jean Barber, Gordon Klang, Sally Greenberg, and Jerry Moeller of OPM; Jim Barie of OMB; Al Cohen and Angie Garcia of USIA; Edna Boorady and Tom Cox of AID; Ross Cook, Lew Davis, and Dick Smith of the Foreign Agricultural Service; and Ron Whitworth of the Department of Commerce. Congressional Staff Members Jerry Christianson, Andy Feinstein, David Keaney, Janean Mann, Bill Moermann, Pierce Myers, Ginny Schlundt, and Paul Smith were partners together with Jim Michel, State's Deputy Legal Adviser, in a close, generally cooperative, occasionally confrontational, but always rewarding experience of managing passage of the Foreign Service Act of 1980.

Others had a more direct role in producing the book. Jessica Dietchman, Catherine Fish, Hazel Pinkerton, and Ann Prosser, all of the Bureau of Personnel, saw the typing and editing of the manuscript through successive drafts in addition to carrying out their normal responsibilities with a high degree of professionalism, and did so with unfailing good cheer and support. Sandy Thatcher of Princeton University Press provided the right degree of encouragement, criticism, and sound advice. I owe a special debt to those individuals who read all or part of the manuscript in its earlier forms: Harry Barnes, Paul Boeker, James W. Fesler, Jim Michel, Jerry Moeller, Frederick C. Mosher, Michael K. O'Leary, Ron Palmer, Ben Read, Jay Shafritz, and Peter Szanton. Their comments and corrections have helped substantially in bringing whatever coherence exists; they cannot be faulted for suggestions not accepted.

Most recently, the editors of the *Foreign Service Journal* helped refine the text of Chapter IV while excerpting it for my article, "Staffing for State," which appeared in the December 1982 issue. I have incorporated many of their suggestions in the book, and I wish to thank them for their help.

Finally, my wife Mary, while maintaining a healthy skepticism about such enterprises, nevertheless was understanding of the demands imposed by my work on this book, and a helpmate in countless ways.

W.I.B.
Arlington, Virginia
December 1982

Staffing for
Foreign Affairs

Like most social institutions, departments of the federal government, and the personnel systems which determine who serves them in what ways, are in large measure captives of their past history and their current practices. Unless both a historical context and a current baseline are established, it can be difficult to assess what problems exist, what changes may be called for, or how to set about attempting to make them. Thus, as a way of introducing the issues for those who may be unfamiliar with how the Department of State and the Foreign Service are run, this study begins with a short history of the Foreign Service of the United States. As for current practices, a brief sketch of some typical Foreign Service officer careers, contrasted with those of members of the Civil Service at comparable levels of ranks and responsibility, may also be of some help.

Historically, the American Foreign Service has always been separate from the mainstream Civil Service.[1] When the beginnings of a career Civil Service emerged with the Pendleton Act of 1883, diplomatic and consular personnel were excluded. They continued for some years to be appointed under the spoils system, with staff hired directly by each consular or diplomatic officer. Several executive orders beginning in 1895 required that appointments be made according to merit, and the Consular Reorganization Act of 1906, which placed all such officers on salary rather than paying them by fee, reinforced this trend.

A career foreign service became possible with the Act of February 5, 1915, which provided for the merit appointment of diplomatic and consular officers (in separate services) by class rather

---

[1] For a detailed history of the Foreign Service up to 1960, see William Barnes and John Heath Morgen, *The Foreign Service of the United States: Origin, Development, Functions* (Washington, D.C.: Department of State, Historical Office, Bureau of Public Affairs, 1961). For more recent history, see Chapters I-IV and materials cited therein.

than position, authorized their transfer or rotation from one post to another (although not to assignments in the United States), and allowed for their promotion on a merit basis from one class to another. All this was more flexible than and quite different from the career Civil Service, where appointment was tied to competition for specific positions and transfer was rare.

Nevertheless, pressures on the new system mounted quickly after World War I and showed that more was necessary, leading to a number of proposals for statutory reform. These culminated in the passage on May 24, 1924, of the Rogers Act, the foundation of the modern American Foreign Service. Its central feature was its consolidation of the formerly separate Diplomatic and Consular Services into a unified Foreign Service. In addition, it provided a comprehensive structure of statutory personnel and management authority entirely divorced from those applying to other civilians employed by the federal government. It also provided a separate retirement system, with such distinctive features as additional credit toward retirement for service at unhealthful posts. Moreover, it authorized home leave in the United States, at government expense. More limited changes followed, up to World War II, including the incorporation of the Foreign Services of the Departments of Commerce and Agriculture into the regular Foreign Service in 1939.

Postwar conditions once again imposed a new role on the United States, and with it came a need for further change in the Foreign Service. The result was the Foreign Service Act of 1946, modeled largely on the Navy Officer personnel system. Developed primarily by a group of Foreign Service officers in the State Department, it remained the basic legislation governing the Foreign Service until 1980.[2] The Act emphasized the separateness of the Foreign Service from the Civil Service as a whole, the mobility of its personnel, rank-in-person as opposed to rank-in-job, rotation from post to post, discipline for the good of the Service, and the development of careers as opposed to the hiring of experts with

[2] For an excellent case study of the passage of the Foreign Service Act of 1946, see Harold Stein, "The Foreign Service Act of 1946," in Stein, ed., *Public Administration and Policy Development: A Case Book*, Inter-University Case Program (New York: Harcourt, Brace & World, 1952), pp. 661-737.

special competence. The Foreign Service also had its own unique provisions for the termination of employment, its own travel regulations, retirement system, medical program, and other distinctive features. All were premised on the Foreign Service career being quite different from that in the Civil Service.

From the late 1940's until the late 1970's, numerous minor changes were made in the Foreign Service Act, but the basic structure remained intact. The Foreign Agricultural Service once again became a separate entity in 1954 (only to be reincorporated in the Foreign Service in 1980); the strict division between the State Department's Civil Service cadre in its Washington headquarters and the Foreign Service was removed by the Wriston program of the mid-1950's (which incorporated many of the former into the Foreign Service and introduced routine rotation between posts abroad and Washington); and ultimately, in 1968, a parallel Foreign Service system for the United States Information Agency (USIA) was created by P.L. 90-494, which provided a specialist career officer category that was also employed by State.[3]

This partial integration of the Foreign and Civil Service components was the origin of a major problem. Because the Civil Service system was felt to be excessively cumbersome, and because the statutes did not prohibit it, State and USIA began, in the early 1970's, to move toward a "single system" at the officer level, with all employees except support staff being included in the Foreign Service rather than divided into Foreign and Civil Service cadres according to whether or not they would be spending a substantial portion of their careers at posts abroad. The idea of a single service had considerable history, being first endorsed by the First Hoover Commission and later by the Rowe Committee in 1950, the Wriston Committee in 1954, and the Herter Committee in 1962. Alas, events were to prove that this was a misguided approach. The earlier thinking, that Foreign and Civil Service constituted separate, but closely related occupations, proved to be right. Early practice had emphasized too much distance

[3] The short survey of the history of the Foreign Service in the preceding paragraphs owes a heavy debt to an unpublished summary prepared in the early 1970's by James H. Michel, then an Attorney-Adviser, later Deputy Legal Adviser, and a principal architect of the Foreign Service Act of 1980.

between the two; that of the 1950's, 60's, and 70's glossed over too much.

Thus, by the mid to late 1970's, when the events covered in this book began, the Foreign Service was in serious trouble, even if one discounted all the changes in its mission and in the world environment. These problems led to the drive for reform which began in 1975, was short-circuited by 1977, revived in 1978, and successful (in legislative terms, at least) with passage of the Foreign Service Act of 1980. The basic concept, that there are important differences between the Foreign Service abroad and those concerned with foreign affairs in Washington, remains, accompanied by a recognition of the need for both cadres to develop a symbiotic relationship.

The differences between the two services can perhaps be clarified by a comparison of likely careers within each category. Although "high-flyers" in the Civil Service may move from job to job almost as frequently as rotational Foreign Service officers, what is striking is how closely they stay in the same occupation, when compared with FSO's. Consider first some successful FSO careers, drawn from actual examples.[4]

A very successful Political Officer:

Age	Rank	Job
23		College A.B.
24	FSO-7	Bombay—Consular Officer
27		Prague—Political Officer
28	FSO-6	
29		Munich—Russian area and language training
30	FSO-5	Moscow—Publications Procurement Officer
32	FSO-4	
33		Washington—Department—International Relations Officer (Bureau of European Affairs)

---

[4] The examples listed follow actual cases closely but are somewhat modified to provide a degree of anonymity. They are drawn from Bureau of Personnel records and the author's personal knowledge. Rank is by the old scale.

Age	Rank	Job
35	FSO-3	
36		Training—National War College
37		Kathmandu—Deputy Chief of Mission
40	FSO-2	
41		Washington—Department—Romanian language training, university MA
42		Prague—Deputy Chief of Mission
44	FSO-1	
45		Washington—Department—Supervisory Personnel Officer
46		Deputy Executive Secretary
48		Ambassador to Class III Post
51		Washington—Department—Assistant Secretary
52	FSO Career Minister	
55		Ambassador to Class I Post

A successful Administrative Officer:

Age	Rank	Job
25		College A.B.
25-27		Private employment
27-30		Washington—Department of Health, Education and Welfare—Personnel Specialist
30	FSO-7	Mexico City—FSO Generalist Officer
32	FSO-6	Rio de Janeiro—Personnel Officer
34	FSO-5	Brussels—Assistant General Services Officer
35		Brussels—General Services Officer
36	FSO-4	
38		U.S.—University training

Age	Rank	Job
39	FSO-3	Washington—Department—Administrative Officer
40		Bonn—Administrative Officer
43	FSO-2	Madrid—Administrative Counselor
47		Washington—Department—Office Director, Bureau of Personnel
48	FSO-1	Deputy Assistant Secretary for Personnel

And a more junior Economic Officer, with Administrative backup skills:

Age	Rank	Job
21		College A.B.
23		University M.A.
23-25		Nigeria—Peace Corps Volunteer
26	FSO-7	Washington—Department—Temporary duty
27	FSO-6	New Delhi—FSO General
28		New Delhi—Consular Officer
29		Washington—Department—Temporary duty
29		Ouagadougou—Economic—Commercial Officer
30	FSO-5	
31		Washington—Department—FSI training
32		Economic Officer
34	FSO-4	Brussels—Economic—Commercial Officer
37		Kigali—Deputy Chief of Mission
39	FSO-3	Washington—Department—Management Analyst, Bureau of Personnel
41		Deputy Executive Director, Geographic Bureau

Notice that each of these careers, even that of the Administrative Officer, shows considerable diversity of occupation and a promotion pattern which is independent of assignment or selection for a new position. Examples of Civil Service employees, every bit as involved in the conduct of the nation's foreign affairs, show much less diversity, whether or not there is rotation from job to job.

First, a highly successful Policy Officer:

Age	Rank	Job
20-24		College A.B., University M.A.
26	GS-9	Washington—Department—International Economist
27	GS-11	
29	GS-12	
31	GS-13	
33	GS-14	
35	GS-15	Development Loan Fund, General Financial Officer
38	GS-15	Department—Special Assistant to Under Secretary of State for Economic Affairs
38	GS-16	Special Assistant to Under (i.e., Deputy) Secretary of State
39	GS-17	
40	GS-18	
43	GS-18 (equiv.)	Deputy Assistant Secretary of State for European Affairs
49	GS-18 (equiv.)	Acting Assistant Secretary of State for European Affairs
50	GS-18	Deputy Assistant Secretary of State for European Affairs
51	GS-18	Special Assistant to Secretary of State and Executive Secretary of the Department
54	GS-18	Director, Foreign Service Institute
56	Senior Executive Service (Charter member)	

If anything, this pattern shows more variety, after advancement to senior policy levels, than normal. Now consider an equally successful officer, a lawyer in the Department of State whose career follows a more typical pattern, staying entirely within one bureau:

Age	Rank	Job
22		College A.B.
25		Law school, LL.B.
25	GS-9	Washington—Department—Attorney
26	GS-11	
28	GS-13	Attorney-Adviser
30	GS-14	
31	GS-15	
35	GS-15	Assistant Legal Adviser for Politico-Military Affairs
35	GS-16	Deputy Legal Adviser
39	GS-17	
40	Senior Executive Service (Charter member)	
41	SES	Acting Legal Adviser

There is a clear difference between those who serve abroad and the Washington headquarters contingent, and personnel systems should reflect such differences in the conditions of employment and service. This book deals with how such differences should be managed. By design, relatively more emphasis is given to the Foreign Service component, because it is less known generally and most discussion of it has taken a quite different and narrower perspective than the one employed here. But despite the emphasis given in this book, both systems are fundamentally important for conducting the nation's foreign relations.

CHAPTER ONE

Defining Personnel Needs: The Future Foreign Affairs Environment

Personnel systems—the means of providing people to staff organizations[1]—should not be independent of purpose. They cannot exist in a vacuum, attuned only to the desires of their own members or administrators. They must also serve the larger organization; they must provide people who have the skills, experience, and motivation it needs to carry out its mission. In the government's internationally oriented agencies, this minimum condition has too seldom, given the stakes, been met.

It is basic that managers of the government's foreign affairs personnel systems should understand the total policy environment with which they and the people they provide must contend. But the past shows how difficult this has been, and it seems certain to become more so. There has been a profound evolution in the nature of international relations and of American society itself, with major implications for these personnel systems. The way they must be managed, the kinds of people they must provide, how those people must be treated, and how the several governmental personnel systems must relate to each other—all this has changed as well.

---

[1] A personnel system is defined here as the complex collection of formal and informal procedures and practices—springing from statute, Executive order, regulation, operating procedures, norms, and expectations—by which any organization recruits, assigns, evaluates, rewards, promotes, and separates the people who staff it. In a certain sense, as will be attested to by anyone who has served in an organization with a well-established personnel system, it is larger than the sum of its parts, and seems at times to be a living entity.

A MOST LIKELY FUTURE

One view of the future, as sensible as any, has been summarized in a staff report of the Commission on the Organization of the Government for the Conduct of Foreign Policy (the Murphy Commission), which reflected the substantial if not complete consensus of a number of academics and government experts:[2]

1. *The most pervasive factor in shaping international affairs in the coming decades will be the growing interdependence* of societies and nations and their reactions to that interdependence. Separate states, even the largest, will not be able to meet their basic needs for well-being independently.

2. It follows that *the capacity to shape significant events will depend on collaboration* among states. . . .

3. *The requisite cooperation must inevitably include a wide range of other nations.* . . .

4. *The required collaboration will have to take many forms.* . . .

5. *Such intimate cooperation will be inherently difficult,* especially for the democratic states. . . .

6. *Compounding the difficulty will be the weakness or instability of governments* or confusion about their purposes over the decades ahead. Social and political tensions will profoundly modify the institutions and outlook of the major states. . . .

7. In this perspective, *the tasks of U.S. foreign policy in the coming decades will be two-fold: to help build the processes and institutions for world collaboration* and *order,*

[2] Peter L. Szanton, "The Future World Environment: Near-Term Problems for U.S. Foreign Policy," in "Foreign Policy for the Future," Appendix A to the *Report of the Commission on the Organization of the Government for the Conduct of Foreign Policy*, Appendix Volume I (Washington, D.C.: U.S. Government Printing Office, 1976), pp. 8-10. Emphasis in original. This section is in Szanton's words a "lightly edited version" of a paper prepared for the conference by Robert R. Bowie, "The Tasks Ahead for U.S. Foreign Policy," which appears in the same volume on pages 20-31. To the author, at least, this summary retained its validity as of 1983. The Commission is henceforth cited as the Murphy Commission, after its Chairman, Ambassador Robert D. Murphy. The main commission report was issued as *Report of the Commission on the Organization of the Government for the Conduct of Foreign Policy* (Washington, D.C.: GPO, 1975).

and *to foster the evolution of the major states in ways conducive to a cooperative order.* . . .

8. In order *to undertake those tasks successfully, U.S. policymaking will have to embody two features* not easy to combine: (a) *clear direction and continuity over time*; and (b) *extensive participation.*

9. *The leadership must come from the President but these tasks cannot be performed as solos.* . . . The critical problem is how to extend his reach by utilizing and organizing the efforts of others. To do so will require the reversal of the increasing tendency over the last decade to concentrate the making and executing of policy into a few hands.

10. *Foreign Policy will have to be based on a coherent strategy or framework widely understood and supported.* . . .

These changes must affect the whole foreign policy-making apparatus of the American government and society. For current purposes, however, the focus of this chapter is upon the demands they will make on career foreign affairs officials and the personnel systems which supply them. These officials do not formally "make" foreign policy, but they are critical in the process, as custodians of the government's expertise and as its institutional memory.[3] They provide continuity of communication with other governments, international organizations, domestic constituencies, and the Congress. How well they meet such demands will have a major effect on the ability of political leaders to conduct an effective foreign policy.

New Issues and Old

To say that we are now entering an era of "complex interdependence"[4] is by now a cliché, as is the growing realization

---

[3] See Hugh Heclo, *A Government of Strangers: Executive Branch Politics in Washington* (Washington, D.C.: Brookings Institution, 1977), pp. 103-5, for the extremely limited tenure of political executives, typically two years or less in recent years, which of course means that if there is *any* such memory, it must come from the careerists.

[4] Robert O. Keohane and Joseph S. Nye, *Power and Interdependence: World Politics in Transition* (Boston: Little, Brown, 1977), p. 23. The defining char-

that the future will differ significantly from that assumed in power-oriented models of the international system. Anyone who has ever waited in a line for gasoline or become concerned with Three Mile Island, the MX missile, the effect of synthetic fuel production on the ecology of the American West, or of grain embargoes on the Soviet Union, is likely to accept this fact. When complex interdependence prevails, there are multiple channels of communication connecting societies, many of which are nongovernmental. There are, similarly, numerous international issue-agendas, many of which in earlier times would have been considered solely as matters of domestic policy. As a consequence, they are taken up by many parts of government, not just foreign offices.

The term "global issues" has also been used to categorize such problems. By whatever name they are known, they are particularly difficult for foreign affairs bureaucracies, which are attuned to more traditional political and military strategic issues, to deal with. These new issues typically include:

—situations which could have catastrophic effects if left unattended, but with uncertain probabilities and long time-horizons which defuse a high sense of urgency;

—future uncertainties which are highly dependent upon changes and developments in science and technology;

—issues with major domestic as well as foreign policy implications, meaning that they cross jurisdictional lines and raise difficult problems *within* governments as well as without; and

—nontraditional modes of confrontation and resolution, featuring diplomacy carried out multilaterally rather than in the more comfortable one-state-to-another fashion to which foreign offices are best suited, as well as a greater linkage of specific issues with more general conditions, such as the global inequity between wealthy, industrialized countries and poorer countries.[5]

---

acteristics are paraphrased from pages 24-25. For another analysis of changes in global society, see Zbigniew Brzezinski, *Between Two Ages: America's Role in The Technetronic Era* (New York: Viking, 1970), in particular Part I, "The Global Impact of the Technetronic Revolution."

[5] This listing follows closely that provided by Keohane and Nye in "Organizing for Global Environmental and Resource Interdependence," in "The Management

Examples of the kinds of issues which are increasingly global include world population growth, nuclear power, satellite communications, ocean pollution, law of the sea, global food management, and intentional and unintentional atmospheric modification. Others include environmental degradation, the transfer of technology, the utilization and distribution of mineral resources, and, cutting across many of these, global energy production and allocation. Such issues require a significant reordering of the thought processes of governments and societies. They can no longer be treated as exceptions.

Obviously, these new or newly important issues have not displaced the fundamental concerns of security and power. Rather, they are an additional complexity in international relations. Thus, proposals that the old organizational and personnel systems now used to carry out foreign policy should be completely replaced are misguided.[6]

A closely related change is the larger part which economic considerations must play in foreign policy. This is underscored by the transformation of the U.S. role in the international marketplace from a position of almost unparalleled dominance in the years immediately after the Second World War to circumstances in which we are arguably more affected by others than affecting them. Yet even as our role has diminished, the sheer volume of foreign trade has increased. After relatively static growth from 1950 to 1960, the percentage of the GNP devoted to exports more than doubled by 1978 (from 5.7% to 12.9%), and imports grew by even more (from 4.6% of the GNP to 12.1%).[7] And if one

---

of Global Issues," Appendix B to the Report of the Murphy Commission, Appendix Volume I, p. 48. See also George W. Ball, *Diplomacy for a Crowded World* (Boston: Atlantic, Little, Brown, 1976), pp. 231-98, for a survey of a number of such issues.

[6] See Adam Yarmolinsky, "Organizing for Interdependence: The Role of Government," in Interdependence Series No. 5, Aspen Institute for Humanistic Studies, Program in International Affairs (Princeton, N.J.: Aspen Institute, 1976); and the National Policy Panel, United Nations Association of the United States of America, *Foreign Policy Decision Making: The New Dimensions* (New York: United Nations Association of the United States of America, 1973), for examples of arguments which, in the author's opinion, go too far in this direction. The latter report is cited henceforth as UNA/USA.

[7] Statistics derived from *Statistical Abstract of the United States*, 102nd edition,

looks at the quantum leap in import figures because of the dramatic increases in petroleum prices after 1973, our greater degree of involvement in the world economy becomes even more obvious. But along with this greater involvement has come a lesser degree of control. Multinational corporations are now a major factor in international economic interactions, posing complicated new problems of monitoring and control beyond the ability of any single government to solve.[8] Inflation at home has been exacerbated by foreign-determined prices for petroleum and other critical raw materials. And the U.S. market has increasingly become a prize for aggressive producers elsewhere, leading to demands for protection against dumping and for import controls. Perhaps most important are major monetary changes, such as the generally weaker position (over the longer term) of the dollar against other currencies and the breakdown of the international monetary regime which lasted for twenty-five years after World War II.[9]

It is sometimes argued that this kind of economic interdependence is hardly new, and that it is therefore unnecessary to be particularly concerned about the way the government is organized and staffed to deal with such issues. For example, it was written in 1922 that

> our people have been taught by events to realize that with the increased intercommunication and interdependence of civilized states all our production is a part of the world's production, and all our trade is a part of the world's trade, and a large part of the influences which make for prosperity or disaster within our own country consist of forces and movements which may

---

U.S. Department of Commerce, Bureau of the Census (Washington, D.C.: GPO, 1981), Table 702, p. 422.

[8] See Joseph S. Nye, Jr., "Multinational Corporations in World Politics," *Foreign Affairs* 53 (October 1974), passim.

[9] See Keohane and Nye, *Power and Interdependence*, for analysis of the monetary issue. They define an international regime as "procedures, rules, or institutions," or "governing arrangements" by which governments control interstate relations (p. 5). The strength of the dollar against major world currencies in the 1981-82 period, due in large measure to high U.S. interest rates, was hardly a sign of continuing economic strength.

arise anywhere in the world beyond our direct and immediate control.[10]

Yet the proliferation of governmental and nongovernmental actors, the emergence of north-south issues, new technologies, declining U.S. productivity, and the destruction of predictable economic relationships all suggest that even such changes of degree, if large enough and if combined with fundamental changes in the international system, make old models and approaches obsolete. Perhaps these changes can be summarized in a single assertion: "During just that period in which the U.S. government, like all other central governments, assumed full responsibility for the nation's economic stability and growth, its power to fulfill that responsibility through autonomous action slipped away."[11]

MULTILATERAL AND FUNCTIONAL DIPLOMACY

One irony of twentieth-century international relations is that general-purpose international organizations, originally established largely for political and security reasons, have proved unsuited to manage or prevent the use of military force; but complex issues of scientific, technical, and economic interdependence cannot be resolved without them. Gaining bilateral agreement among all the pairs of nations involved would be impossible.

Regional and special-purpose organizations have proliferated, supplementing general organizations like the United Nations. Their record is mixed, but one lesson already learned is that all states must learn how to operate through them to pursue their national interests. It is hard to disagree with a private study conducted by a Foreign Service officer with intimate experience in multilateral diplomacy:

> If the United States persists in believing that it can protect its interests through traditional bilateral diplomacy alone or through special arrangements with small groups of like-minded coun-

[10] Elihu Root, "A Requisite for the Success of Popular Diplomacy," *Foreign Affairs* 1 (September 1922), 6.

[11] Graham Allison and Peter Szanton, *Remaking Foreign Policy: The Organizational Connection* (New York: Basic Books, 1976), p. 46.

tries, we will seriously jeopardize our longterm interests. The United States must overcome a natural distaste for negotiating with a large number of individually weak and sometimes irresponsible countries.[12]

The trend is emphasized by the recent increase in U.S. participation in international organizations and conferences. As of September 1979, it was a member of sixty-two permanent international organizations and a contributor to fifty-two special programs, few of which even existed until after World War II.[13] Official U.S. participation in international meetings has similarly expanded, from 141 in 1946 to 394 in 1960, 588 in 1968, 817 in 1975, and 921 in 1980. In fifteen years, the total number of delegates participating in such meetings—representing no less than forty-six agencies of the U.S. government—expanded from 2,378 in 1964 to 3,656 in 1974, and to 4,525 in 1980.[14]

A caveat is in order. Some assert that the growth of multilateral relationships will make bilateral ones obsolete. But nation-states remain *the* autonomous institutional actors in the world of politics; international organizations do not qualify even as embryonic world governments. Bilateral relationships have been expanding at the same time as multilateral ones. The number of states with which the U.S. has formal diplomatic relationships has more than doubled in recent years to 149 countries as of May 1982,[15] and the content of such relationships is typically much broader and more

[12] Otho E. Eskin, "Notes on the Management of Multilateral Diplomacy" (unpublished ms., Washington, D.C.: Department of State, 1977), p. 1. Eskin was staff director of the National Security Council Interagency Task Force on the Law of the Sea, and his experience in that capacity is the basis for the case he analyzes.

[13] Statistics summarized from "United States Contributions to International Organizations," Report to the Congress for Fiscal Year 1979, 28th Annual Report (Washington, D.C.: Department of State Publication 9140, International Organization and Conference Series 149, 1980).

[14] Keohane and Nye, *Power and Interdependence*, Table 8.1, p. 241, augmented by 1978 and 1980 figures supplied by Bureau of International Organization Affairs, Department of State.

[15] *Key Officers of Foreign Service Posts*, Department of State Publication 7877 (Washington, D.C.: Foreign Affairs Document and Record Center, Department of State, revised May 1982), p. viii.

varied than in earlier periods. Where the Department of State was virtually the only U.S. agency represented in most overseas missions forty years ago, at last count representatives of some twenty-five agencies now serve in missions abroad.[16]

In short, bilateral and multilateral relationships must be seen as mutually reinforcing. It will be increasingly necessary, with the relative decline in U.S. power (see below), to seek support for American positions on multilateral issues through the bilateral persuasion of other nations. And, since many of the issues in question will be highly technical (law of the sea, food production, resources), greater specialized competence will be required among those carrying out bilateral relationships than typically now exists.

Critiques of the weakness of State's "functional" bureaus (e.g., Economic and Business Affairs, Politico-Military Affairs, Oceans, International Environmental and Scientific Affairs), asserting that the Department is not equipped for these new kinds of responsibilities, are common.[17] These assessments are strongly challenged by some of the Department's most respected senior officers, but they too would agree about the importance of such competence.[18]

George Kennan may have made the definitive statement about the relationship between traditional diplomacy and the new functional needs:

[16] U.S. Congress, Senate Committee on Governmental Affairs, "Organization of Federal Executive Departments and Agencies," chart (Washington, D.C.: GPO, 1982). Data as of January 1, 1982.

[17] See Allison and Szanton, *Remaking Foreign Policy*, pp. 135-37, and many of the studies carried out for the Murphy Commission, in particular that of Keohane and Nye previously cited; Edward K. Hamilton et al., "Cases on a Decade of U.S. Foreign Economic Policy: 1965-1974," Appendix H, Appendix Volume III; and Graham T. Allison et al., "Findings, Recommendations and Case Studies on the Adequacy of Current Organization: Defense and Arms Control," Appendix K, Appendix Volume IV.

[18] For example, in late 1980, after reading an earlier version of this work, Paul Boeker, former Ambassador to Bolivia, then Director of the Foreign Service Institute and one of the Department's acknowledged economic stars, took strong exception with the critiques cited in the previous note, stating, "I think you will find that Treasury, Agriculture, Commerce, etc. consider State/EB a strong organization. Here there has been a major change since Murphy Commission days."

. . . no one questions the need for expert assistance in the conduct of foreign relations in this age. Many of the problems that arise have highly complex technical or scientific implications of which the policy-maker needs unquestionably to be informed. But the generalist—the person of wide cultural horizons and knowledge of the world at large and experience with its bitter political problems—is needed, too. And of the two, the generalist occupies the more central and essential position; for without his guidance and coordination of their efforts the experts, however admirable, would produce only chaos.[19]

While one may question the relative weights Kennan assigns, it is almost indisputable that the "comparative advantage" of the Foreign Service (although it has many additional responsibilities) lies in its generalist talents and in its knowledge of foreign societies and cultures. How best to link this vital resource to knowledge of specific issues and to the domestic policy process is a major concern of this book.

THE DIMINISHING U.S. POWER ADVANTAGE

Accompanying the emergence of new issues of interdependence is a decline in the usefulness of military force:

The security of the United States and its allies is still subject to threats, but many are not susceptible to standard military response. For the United States, as for our major allies, the most likely external threats of the next decades concern the denial of important resources (or their supply only at prohibitive prices), or severe environmental change, or attack by terrorists. None are likely to be relieved by conventional military strength. Thus a paradox emerges: much of our military strength is essential without being usable.[20]

[19] George F. Kennan, "Reflections: Foreign Policy and the Professional Diplomat," *Wilson Quarterly* 1 (Winter 1977), 134-35.

[20] Allison and Szanton, *Remaking Foreign Policy*, p. 55. On the changing nature of public opinion and decline of support for an interventionist role for the U.S. abroad, see Bruce M. Russett, "The Americans' Retreat from World Power," *Political Science Quarterly* 90 (Spring 1975), 1-21. One can of course question,

For the United States, which had hegemonic military power in the first years after World War II, in turn breeding an illusion of omnipotence and perhaps of omniscience, the change in relative world power is profound (even if in absolute terms its military strength is considerably larger). There are now many more players, who are playing with new kinds of chips and participating in a "game" in which autonomous action is not likely to produce the desired results. The U.S. controls a much smaller proportion of the total usable power which can be employed in international politics, but it is not alone in this situation. The great powers share a common problem: "The 'world leaders' have much more difficulty working their wills in many areas or in mobilizing support of their 'allies.' Smaller nations reach for new goals and maintain power through combinations of insurgent force, armed threat, terrorism, economic pressure, and shifting associations in the United Nations."[21]

This inevitably means that the United States has a considerably reduced margin for error. In the past, American mistakes could often be overcome by brute strength, by applying overwhelming resources to carry out corrective actions. This is no longer true. Knowledge, finesse, persuasion, and coalition-building play a much greater role; unilateralism is less and less a viable basis for national policy.[22] The future foreign policy process—and the qualities needed by personnel who are a part of it—must reflect these new circumstances.

Three aspects of this process warrant special comment. First, given a world environment in which problems are likely to be more difficult, harder to understand, and (to anticipate the next section) of concern to a much larger number of actors and interests, policy consistency is likely to be elusive. This will place a pre-

from the perspective of the early 1980's, how permanent this attitudinal change may be. Britain's Falklands War with Argentina and the U.S. role in the evacuation of the PLO from Lebanon give pause.

[21] James W. Clark, "Foreign Affairs Personnel Management," in "Personnel for Foreign Affairs," Appendix P to the Murphy Commission Report, Appendix Volume VI, p. 183.

[22] Ball, *Diplomacy*, pp. 3-17, provides a critique of the unilateralist approach to foreign and national security policy.

mium on what might be called policy synthesis and monitoring, that is, the capability of the government to evaluate the likely effects of past or proposed policy actions, combined with the ability to use this knowledge to produce a coherent future policy. Conscious integration of these complex factors will be required.

At least as important will be the need to recruit and to train people with the knowledge and understanding to do this work. It has been said of the current era that "events have outrun understanding."[23] It will be extremely difficult to find such knowledgeable people. One irony of recent personnel management for foreign affairs is the emphasis given to producing managers at just that time when management, in the traditional sense of marshaling people and resources to carry out programs, has become relatively less important as the size of overseas programs diminishes.[24] Less attention has been given to the more intractable problem of producing "policy managers" who are knowledgeable enough about the intricacies of the total issue-agenda, broad-gauged enough to weave the many strands together, and able to think creatively and boldly about how to preserve U.S. interests. This may be the single most critical talent which the government will require. Foreign affairs agencies may be devoting too much effort to preparing for a world which has largely disappeared.

A second area where improvement is needed is in the gathering of information and the development of coherent explanations. Research undertaken for the Murphy Commission revealed many areas where "policymakers have failed to understand why foreign governments were taking certain actions, or to anticipate the impact of a U.S. action, and thus have designed actions aimed at one objective which in fact triggered contrary actions by foreign

[23] David E. Bell and Adam Yarmolinsky, "Comment," UNA/USA Report, p. 102.

[24] See, for example, State's innovative professional development program proposed in 1980, "Career Development Training for Foreign Service and Department of State Personnel," prepared by the Foreign Service Institute under the leadership of its Director, Ambassador Paul Boeker, which is only the latest of many reports emphasizing management rather than substantive expertise. By late 1982, there was justified skepticism that Boeker's program could survive his departure, given budgetary limitations and some real reservations on the part of State's new leadership that his premises were right.

governments.''[25] Subsequent events such as the revolution in Iran show that the problem has not disappeared. The Commission argued that the major function of the Department of State in particular—of both embassy personnel abroad and the Washington establishment—will be foreign assessment, or "analysis of probable host country responses to emerging issues of concern to the U.S.," including not only factual information but also "predictions and proposals on specific issues." The Department's goal should be to explain why foreign governments act as they do, to predict the most likely impact upon individual countries of proposed U.S. actions, and to present such information in a way that suggests "how U.S. initiatives can be designed or modified to have their desired effect."[26]

At times, State will find itself, by virtue of its superior knowledge of the relationships between domestic policy and events abroad, playing the uncomfortable role of explaining the interests of other nations in possible U.S. actions. This will not be popular, but it will be essential. *Some* part of the government must provide the rest of it with "detailed understanding and judgment of the dynamics of foreign societies and governments and multilateral

[25] Quoted from Murphy Commission Report, p. 40. In addition to the studies previously cited, other major components of the Murphy Commission research program included National Academy of Public Administration (Roy W. Crowley, Executive Director), "Making Organizational Change Effective: Case Studies of Attempted Reforms in Foreign Affairs," in Appendix O, "Making Organizational Change Effective: Case Studies," Appendix Volume VI; Abraham F. Lowenthal et al., "The Making of U.S. Policies Toward Latin America: The Conduct of 'Routine' Relations," in Appendix I, "The Conduct of Routine Relations," Appendix Volume III; Lloyd I. Rudolph, Susanne Hoeber Rudolph et al., "The Coordination of Complexity in South Asia," in Appendix V, "Coordination in Complex Settings," Appendix Volume VII; Atlantic Institute for International Affairs (John W. Tuthill, Executive Director), "Problems in the Organization of United States Foreign Policy: Comparative Foreign Practices," in Appendix R, "Comparative Foreign Practices," Appendix Volume VI; and Alexander L. George et al., "Towards a More Soundly Based Foreign Policy: Making Better Use of Information," in Appendix D, "The Use of Information," Appendix Volume II. A complete listing may be found in the Murphy Commission Report, pp. 275-78. An expanded and revised version of the George study was later published as Alexander L. George, *Presidential Decision-Making in Foreign Policy* (Boulder, Colo.: Westview Press, 1980).

[26] Murphy Report, p. 118.

groupings and agencies,''[27] and their relationship to events at home.

Intimately related both to policy synthesis and monitoring and to foreign assessment is a third element of the policy process which has major implications for personnel systems of the future: policy planning. There is great skepticism in government about the utility of advanced planning in foreign affairs. Planning is suspect for both intellectual and practical reasons. Intellectually, it is virtually impossible to account for all possible contingencies, and what usually passes for planning is often just projection of current conditions into the future. Practically, those who do the planning are almost never those who make the critical decisions, and planners almost invariably become either so removed from the true decision-makers that they are irrelevant or so close to the policy process that their involvement in current operations deprives them of the time for contemplation and reflection so critical for planning.[28] While from time to time the policy planning staff in the Department of State makes useful contributions (not always as planners), its record has been mixed, and it has seldom if ever been the source of overall strategic planning for the Department, much less for the government as a whole.

Unfortunately, the fact that planning is difficult does not mean that it can be dispensed with. There are many definitions of what policy planning should be, but the following suggests the elements usually included:

the conceptualization of foreign policy by the continuous defining and redefining of the U.S. external role and goals (i.e.,

[27] Ibid., p. 41. See also Allison and Szanton, *Remaking Foreign Policy*, pp. 125-26, for a closely related answer.

[28] George F. Kennan, *Memoirs 1925-1950* (Boston: Atlantic, Little, Brown, 1967), pp. 467-68, gives perhaps the most telling discussion of the difficulties involved in foreign policy planning. See also Robert L. Rothstein, *Planning, Prediction, and Policymaking in Foreign Affairs* (Boston: Little, Brown, 1972); Lincoln P. Bloomfield, "Organizing for Policy Planning," in Appendix F, "Policy Planning," Murphy Commission Appendix Volume II, pp. 211-22, and the commentaries on this paper by Robert R. Bowie, Chester L. Cooper, and Henry Owen, pp. 225-35. The Commission's findings about policy planning may be found in its report, pp. 143-50.

the "national interest") and the shape of the international system, including past strategies, with emphasis on *emerging and over-the-horizon problems and opportunities, without limitation of subject matter or area, free to challenge conventional premises and assumptions on the most fundamental level if necessary,* and at the same time, *linked to authority in such a way as to insure access to both information and top decision-makers.*[29]

To be in any way effective, policy planning cannot be the exclusive property of any one department, or even of the Executive branch as a whole. It must also combine an extensive knowledge of the international environment and of the intricacies of highly complex and technical issues with political savvy, and it must rely not only on experience and judgment but also on the best available analytic techniques (which have not found much favor among foreign affairs planners).[30]

Any effective policy planning mechanism must be staffed extensively from the career foreign affairs services, although outside perspectives will also be needed. But no systematic programs now exist which can routinely provide career foreign affairs officials with the requisite combination of experience, formal training, and integrative capacity to carry out such arduous tasks. While some individuals, of course, develop the needed skills today, this is the result of individual interest and chance. Such random methods of learning are not likely to suffice in the future. There must be conscious professional development to ensure that the requisite competencies are at hand when needed.

A Broader Foreign Policy Process

The expansion in the number of participants in international politics—newly independent nations, new multilateral organiza-

---

[29] Bloomfield, "Organizing for Policy Planning," p. 215. Emphasis in original.

[30] For an elaboration of this last point, see Warren R. Phillips and Richard E. Hayes, "Utilization of Computer Technology and Formal Social Science in Foreign Policy Decision Making," in Appendix G to the Murphy Commission Report, "Analytic Techniques for Foreign Affairs," Appendix Volume II, pp. 241-60.

tions and mechanisms, and a proliferation of nongovernmental actors—is paralleled at home.

It seems inescapable that major decisions in foreign policy will increasingly be made at home. Although from time to time efforts are made to give U.S. representatives abroad more responsibility, there are a host of countervailing pressures—technology, complexity, interdependence, and most of all the recent erosion of the distinction between foreign and domestic policy. At the same time, many interests and individuals formerly little concerned with foreign affairs have become important in the policy process, as have virtually all agencies of the government. The authors of one recent study concluded that the overriding organizational problem for the American government will be "how to conduct effective foreign policy when power is broadly dispersed."[31] Certainly, the difficulties of administration after administration over who runs foreign policy support the thesis.

The reason for this lack of overall direction is simple: there are more "players" concerned with more issues. There are new dimensions to policy-making in Washington stemming from the ever larger number of concerned agencies, the immediacy of domestic issues, much wider and much less deferential congressional interests, pressure groups, ethnic politics, and the increased use of the techniques of public relations. There are no better examples than the areas of energy, food, the Middle East, and Mexican, Cuban and, Haitian refugees—complex issues for which it is arguable that preliminary negotiations between agencies and interests in the U.S. may be even more strenuous than negotiations with foreign governments. Domestic policies applied to these areas may produce international *causes célèbres*, just as international events spill over to domestic politics. Attempting to confine such issues to either the domestic or foreign category is now impossible. The international agenda has been annexed to the domestic one, bringing together all those interests and actors who participate in both spheres.

An informal study prepared within the State Department for

[31] Allison and Szanton, "Organizing For the Decade Ahead," Chapter Six in Henry Owen and Charles Schultze, eds., *Agenda for the Decade Ahead* (Washington, D.C.: Brookings Institution, 1976), p. 228.

the Murphy Commission in 1974 amplified these developments, in an analysis which is still valid:

> . . . we find a natural and increasing concern with foreign policy issues in an ever wider number of domestic groups. Environmentalists, farmers, workers, white collar groups and the public at large will assert an increasing interest and voice in foreign affairs.
>
> This democratization of foreign policy is a desirable development, but now we confront the difficult problems of strengthening the ties between citizens and policy-makers. While foreign affairs impinges more and more on the lives of individual Americans, this occurs in ways that are less and less understandable in traditional terms. . . . Not for the first time in American history, we will have to try to develop policies that can command public support over the long haul without the spur of a particular enemy to be defeated, or a specific cause or ideology to be contained.[32]

Within the Executive branch, successive waves of formerly unengaged departments and agencies have become involved in foreign affairs. Through most of our history, only the Department of State can be said to have had a continuing interest in foreign affairs and to have had anything resembling a professional foreign affairs staff. In the thirties and forties, the old-line departments, especially War, Navy, Treasury, and Agriculture, and some newer ones like Commerce, began playing stronger roles, as a necessary adjunct to carrying out their domestic duties. All other cabinet departments followed, in one way or another.

The next wave came with the birth of a new set of agencies created to carry out operational and specialized programs in such areas as foreign assistance, intelligence, and cultural and informational affairs. Close behind followed the new scientific and

---

[32] "Department of State Submission to The Commission on the Organization of the Government for the Conduct of Foreign Policy" (multilith, February 1974), pp. 8-9. Due to internal ambivalence in State and the Administration about the Commission, this document was never formally cleared within the Department and thus was not an official statement of policy, but it was provided informally to the Commission as background.

technologically oriented agencies which necessarily exhibited high interest in international activities: ERDA (now DOE), NASA, EPA, Drug Enforcement Administration (DEA). Altogether, the Murphy Commission estimated that more than 20,000 civilian professionals work full time in foreign affairs, excluding both support activities and the intelligence agencies, which add at least that many more. Only about 4,000 of these are employees of the Department of State.[33] Another revealing figure is that as of January 1, 1982, there were 126,520 civilian Executive branch employees (professional and support) outside the United States (64,879 U.S. citizens, the remainder local nationals), representing twenty-five departments and agencies. Only 15,339 of these worked for State (Americans and foreign nationals combined), and it is not uncommon to find that as few as 15 percent of the employees of a particular overseas mission are State Department Foreign Service personnel.[34]

These developments, and especially the fragmentation within the Executive branch, have been the focus of major attention since World War II and, by virtue of the way these departments and agencies conduct their business with one another, the cause of the concern with "bureaucratic politics" in the foreign policy process.[35] One manifestation is that the typical agency has a strong

[33] See Table 2 for a more detailed summary. (The count excludes employees in the federal government who do not have direct foreign affairs responsibilities, mostly in the administrative area.)

[34] "Organization of Federal Executive Departments and Agencies" (see note 16). State Department percentage of total mission population figures provided by Office of Management Operations, August 1980, as of December 31, 1979. By region, State personnel as a percentage of all U.S. citizen personnel ranged from 13.7% in Africa to 49.5% in Europe, with an overall average of 25.3%.

[35] Richard Neustadt's *Presidential Power* (New York: Signet, 1960) is perhaps the seminal work in this area, but those who have written on it are countless. See, for more recent examples, sources listed in Chapters I and II of the author's *Foreign Policy and the Bureaucratic Process* (Princeton, N.J.: Princeton University Press, 1974); Destler, "National Security Advice to Presidents: Some Lessons from Thirty Years," *World Politics* 29 (January 1977), 143-76; and the exchange between Destler and Szanton on the proper role for the President's National Security Advisor in *Foreign Policy* 38 (Spring 1980): Destler, "A Job That Doesn't Work," 80-88; Szanton, "Two Jobs, Not One," 89-91. See also, on bureaucratic politics, Neustadt; Halperin; Allison, *Essence of Decision: Ex-*

preference for conducting its own affairs overseas as autono-
mously as possible, with minimal interference from State.[36]

None of this is unfamiliar; but as the domestic-foreign dichotomy fades, new agencies not experienced in international affairs
become involved, necessitating both better coordination of the
overall policy process and changes in the way the agencies themselves conduct their business. Perhaps the most difficult lesson is
that policies which make great political sense when directed to
the domestic scene may have unacceptable international costs.

Beyond the Executive branch, much the same dispersion of
power is apparent. Despite occasional forays into major issues of
foreign policy, the Congress has usually desired, until recently,
little more than to be informed, and not to be a major partner.
This has been singularly true in the national security area, where,
"particularly during the Cold War . . . Congress tended to reinforce the prevailing inclinations of the Executive branch rather
than to temper them by exploring alternative policies. For many
years this was especially true of strategic weapons policy. Whatever proposals the President advanced Congress inclined to en-
large rather than to refine."[37]

This is no longer accurate. SALT II, the Panama Canal issue,
and AWACS sales were prime examples. Partly because of the

---

plaining the Cuban Missile Crisis (Boston: Little, Brown, 1971); and Charles E.
Lindblom, *The Policy-Making Process*, 2nd ed. (Englewood Cliffs, N.J.: Prentice-
Hall, 1980).

[36] The Carter reorganizations of foreign assistance, international communications and information, and foreign trade units of the Executive branch give recent
evidence, but the feeling goes back to the early postwar period, as for example
the establishment of a separate mechanism to carry out the U.S. part in the Marshall
Plan, or the successful effort in 1954 by the Department of Agriculture to establish
a separate Foreign Agricultural Service. On the Marshall Plan, see Joseph Marion
Jones, *The Fifteen Weeks*, 2nd ed. (New York: Harcourt, Brace & World, 1964).

[37] Alton Frye, *A Responsible Congress: The Politics of National Security*, Council on Foreign Relations (New York: McGraw-Hill, 1975), p. 2. Frye advocates
a stronger congressional role; for an exposition of the contrary position, see John
Lehman, *The Executive, Congress and Foreign Policy: Studies of the Nixon
Administration* (New York: Praeger, 1976). See also Bayless Manning, "The
Congress, the Executive and Intermestic Affairs: Three Proposals," *Foreign Affairs* 55 (January 1977), 306-24, and the several studies on the role of Congress
in foreign policy in Murphy Commission Appendix Volume V.

deep trauma of Vietnam, and with the realization that "the constitutional system itself must be insulated from the perils of an overweening Presidency,"[38] the Congress has become much more assertive, at least for the moment, about playing what the majority of its members of both parties now conceive to be its proper role in the making and carrying out of foreign policy.

With the increasing likelihood that any negative impacts of foreign actions—especially economic—will be felt directly by constituents at home, the primordial congressional interest in being reelected (it has been argued that this is the members' only fundamental interest)[39] will be engaged. Better and closer Executive-Legislative relationships and exchanges of information, as well as considerable statesmanship on the part of individual Members of Congress, will be required if national policy is to be squared with the longer-term interests of *the nation*, rather than the shorter-term interests of members.

One final circumstance of the current foreign policy process also has major implications for foreign affairs personnel systems: the relationship between career officials and the temporary political executives appointed by the President. There is cause for concern in this area:

> The need for working relations between political and bureaucratic executives is greater now than ever before. . . . Political administrators have to cope with a proliferation of government activities and organizations. They need to work together across agency lines on policy problems that have become increasingly interdependent. The momentum growing from an ever-larger base of government programs tests any political leader's capacity to come to grips with the executive branch establishment. And as healthy as it may be for democracy, the increasing permeability of national policymaking promises to strain the abilities of any prospective government manager. Facing this operating environment, political executives who merely do as

---

[38] Frye, *A Responsible Congress*, p. 225.

[39] For explication of this hypothesis, see David R. Mayhew, *Congress: The Electoral Connection* (New Haven and London: Yale University Press, 1974).

well as their predecessors in dealing with the bureaucracy are likely to fall consistently behind the pace of events.[40]

It was argued earlier that the government will need higher levels of expertise if it is to cope with the staggering array of problems, and that this competence will come primarily from career foreign affairs officials. But expertise must be used to have any impact, and whether it will be deployed to full effect depends heavily on the relationships between career officials and political appointees. Some argue that this has been less a problem in State than elsewhere, perhaps because political appointees in that Department have been of high quality, often known and respected by the career service.[41] There has been a tendency, however, even in State, particularly in the early period of an administration, for political leaders to be highly suspicious of "the bureaucrats" and to attempt to go it alone or to build their own policy shops of trusted associates from the outside. This can lead to mistakes which the reduced national margin for error may no longer be able to tolerate.

The lesson is clear: career foreign affairs officials must adapt to the broader foreign policy process. They must become more attuned to the interplay of domestic and foreign policy, which means that they must devote the same kind of attention to the domestic political scene and to issues which transcend the narrowly political and military that they purportedly give now to developments in foreign countries. As an important part of this process, they must gain a greater familiarity with the concerns and procedures of the Congress, and to the degree possible they must help to minimize the negative aspects of the inherently adversarial nature of Executive-Legislative relationships. Finally, they will need to be more responsive to the legitimate concerns of political executives, displaying the kind of "neutral competence"[42] which will win trust and support. Foreign affairs professionals will no longer be able to function in isolation, re-

---

[40] Heclo, *Government of Strangers*, p. 236.

[41] Comments by Paul Boeker on an earlier version of this chapter, November 1980.

[42] For elaboration of this need, see Heclo, "OMB and the Presidency—The Problem of 'neutral competence,' " *Public Interest* 38 (Winter 1975), 80-98.

garding critical international issues as their exclusive territory and only grudgingly accepting the interest and participation of the broader government and society.

ASIDE: AN INTERNAL STATE VIEW

It is interesting to compare this picture of the future of foreign affairs with the perceptions of those charged with managing the personnel system of the Department of State, as evidenced in the results of an exercise conducted at a Bureau of Personnel conference held in the fall of 1978. The question posed was the probable content of State Department activities in 1985. After extensive discussion among the Bureau's leaders (office directors, planners, senior officials, and a few others), the consensus was that the major functions of the Department would be (in order of importance):

1. Planning, coordination and management of foreign affairs
2. Monitoring and coordination of implementation of foreign policy initiatives
3. Creation or formulation of foreign policy initiatives
4. Representation of U.S. government interests to foreign governments
5. Recording and interpreting political/economic dynamics of foreign countries
6. Commercial functions and economic analysis
7. Facilitating and providing support services for overseas activities of other U.S. government agencies
8. Information and support services for travelers and tourists; consular and legal services.[43]

What is interesting in this list is the mix of the old and the new: the planning and oversight functions advocated in this chapter rest side by side with the long-sought goal of dominating the determination of policy, on one hand, and with the more pedestrian functions of providing support and services, on the other. This is

[43] The larger question for the conference was essentially the same as that of this book: What does the future imply for personnel systems for foreign affairs? The list was later circulated in an internal bureau memorandum but not published or given distribution elsewhere. The author participated in the conference.

probably a realistic list, but it emphasizes the primary dilemma of personnel management for foreign affairs: how to design a personnel system which produces individuals able and willing to range from participation in the paramount policy processes of government on one hand, to the provision of routine services on the other.

IMPLICATIONS FOR FUTURE FOREIGN AFFAIRS PERSONNEL SYSTEMS

It should be apparent that the evolving nature of the foreign affairs environment has major implications for the kinds of people needed to help develop and carry out national policy.

Specialization

A first lesson provided by the new international agenda is that the Department of State as well as other parts of government will need a wider range and depth of technical and specialized competence than heretofore, deployed primarily in Washington but to some degree also available for assignment abroad. Abroad, technical reporting, representation at scientific meetings, and effective negotiation on increasingly complex issues will be needed. At home, a cadre of specialists will be required, fully at home in the rough and tumble of Washington policy-making and possessed of both professional and bureaucratic skills. An unresolved question is the degree to which this kind of talent should be concentrated in the Department of State, in addition to being located in the more functionally oriented departments and agencies. The British have increasingly opted for placing it in the issue oriented ministries rather than in the Foreign Ministry,[44] but in a less cen-

---

[44] For a discussion of the British approach, see Geoffrey Moorhouse, *The Diplomats: The Foreign Office Today* (London: Jonathan Cape, 1977), pp. 388-92 and passim. More generally, all Foreign Services seem to be confronting the same problems, as judged by the number of representatives of other countries who have requested information on U.S. thinking. Between 1978 and 1982, the author personally saw representatives of Canada, the United Kingdom, France, Sweden, West Germany, South Korea, Australia, New Zealand, and Brazil, and in each instance the agenda of problems faced was remarkably similar.

tralized system such as that of the United States it seems likely that the Department of State must have considerable functional competence if it is to play the needed role of viewing foreign policy as a whole, in contrast to the narrower perspective which necessarily predominates in other agencies with mandates limited by subject area.

Diplomatic Functions

This greater emphasis on specialized competence does not mean that the more traditional diplomatic functions will lose their importance; in fact, better performance in this area will be essential as well.[45]

Reporting of a high quality will be fundamental in carrying out the critical foreign assessment function described above, although it will need to be keyed much more closely to the policy process than is often the case today. Such reporting will be done in part by specialists, but primarily will continue to be the responsibility of broad-gauged generalists able to synthesize the meaning of the whole range of activities and developments in the host country or international organization in question, even with respect to difficult technical issues.

Much will be the same with respect to perhaps the most traditional of all diplomatic functions, representation of U.S. interests abroad and negotiation with other nations. The range of bilateral topics will change to reflect new times, but the number of such issues will expand, not contract. Moreover, representation and negotiation in multilateral settings will vastly increase.

Support can be found both for the proposition that it will be necessary to develop a new cadre of diplomats who spend virtually all their careers working in the multilateral area, and for the contrary argument that since bilateral and multilateral diplomacy will depend increasingly on each other, diplomats should serve in both contexts to the extent possible. The diplomatic generalist,

[45] See, for a view close to that suggested here, E. Raymond Platig, "Educating Diplomats for the 21st Century," unpublished paper prepared for the XIIIth World Congress of the International Political Science Association, Rio de Janeiro, Brazil, August 9-14, 1982.

able to report developments abroad accurately, and to convey U.S. positions and concerns to others, will be a critical element in the conduct of foreign policy in a way that has seldom been true in the past, current mythology notwithstanding.

Policy Development and Integration

Providing another type of generalist may be the single most difficult personnel problem the government has to face. This is the policy generalist, whose critical skill is that of being able to integrate a diverse range of interests, bureaucratic considerations, political pressures, and goals in such a way as to provide coherent and pertinent policy recommendations to political leaders. The policy generalist is at the heart of the policy process, whereas his or her diplomatic counterpart operates abroad more in the areas of inputs (reporting) and outputs (negotiation, representation). It has almost always been assumed that long experience in diplomatic activities is the best preparation for demanding policy development roles; but the new issue-agenda, coupled with the very different operating environment which exists in Washington compared with that typically encountered overseas, suggests that this assumption needs to be reexamined. It is more likely that no single type of career can guarantee the development of effective policy generalists, and that a major effort will be needed to seek out individuals with the requisite qualities of mind, whatever their previous experience.

In light of this background, it is time now to turn attention to what "is," compared with what "must be."

CHAPTER TWO

The Need for Change:
Failures of the Current System

Adapting foreign affairs personnel systems to meet the new requirements would be a significant challenge even if these systems were now operating at peak efficiency. Unfortunately, current performance is seriously flawed. The faults are due partly to structural deficiencies, partly to poor management, and partly to factors beyond department or agency control; but they also derive from operational challenges and societal and governmental trends which complicate the problem of providing the right individuals with the right experiences in the right places at the right times.

This chapter examines how well the current systems provide the competences necessary for success in the development and conduct of U.S. foreign policy.

Of necessity, this chapter and the preceding one give limited coverage to one category of foreign affairs officials and employees: those in such functions as administration and consular work, who are not normally considered to have direct foreign policy functions but who nevertheless devote their working lives to the support of American diplomacy and international programs. Their efforts are critical to the work of the Service and worthy of separate, full consideration. Most of the problems taken up in subsequent chapters, however, apply equally to the entire Foreign Service, as does the new Foreign Service Act, discussed in Chapter VI.

WHAT COMPETENCES? THEORY

The competences that seem to be needed in the foreign affairs community will vary according to the relative weight an observer places on the importance of the new foreign policy agenda compared with the old.[1] Those who give high importance to the new will be most concerned about expertise in technical, scientific, economic, and other functional areas, while those who either downplay the importance of this agenda or find that it varies in content but not in form from the old agenda will emphasize generalist, diplomatic skills, that is, techniques of negotiation, representation, and reporting rather than knowledge about the content of specific issues.

These differing emphases are paralleled by two others. The generalist point of view, essentially synonymous with the core values of the FSO "subculture" (a term sometimes used only half facetiously by its members), is rooted in overseas responsibilities. This branch of the foreign affairs community values individuals who are conversant with the whole range of U.S. policy, particularly as it may affect the foreign government to which they are accredited, and who have personal relationships and contextual knowledge which will facilitate accurate reporting, including predictions of how a government will react in a wide variety of circumstances. A premium is thus placed upon experience (rather than academic training), "feel," and intuition as preferred elements of problem solving. Rigorous analysis ranks lower on the scale.

In contrast, the functional or specialist perspective, that of the Washington community of foreign affairs experts reflects its very different milieu. Formal training is valued more highly (although experience is by no means ignored), and the more technical and narrower nature of individual responsibilities combine to place a greater weight upon analysis and formal problem-solving approaches. At the same time, analysis may be influenced by the bureaucratic forum in which it is undertaken as well as by domestic political interests; and it is likely to become a weapon used to further agency or client group interests in the fray over the development of policy.[2]

These stylistic differences underscore the obvious but fre-

---

[1] This section follows closely William I. Bacchus, "Foreign Affairs Officials: Professionals Without Professions?" *Public Administration Review* 37 (November/December 1977), 641-50.

[2] Lindblom, *Policy-Making Process*, pp. 30-34 and passim, develops the idea of the relationship between analysis and the bureaucratic politics of policy-making.

quently neglected fact that two very different forms of activity are involved. As Harold Nicolson argued, policy and negotiation should not be confused with each other, nor should these "two branches" of the subject be called by "the same ill-favoured name of 'Diplomacy.' " Foreign policy was for the Executive (i.e., political leadership) to decide; in contrast, its execution was best "left to professionals of experience and discretion."[3]

The FSO corps is oriented toward diplomacy in the second sense. By training and predilection its members are best equipped for negotiation and for carrying out national policy abroad, not for the rough and tumble that characterizes the modern policy-making process in Washington. Accustomed to living at post, where a sense of unity is more likely to prevail, together with relatively smooth working relationships with representatives of other agencies at the mission, Washington can be a shock to FSO's. Success in the core Foreign Service activities of negotiation, representation, and reporting requires a compromising style and at times a passive, nonaggressive approach.[4]

In contrast, most of the Washington-based foreign affairs bureaucracy is more directly concerned with policy determination, even though its role may largely be that of providing analysis, alternatives, and argumentation for politically appointed policy makers. Because these officials almost invariably represent specific agency and departmental viewpoints, usually along narrow, client-oriented, functional lines, the policy process often features intense advocacy, aggressive behavior, and a disinclination to compromise. While this style is normally well attuned to the dynamics of the situation at hand—to sorting out the domestic political implications of proposed policies, to digging out facts and analyzing specific issues—too often its practitioners do not know or care enough about overseas ramifications of what is done

[3] Harold Nicolson, *Diplomacy*, 3rd ed. (London: Oxford University Press, 1963), p. 3.

[4] For development of this theme, see Chris Argyris, *Some Causes of Organizational Ineffectiveness Within the Department of State*, U.S. Department of State, Center for International Systems Research, Occasional Paper 2 (Washington, D.C.: GPO, 1967).

at home, and are ill informed about the ease or difficulty of implementing a given policy abroad.

There has been a long, inconclusive generalists-versus-specialists controversy about the appropriate nature of the FSO corps, for which, of all groups of career foreign affairs officials, the question of the mix of skills needed is most difficult to answer (see Chapter IV). If, as argued here, duties in Washington are very different from those in the field, and FSO's must serve in both locales, the question arises of which cluster of skills should be emphasized in recruitment and career development.

Quite different answers have been given through the years. In the mid-1960s John Harr found in his comprehensive survey that FSO's strongly endorsed management, negotiating, and reporting as the central functions of the diplomatic profession, and placed considerably less emphasis on policy development.[5]

William Macomber, as Deputy Under Secretary of State for Management, came to hold a broader view. He emphasized not only the need for traditional diplomatic skills such as reporting, negotiating, and persuading but also in particular the need to be able to analyze objectively and to develop sound and creative policy choices. These skills were needed by all officers, independent of speciality. In addition, substantive knowledge, in many cases of a specialized nature, was in his view essential.[6]

Later, in 1976, a staff study conducted by several mid-rank FSO's for a working group on professional development sponsored by then Director General of the Foreign Service Carol C. Laise attempted to isolate qualities and skills needed by the "ideal" foreign affairs executive, based in part upon those of a group of senior officials generally agreed to have been successful. The list emphasized management and operational skills, persuasiveness, and the ability to negotiate, with less concern about expertise or analytic skills.[7] By the summer of 1979, State's Bureau of Per-

[5] Harr, *Professional Diplomat*, pp. 242-44.

[6] William B. Macomber, *The Angel's Game: A Handbook of Modern Diplomacy* (New York: Stein and Day, 1975), pp. 39-78.

[7] Professional Development Working Group, Department of State, "Final Report and Action Recommendations," Tab 3, "Characteristics of the Senior Foreign Affairs Executive," unpublished, Department of State, Bureau of Personnel, 1976.

sonnel was advocating a "major-minor" career pattern requiring experience in depth in both a primary and secondary "cone." (The FSO corps in recent years has been subdivided into four broad cones: political, economic/commercial, consular, and administrative, reflecting broad subdivisions of work but not deep specialties for FSO's.) The major-minor pattern was not intended to develop specialized skills but to ensure that individuals reaching the top will have had a wide breadth of experience.[8] By late 1980, yet another scheme had evolved, one would have established a set list of criteria to be met before an officer would be eligible for promotion to senior levels, including, for FSO's, language competence, set periods of service in primary cone jobs, at least one tour each in "policy content" and "supervisory" jobs, and one tour at a hardship post.[9]

What is striking about these and other self-analyses is the degree to which the generalist point of view persists, augmented by an increasing concern with program management. Few of the qualities cited suggest that some senior positions may differ dramatically from others and may therefore require individuals with different configurations of skills. Moreover, analytic, conceptual, and integrative skills critical for policy development are almost invariably downrated. As long as such lists of qualities reflect what the Service itself thinks it needs, it is not likely to recruit or develop individuals with specialized expertise or with the combative style needed in Washington.

That generalists are still preferred is reflected by the recruitment process. Broad formal education is clearly an asset in doing well on the FSO examination; technical training is less valuable. Even more telling than the continued preponderance of history and political science majors among new FSO classes is the lack of an effective system designed to put to use specialized expertise that some new FSO's do bring with them, although conceivably the

[8] Harry G. Barnes, Jr. (Director General of the Foreign Service), "Foreign Service Structure: Modifications of the FSO Cone System," unpublished Draft Action Memorandum to Ben H. Read (Under Secretary of State for Management), July 27, 1979. This plan was overtaken, and not implemented.

[9] Announced by cable to the field in August 1980, modified on the basis of impassioned responses by a second cable in December, and in limbo as of fall 1982.

cone system could be refined to serve this purpose. Experience gained on the job (sometimes augmented by service–conducted training) still counts for more than skill-related formal education.

Another problem is the bifurcation of the FSO career. The system recruits at the bottom, giving primary emphasis to generalist qualities thought to be necessary for those who will serve abroad, a quarter-century later, as Ambassadors. However, many of the mid-level policy related jobs through which FSO's pass in the intervening period are best filled by persons with specialized expertise. This is particularly true in the functional bureaus of State, such as those dealing with economics, environmental and scientific affairs, and political-military affairs. Without such expertise, State cannot play the comprehensive role of policy integration earlier suggested to be vital. Table 1 indicates the degree of mismatch in staffing, by State's own definition of job requirements compared with incumbent skills: the situation has not notably improved between 1976 and 1982. (The picture overseas, while better, still shows the same problems.)

Traditionally, there has been little incentive for FSO's to acquire deep competences. Since they are evaluated as generalists for promotion to senior ranks, the best strategy for the individual is to become sufficiently specialized in order to survive in the middle ranks, where promotion is based on functional competition, without becoming overly narrow. This perception of self-interest leads to the underutilization of skills; for example, it is seen as safer to be a "generalist" economic officer than a more specialized fisheries or resources officer, even when there may be a more critical need for the latter. Service in specialized areas over the extended period necessary to develop professional-level expertise is not likely to establish the credentials required for promotion to senior ranks, nor even to provide the generalist skills required at that level. Individual incentives are not consistent with system needs.

The rest of the foreign affairs community is by no means fully equipped for its evolving responsibilities, but in many respects its problems are less complex, both in State and in other agencies. Focusing on more limited technical areas, hiring and promotion can be conducted on the basis of qualifications needed for specific positions, or at least for a series of positions all within the same

TABLE 1

Matching Skills and Job Requirements (Department of State—Domestic Positions)

Organization	Officer Positions w/"High Interest"[1] Skill Codes		Filled w/Identical Skill Codes (Primary)		Filled w/Identical (Secondary) or Related[2] Skill Codes		Filled w/Unrelated Skill Codes		Vacant	
	1976	1981	1976	1981	1976	1981	1976	1981	1976	1981
Functional Bureaus										
PM (Politico-Military)	29	38	8	2	13	28	4	6	4	2
OES (Science)[3]	34	7	17	3	4	1	6	2	7	1
EB (Economics)	117	124	56	49	46	54	9	11	6	10
IO (International Organizations)	30	19	11	0	8	13	11	4	0	2
Geographic Bureaus										
AF (Africa)	9	9	4	3	1	3	3	3	1	0
ARA (Latin America)	15	19	7	7	7	8	0	4	1	0
EA (Asia and Pacific)	14	23	2	9	6	12	6	2	0	0
EUR (Europe)	36	48	6	6	22	38	8	4	0	0
NEA (Near East and South Asia)	24	38	5	7	12	25	6	5	1	1
TOTAL	308	325	116 (37.7%)	86 (26.5%)	119 (38.6%)	182 (56.0%)	53 (17.2%)	41 (12.6%)	20 (6.5%)	16 (4.9%)

[1] "High Interest" Skill Codes:

5010 Economic/Commercial Officer
5055 Trade Promotion Officer
5105 International Economist
5107 International Economist—Trade
5108 International Economist—Commodities
5110 Int'l Economist—Defense Economics
5120 Financial Economist
5230 Int'l Transportation and Communications Officer
5231 Int'l Trans./Comm. Officer—Civil Aviation

5250 Fisheries Officer
5260 Metals and Minerals Officer
5270 Petroleum Officer
5410 Commercial Officer
5411 Market Research Officer
5530 Political/Economic Officer
5570 Political Military Affairs Officer
5610 Labor Political Officer
6150 Physical Science Officer

[2] Secondary skill codes represent an individual's "back up" competences. A related skill code is one in the same general occupational category, which nevertheless does not match the code for a specific job (e.g. a 5010 Economic officer in a 5250 Fisheries position).

[3] By 1981, OES was emphasizing FSO staffing, reducing heavily the number of positions with "high interest" codes.

occupation.[10] There is easier access from outside at the middle as well as junior levels, and it is thus possible to respond to changing needs with less difficulty than in a bottom-entry system like the FSO corps. Furthermore, it is the organization rather than the profession itself which controls entry, making it easier to change standards in response to new circumstances.

The personnel implications of the evolving, more technical international issue-areas are not yet clearly recognized by the government. In the State Department, some FSO's gain specialized skills through multiple assignments dealing with one set of issues and accompanied by short-term training, but within the overall context of generalist career patterns. While some corrective actions have been taken to meet new demands, they reflect a preference for minimizing the new agenda's impact on the existing structure and mores of the FSO culture, rather than a true appreciation of needs. At the same time, the department also acquires some policy expertise through non-FSO appointments. Specialists from the private sector or elsewhere in government are appointed in limited numbers both temporarily (for periods of five years or less) and permanently, under both the Foreign and Civil Service systems. Unfortunately, the possible benefits of such appointments in the past have been lessened by an insufficient control over the quality of appointees and a too common assumption that only FSO's really understand foreign affairs.

Be that as it may, the underlying concept for this mixed staffing approach is apparently that many or most FSO's might eventually become "generalist/specialists," while "deep specialists" would be employed in other categories. While one may doubt the efficacy of this strategy, it has a certain plausibility as long as FSO's must fill more generalist roles abroad at the same time the Department of State has an urgent need for more functional competence at home. From the standpoint of the FSO corps, however, this pattern of hiring may risk increasing the FSO's irrelevance in Washington. It is plausible that influence and responsibility will in the future

[10] Most of the foreign affairs community is staffed through the competitive Civil Service, which is "rank-in-job." The Foreign Service, by contrast, is "rank-in-person," although groups other than FSO's and FSIO's are still specialists. (See Chapter IV.)

flow more heavily to subject matter experts, to non-FSO's in State as well as to officials and analysts in other agencies.

Whether or not the FSO corps is able to adapt sufficiently to retain some portion of the Washington action, a major problem will remain. It will still be necessary to mesh the quite different overseas-generalist and headquarters-specialist perspectives. Policy synthesis will be at a premium, and it is unclear that either the FSO corps or the policy analyst/specialist group will be able routinely to provide sufficient individuals with the necessary integrative ability to excel at senior-level responsibilities.

More generally, what is lacking is a means of systematically linking personnel practices with what various parts of the Executive branch require.[11] Without such linkages, shortfalls in competence are almost inevitable.

WHAT COMPETENCES? REALITY

In the absence of better agreement on roles, it is almost impossible to be definitive about whether there is enough of various kinds of competences in the foreign affairs community. Nevertheless, obvious deficiencies exist in spite of some recent improvements. There are weaknesses in meeting not only the technical and specialized demands generated by the new issue-agenda but also the more traditional requirements of diplomacy and of policy-making.

Specialist Competence: Politico-Military

In State, the area of national security and politico-military affairs is a good example of both the problems and the disagree-

[11] For a discussion of "position management" as one means of bridging this gap, see Jay M. Shafritz, *Public Personnel Management: The Heritage of Civil Service Reform* (New York: Praeger, 1975), especially chapter 4. In the introduction (p. iv), Dale S. Beach has captured a major part of the problem: "Personnel specialists have succumbed to 'goal displacement.' They have become so enamored with administering employment examinations, analyzing and classifying jobs, are designing performance rating plans (that is, the procedural control functions of personnel) that they have lost sight of the fact that agency mission, efficiency, and high performance are important goals."

ments. In 1975, the Murphy Commission, drawing on its own extensive research study as well as independent investigations, concluded State was inadequately organized and staffed to meet its responsibilities in the defense policy area, asserting that "attitudes toward management, quantitative analysis, budget processes and toward military expertise all contribute to the problem. . . . *Current recruitment and training patterns in the Foreign Service do not routinely produce competent analysts of national security policy issues. Moreover, restrictions on lateral entry inhibit their recruitment from the outside.*"[12] More directly, Allison and Szanton quote one recent Director of Politico–Military (PM) Affairs in State as saying, "There are not a half-dozen people in the building who have any understanding of the strategic consequences of the SALT agreements."[13] By mid-1982, there had been good *outside* recruits through the efforts of Secretary Vance and PM Directors Leslie Gelb in the Carter Administration and Richard Burt at the beginning of Reagan's, but the situation with respect to FSO's was still essentially the same. Some FSO's with the requisite skills did join PM, but they had developed them on their own, and not because of the system.[14]

In contrast, the viewpoint of the career Foreign Service, as reflected in a 1976 report, was much more sanguine: "In PM, four deep specialists in nuclear policy and arms control seem to be all that the bureau needs within its 44 officer positions." In addition, it was argued the bureau needed about fifteen political officers with a concentration in political/military affairs (for whom the accumulation of knowledge from one or two prior political-

[12] Murphy Commission Report, pp. 79-80. Emphasis in original. The major research study mentioned was that conducted by Allison, previously cited. Interestingly, the quoted comments were drafted by a former FSO who served as a consultant to the Commission and who, with the change of administrations, subsequently became an Assistant Secretary of State.

[13] Allison and Szanton, *Remaking Foreign Policy*, p. 136.

[14] Interviews with both operating officials and those responsible for staffing the Bureau of Politico-Military affairs. FSO's, in the opinions of those interviewed, generally continued to lack competence in systems analysis and knowledge of the defense community. Little incentive existed for them to develop such skills, since there were few overseas positions requiring them and since PM was therefore not well positioned to help its "alumni" find attractive follow-on assignments.

military assignments—two/four years—was deemed sufficient) and about an equal number of officers with traditional Foreign Service backgrounds in analysis and drafting, who did not need any specific political/military qualifications.[15]

This disparity in the assessment of needs is typical of a phenomenon the author has observed over a number of years: outsiders are as a rule much more critical of State's functional competence than are those in the Foreign Service. Part of this comes from different views of the role of the Department, part from different evaluations of the need for specialists as opposed to generalists, and part from self-interest. Virtually every discussion of the need for more specialists in State quickly comes to the point that recruiting more specialists may hurt assignment and promotion opportunities for FSO's (who, we have seen, have no major incentives to become true specialists themselves).

Specialist Competence: Economic

In economics, the picture is largely the same. The same internal State study previously quoted rather smugly concluded that in the Bureau of Economic and Business Affairs (EB), "out of a total complement of 149 officers the need for such specialists seems to be limited to three positions in the Office of International Communications Policy and to an occasional temporary need for an econometrician or other highly-specialized economist."[16] In contrast, Allison and Szanton found that the Bureau of Economic and Business Affairs was "grossly undersupplied with trained economists (3 Ph.D.s in economics out of a professional staff of 126)."[17]

State is justifiably proud of the major improvement it has achieved in overseas competence in recent years—owing to the twenty-six-week course in economics provided at the Foreign Service Institute, but this has not had the same impact in the domestic policy arena.

The major research study conducted for the Murphy Commis-

[15] Professional Development Working Group. The quotation is from "Executive Summary and Recommendations," p. 2; the rest of the paragraph is drawn from Tab 1, "Summary of Research in Operating Bureaus," p. 3.

[16] Professional Development Working Group, Executive Summary, p. 2.

[17] Allison and Szanton, *Remaking Foreign Policy*, p. 136.

sion on the conduct of international economic policy led to the
conclusion that

> . . . the State Department is dangerously under-equipped to
> play even a supporting role with respect to most issues which
> require professional training in economics. Some of this reflects
> questionable organization and the leadership's preoccupation
> with "political" issues, but the most important factors, in our
> judgment, lie in the traditions and incentives of the Foreign
> Service. These problems are so entrenched and have so long
> resisted reform that several knowledgeable observers believe
> that the only real alternatives may be the European model, in
> which responsibility for foreign economic matters is usually
> vested in the Finance Ministry rather than the Foreign Office.
> Indeed, it is no accident that case after case shows that in the
> present-day American system, a vacuum of leadership in for-
> eign economic policy is much more likely to be filled by Treas-
> ury than by State.[18]

Other studies conducted for the Murphy Commission substantiate
the weak performance of State in these critical economic issues.[19]
Rightly or wrongly, it came as no surprise when, in the fall of
1979, the Carter Administration placed into effect plan for reorganization which stripped State of a major role in commercial
representation and trade development.[20]

In 1980, when I circulated an initial version of this section in
the Department of State, it elicited strong comments from those
who, while admitting that State was not playing as prominent a
role as they felt desirable in foreign economic policy, took strong
exception to the assertion that the fault could be traced to the lack

[18] Hamilton et al., p. 14 (see note 17, Ch. I). At about the same time Maxwell
D. Taylor made virtually the same argument. See his *Precarious Security* (New
York: W. W. Norton, 1976), pp. 108-9.

[19] See Mortimer D. Goldstein, "Personnel for U.S. Economic Activities Overseas," and Sidney Weintraub, "The Personnel System for the Conduct of Foreign
Economic Policy," both in Appendix P to the Murphy Commission Report,
"Foreign Economic Policy," Appendix Volume III, pp. 310-27 and 328-35,
respectively.

[20] Reorganization plan No. 3 was transmitted to the Congress in September
1979 and was implemented by Executive order 12188 of January 2, 1980.

of economic competence. One comment came from a highly regarded economic officer with a strong governmentwide reputation:

> . . . The easy explanation [lack of competence = low influence] is, however, wrong. State's economic competence has improved over a decade, including since Murphy Commission judgments, and *is* competitive with other agencies and infinitely better than Commerce's. The trade function was given away, for political reasons. . . . The "charge" against State was rather lack of interest at the top in trade promotion (a more accurate indictment than lack of staff competence).[21]

Even with improvements, however, it is far from clear that "better than Commerce" is good enough, as a study commissioned by State itself indicated in its conclusions in late 1980:

> Sustained effort over many years has enabled the Foreign Service to build an economic staff equal in competence to that found in any other part of the Government. There are nevertheless deficiencies which badly need remedying. The State Department needs a greater capability for in-depth professional economic analysis useful for both long-term planning and crisis management. It needs to assure a larger and more timely flow of economic information to, and advice from, the field as well as better evaluation of economic reporting. Its economic officers need to be offered more opportunities to become better informed about the domestic economy and its institutions, about the workings of the Congress and about the problem faced by the domestic economic agencies of the Executive Branch when seen from inside. In many cases economic staff in the field, especially in the developing countries, needs strengthening.[22]

More will certainly be required.

[21] This officer had an intimate knowledge of the trade reorganization issue.

[22] "Recommendations Concerning the Economic Function, Organization and Personnel of the Department of State and the Foreign Service," November 1980, transmitted by the Economic Functions Study Group (Edwin M. Martin, John M. Reddy, and Frances M. Wilson) to Secretary of State Muskie, December 8, 1980. Unpublished. Quotation from page 2 of "Summary of Conclusions and Recommendations." This study became known as the Martin Report, after the study group's chairman.

Specialist Competence: Science and Technology

In the area of science and technology, especially involving the global issues discussed in Chapter I, the Department of State seems more willing to admit that there may be shortfalls, although State is divided internally over what to do. Even so the outlook is mixed. There is general agreement that the Bureau of Oceans and International Environmental and Scientific Affairs (OES) is not equipped to fulfill its responsibilities. The previously cited study of the Professional Development Working Group concluded:

> For the present, OES clearly needs much more specialized expertise than the Department's current career service can provide. Perhaps roughly half of the officers there need to be deep specialists. The rest of OES's need is largely for generalist/specialists of a type that is as yet in very short supply. This is partly a function of time and slow-to-change values in the Foreign Service. Most officers currently have neither the background nor the interest for OES, nor is there any clear pattern of rewards and incentives to attract them.[23]

Note, however, the assumption that this weakness can eventually be corrected, using the existing system of FSO's supplemented by specialists.

Even though stating that he accepted this analysis, T. Keith Glennon, in an independent study conducted for OES at about the same time, seriously doubted that such an approach could ever be successful:

> . . . OES is seriously undermanned to meet its present responsibilities, let alone those appearing on the horizon. Even a cursory review of the mission statement reveals broad areas which have suffered from a lack of qualified personnel and financial resources.
>
> The legislation of 1974 establishing the present Bureau of Oceans and International Environmental and Scientific Affairs greatly enlarged the scope of its predecessor Bureau (SCI) and

[23] Professional Development Working Group, "Executive Summary: Specialist Paper," p. 2.

significantly changed the status of its activities. The addition of fisheries and wildlife, ocean affairs and population problems to the already formidable array of responsibilities of SCI in science, technology, and environment, has overburdened OES to the point that it can only respond to the most urgent demands placed on it. Consequently, important areas have been largely or totally neglected, and thoughtful long-range analyses and planning have been virtually abandoned to accommodate operational requirements.[24]

Typical of the problem was the circumstance described in an internal memorandum originating in OES at the beginning of the Carter Administration, when some realignment of OES responsibilities was under consideration:

> All future options should include an expansion of the resources supporting international energy technology cooperation. . . . Lack of adequate manpower has resulted in relatively superficial treatment of issues, inadequate attention to energy technology developments occurring outside of the OECD/LDC area, and a disappointingly small number of new initiatives in an area with high potential for political and economic benefit.[25]

OES at the time of the Glennan study had fifty-eight professional officers doing substantive work, thirty-five of whom were classified as Scientific and Technical specialists and twenty-three as Non-Technical Foreign Service Officers. While educational background is by no means a perfect indication of competence, it is distressing that, among the twenty-two (of thirty-five total)

---

[24] T. Keith Glennan, "Technology and Foreign Affairs," A Report to Deputy Secretary of State Charles W. Robinson, October 20, 1976 (Washington, D.C.: GPO, 1976), pp. 41-42. Glennan has been, *inter alia*, the first Administrator of NASA, a Commissioner of the Atomic Energy Commission, U.S. Representative to the International Atomic Energy Agency, and President of the Case Institute of Technology.

[25] Department of State, Internal Memorandum, unpublished, February 1977. For a later but not dissimilar discussion in the environmental field, see *The Global 2000 Report to the President*, A Report Prepared by the Council on Environmental Quality and the Department of State, 2 vols., Gerald O. Barney, Study Director (Washington, D.C.; GPO, 1980).

technical personnel for which information was given, only seven held Ph.D.'s in technical/scientific areas; only three of twenty Foreign Service Officers had scientific academic majors, and none held Ph.D.'s.[26] There was thus a long way to go, even to meet the probably understated needs identified in the Department's own assessments. Subsequent reviews identified at least 200 FSO jobs whose incumbents needed considerable "S and T" competence.

If anything, the problem may have been exacerbated after late 1978, when a new Assistant Secretary, an FSO, concluded that OES should nevertheless be staffed more heavily by FSO's, and not so much by technical experts. The situation was made no better when the 1978 Department of State Authorization Act (Title V) charged State with substantially greater responsibility for co-ordinating science and technology policy in the international area—but gave it no added resources or strategy for carrying out such tasks.[27]

All this leads to one basic point: the Department of State does not have the functional competence—politico-military, economic, or scientific—to play anything resembling an integrative, policy development role with respect to the new issue-agenda. And there is little current indication that significant improvement is likely.

SPECIALIST COMPETENCE: BEYOND STATE

None of this should be taken as meaning that it is only the Department of State which has serious problems in acquiring and keeping the necessary specialized competence. A full review here is impossible, but what follows is illustrative of the problem.

Edward K. Hamilton, summarizing the implications of his previously cited review of the conduct of foreign economic policy, found that

[26] Data from Phillip M. Whitbeck, "Summary of Findings and Recommendations: Report on Personnel Management for the Bureau of Oceans and International Environmental and Scientific Affairs," Appendix G to Glennan, "Technology and Foreign Affiars," pp. 3, 10, 11.

[27] P. L. 95-426, Section 503(b). Initial reports required by this section, filed in January 1980, were, in the author's opinion, carefully elaborate discussions intended to disguise how little had been done—or was possible, given existing budgetary restraints.

beyond the issue of central management of the process, the most striking lesson of the cases is the minuscule and relatively static number of individuals in policy-making or staff positions who feel competent and comfortable dealing with both "political" and "economic" issues. This is particularly true in the Department of State . . . but it is a general truth applicable to all agencies.[28]

He recommended establishment of a comprehensive, governmentwide inventory of individuals with professional economic training and experience; additional training; better arrangements for interchange of such people with selected private sector activities and within government; and other steps designed to upgrade capabilities in this area.

Drawing in part upon this same study, Allison and Szanton found a very uneven pattern of economic competence:

Over the last decade the Department of Agriculture has lost to private competitors its position of preeminence as an analyst of supply and demand in markets for major agricultural products. Commerce, never accomplished at industry studies, has fallen further behind. On the other hand, the new Federal Energy Administration has become the leading source of information and estimates about energy markets.

If the government is to stay at least as well equipped with data and analytic skill as the private sector, the key departments must build and retain the necessary staff.[29]

Foreign Assistance

The problems of the Agency for International Development deserve special comment. Nowhere else in government has there been so much uncertainty. AID's status as a "temporary" agency, in spite of two decades of existence, has meant that it has had no

[28] Hamilton et al., p. 14 (see note 17, Chap. I).

[29] Allison and Szanton, *Remaking Foreign Policy*, p. 158. Of course by the time of this writing FEA had become the Department of Energy, and by 1981 had been marked for extinction, thus demonstrating among other things the difficulty of running a coherent personnel system in the face of organizational instability.

career personnel system. This has made the recruitment and maintenance of the necessary competence difficult.

An internal report commissioned by AID Administrator John J. Gilligan concluded in late summer 1977 that "in the course of this study one theme emerged stronger than any other: *the personnel system does not work to anyone's satisfaction.* This view was unanimous—employees and managers in all parts of the Agency are universally dissatisfied, neither employee nor organization is currently well served."[30]

Among the specific criticisms were several which suggest that the personnel system and the types of people it produced were seriously out of line with the Agency's mission of overseas development:

—the percentage of the workforce in Washington changed from 35% in 1961 to 64% in 1977, "a complete reversal in the ratio of overseas to headquarters personnel."
—in terms of the number of professional staff, "categories corresponding to A.I.D.'s major fields of work—Agriculture, Health, Population and Education—account for 395 or 15%, while the categories for Program/Economics, Administration, Controller, General Service, Audit, Legal and Procurement total 1,646 or 65%."
—there is a need for "more language, area studies, and special technical training, and sufficient opportunity to specialize in a given geographic area."

Although Gilligan was later to lose control of the efforts to reorganize AID and to reform its personnel system (he was eased out early in 1979), the Carter Administration did submit a reorganization plan covering its foreign assistance function in the

[30] Task Force Report for the Administrator, Agency for International Development, "Organization and Structure of A.I.D.," unpublished, Washington, D.C., AID, October 1977. Quotation from page IV-1. Emphasis in original. The points listed are extracted from subsequent parts of the report. For another summary, see John Cramer, "AID's Personnel System is Completely Out of Whack, Task Force Finds," *Washington Star*, September 7, 1977, B-2.

spring of that year.[31] The plan was a compromise, creating a small International Development Cooperation Administration (IDCA) intended to play the primary role in managing development. AID was to become a part of IDCA, but in the opinion of many this plan did not give IDCA's director the strength needed to be successful. It did take AID out of the State Department, although the AID and IDCA directors were charged with taking foreign policy guidance from the Secretary. The whittling away of State continued, to the chagrin of the Foreign Service, even though there had been less and less interest in recent years among FSO's in development, as measured by their willingness to take assignments on detail to AID.[32]

In large part at the instigation of Gilligan and his team, AID was also required by the "Obey Amendment" to the International Development and Food Assistance Act of 1978 to develop an improved and "integrated" personnel system and to provide the Congress with regulations under which that system would be operated by March 15, 1979.[33] AID's plan would have placed its entire professional-level workforce in the Foreign Service system whether or not individuals were likely ever to serve overseas, in order to gain the advantage of having a single, flexible rank-in-person personnel system (see Chapter IV). Ironically, at the same time State and the United States International Communication Agency (successor to USIA as a result of Reorganization Plan No. 2 of 1977) had concluded that their decade-old attempt to use a single system simply would not work, and had decided that it was necessary to run one personnel system for rotational per-

[31] Reorganization Plan Number 2 of 1979, effective October 1, 1979.

[32] For example, as of February 1980, twenty-five AID officers were on detail to State, while only three from State were serving in AID (AID data). These figures parallel those of earlier (and later) years.

[33] P.L. 95-424, Section 401. The regulations were to have the force of law, unless rejected by either house within sixty days of submission. They were submitted on May 1, 1979 (to be effective October 1, 1979), rather than on March 15, owing to considerable dispute within the Executive branch about the direction in which AID should move, which was essentially counter to that being contemplated by other foreign affairs agencies (see the following paragraphs and Chap. VI).

sonnel who served both at home and abroad, and another for those who served only in the United States.

Though pressure from OMB, State, and the House Post Office and Civil Service Committee, AID was forced to abandon its plan and to devise a "dual" system which would place in the Foreign Service those individuals who were going to serve abroad. At the same time, AID developed plans to shift the balance of its staffing efforts more toward Foreign Service personnel, in order to meet the complaint (accepted by all agencies and the various engaged congressional elements) that too many of AID's senior managers had no "hands on" development experience overseas.[34] While these plans seemed a step in the right direction, clearly much time would be needed before AID could gain the competence necessary to do its job with maximum effectiveness.

Defense

There are also weaknesses in the defense area, usually thought of as being the best staffed in government for its responsibilities. Yet in recent years some of its most vital competences have declined. The Murphy Commission argued that the Office of International Security Affairs (ISA) in the Office of the Secretary of Defense (OSD) should be an important participant in shaping military policy and in relating it to the rest of national policy, but that it was not equipped to play such a role: "ISA shares with State the traditional diplomats' weaknesses in quantitative and technical analysis. In recent years, analytic techniques have been one of the Defense Secretary's main tools in evaluating and shaping the defense program and budget, and the role of ISA has been weakest in this area."[35] Allison and Szanton arrive at the same conclusion:

[34] The shift toward more Foreign Service staffing was to occur over a five–year period, as positions became vacant. Of AID's roughly 1,350 officer positions in Washington, 700 were eventually to be staffed by the Foreign Service. Figures from letter to Congressman Obey from Herbert A. Jolovitz, Acting Assistant Administrator of AID for Legislative Affairs, April 23, 1979.

[35] Murphy Commission Report, p. 87.

The Secretary will need the support . . . of a rebuilt office of International Security Affairs (ISA). Recent insensitivity to the linkage between defense and broader foreign policy objectives appears largely attributable to a decline in the quality of Defense's "little State Department," which has primary responsibility for monitoring that linkage. The recent elevation of ISA's chief from assistant secretary to deputy secretary status should be matched by a commensurate rebuilding of its staff.[36]

In a related area, but one outside the Department, there is evidence that

the Arms Control and Disarmament Agency should . . . be strengthened. Operating with a professional staff of fewer than a hundred, ACDA has managed to develop a technical expertise on strategic weapons that is unmatched outside of the Pentagon and the CIA. But its capacity to deal with less central arms control issues, such as military sales of conventional weapons and their effect on regional strategic balances, is far less adequate.[37]

Domestic vs. Foreign Policy

There is one other "missing" competence of major—and increasing—importance. Because of the growing interrelationship between international and domestic policy, the need surely exists among agencies dealing with foreign affairs for greater knowledge about the domestic U.S. political environment, if only because of the need to advocate the nation's overseas interest in the fray of domestic politics. What may be even more difficult, however, is the reverse: it will be necessary for those with domestic responsibilities to become sensitized to the possible foreign implications of what they do. To a degree this has happened; it is best exemplified by the creation of International Affairs bureaus or offices in virtually all the major departments of government and

[36] Allison and Szanton, *Remaking Foreign Policy*, p. 185.
[37] Ibid., p. 184.

in many of the agencies.[38] Such units can serve as links to foreign
policy, but they may not be enough. The merging of foreign and
domestic issues means that the activities of the traditionally domestic units in these departments and agencies will at times have
major international consequences.

DIPLOMATIC SKILLS

Although State and the Foreign Service must play a larger role
with respect to the new issue-agendas, the burden of the Department's current diplomatic responsibilities will remain. The strongest suit of the Foreign Service should be the application of its
foreign-related knowledge across a broad spectrum of issues. But
here, change is essential. Recent critiques almost universally conclude that reporting from overseas needs to be more analytic,
more attuned to U.S. domestic political realities and to the Washington policy context, and better keyed to purposes for which it
is used.[39] The flavor of these critiques has not changed much since
that written in 1969 by a then relatively junior FSO, Michael
Michaud: "Most Foreign Service reporting is not designed consciously to influence the direction of policy, or to provoke a

[38] They include Agriculture (Office of International Cooperation and Development, Foreign Agricultural Service); Commerce (International Trade Administration, U.S. Travel Service, Foreign Commercial Service); Defense (Office of
the Assistant Secretary for International Security Affairs, and many others); Energy
(Assistant Secretary for International Affairs); Justice (Immigration and Natural-
ization Service); Labor (Bureau of International Labor Affairs); and Treasury
(Assistant Secretary, International Affairs, and U.S. Customs Service).

[39] For example, see Henry A. Kissinger, "Reporting from the Field," De-
partment Notice, U.S. Department of State, November 7, 1973; William D.
Coplin, Michael K. O'Leary, Robert F. Rich et al., "Towards the Improvement
of Foreign Service Field Reporting," in Appendix E, "Field Reporting," Murphy
Commission Appendix, Volume II, pp. 139-207; Carol C. Laise, "From the
Director General: Reporting—Cornerstone of the Profession," *Department of State
News Letter*, 188 (March 1977), inside front cover; and Tad Szulc, "Shaking Up
the C.I.A.," *New York Times Magazine*, July 29, 1979, 13ff. Under direct presidential order, the Department of State began an effort late in 1979 to upgrade
reporting competence through increased classroom training and creation of special
"Reporting and Analysis ("RAP") Positions overseas, explicitly designed as a
means of providing additional training in reporting skills.

response from Washington as part of a dialogue."[40] After antic-
ipating the later critiques, most notably that of Kissinger, he
concluded that "the Foreign Service must recognize that its primary duty is not simply to report information, but to make judgments and recommendations."[41]

In 1975, a team of Foreign Service Inspectors reached a similar
conclusion, in spite of the efforts of some embassies and country
directorates to mesh their reporting more closely with policy needs.
As a result of the Inspector's report, an Office of Reports Coor-
dinator was established in the Management Operations Office of
the Department, but this office brought little improvement, and
it was disbanded in 1979.[42]

Added to ambiguity about what reporting should be are weaknesses in competence of those reporting. The mere possession of
a degree in political science or international affairs does not guarantee analytic competence of a high order; and while many FSO's
through sheer ability become excellent reporters, as of 1982 there
was too little systematic instruction or practice. An orientation
toward generalist diplomacy seems to go hand in hand with a
disinclination to become an analyst in the usual sense of that term.

The Foreign Service also lacks competence of an even more
basic type: the language and area knowledge of the FSO corps as

---

[40] Michael A. G. Michaud, "Communication and Controversy: Thoughts on
the Future of Foreign Service Reporting," *Foreign Service Journal* 46 (October
1969), 24.

[41] Ibid., p. 34

[42] Office of the Inspector General of the Foreign Service, Department of State,
"Inspection Report: Foreign Service Reporting Management," multilith, October
1975. Similarly ill-fated was a related project of the Organizational Analysis and
System Integration Staff (OASIS) which involved sampling and a statistical analysis of reports. The OASIS project, among other things, led to the development
of a "Net Efficiency Output Index" for economic and political reports (per capita
net production, or number of reports per reporter), and other highly questionable
measures. Since one of the concerns behind the project was to improve the use
of resources, meaning budgets and positions made available for reporting from
abroad, such techniques seemed almost certain, if taken seriously, to encourage
excessive reporting of information not needed, little time-consuming but important
analysis, and more passive report-writing at the expense of active observation.
Not surprisingly, it all came to naught. In 1982 yet another study, under the
auspices of State's Bureau of Intelligence and Research, was launched.

a whole, in spite of slow and expensive efforts to improve them, are barely remaining constant, relative to needs. This poses a real dilemma. In the field, language competence lags behind what the Department of State itself regards as minimally desirable: as of 1979, only 65 percent (858 of 1,320) of all language-designated positions at posts abroad were occupied by officers with the acceptable level of competence in the *appropriate* language. To be fair, one needs to acknowledge improvement over the years: in 1972, 567 of 1,031 such positions were filled by those who fully met the requirements. Thus, seven years later there were 290 more positions filled appropriately; but since 281 more positions were designated, there was no major change in the percentage of compliance. The 1980 figure was 70 percent.[43] But the fact remains that this deficiency in language skills forces undue reliance upon foreign nationals, and naturally impedes the accurate reporting and assessment of new developments. Of particular concern is that in many cases the most acute shortages of adequately trained personnel involve languages which may be the most important, because of the countries involved. In Iran, the Shah was overthrown in 1979, there were only three Farsi speakers on the entire embassy staff.[44]

Much the same is true of country and area knowledge (as opposed to language). Given the general background emphasis in FSO recruitment, it is only accidental that new officers will have had any extensive area studies in their academic background; and given the oft-cited "needs of the Service," it is by no means certain that officers with such knowledge will be assigned to the

[43] Data provided by the Department of State, Foreign Service Institute, 1980. The 65% compliance is in the normal range, which has varied from 55% to 74% since 1963. The Department rates language competence on a scale of one to five for both reading and speaking ability: "5/5" would be a native-born speaker or equivalent, while "3/3" means good fluency and command, which is the standard for the requirements of a language-designated position to be met.

[44] Szulc, "Shaking Up the C.I.A.," p. 16. For a later but not dissimilar critique of the language and knowledge weaknesses, this time relating to the problems of the American Embassy in Cairo in determining the true situation in the hours after Egyptian President Sadat was shot on October 6, 1981, see Loren Jenkins, "Watch on the Nile: Massive U.S. Embassy Falters at Fact-Finding," *Washington Post*, October 19, 1981.

countries they know most about. Nor does in-house training suffice; most area studies courses at the Foreign Service Institute are limited to two weeks and in any event are focused on broad geographic areas rather than individual countries. The one exception is that hard language courses do contain one-half day per week (for forty-four weeks) of area studies instruction.[45] The only alternative is experience gained on the job, during assignment in a particular country. Knowledge acquired in such fashion may be practical, but is difficult to place in a larger context.

This lack of effective training has led one distinguished career officer—perhaps not accidentally, one who has had extensive service outside State—to propose a

> fairly intensive course of modest length (eight weeks) aimed at expanding area competence, but also at relating that competence to, or rooting it in, broad disciplinary and conceptual frameworks and analytical methodologies. My argument is that this kind of synthesis is necessary if practitioners are to be effective in any geographic area. Knowledge about a geographic area is not *per se* very useful unless it can be related to something larger than itself—comparatively (to data on other areas) and/or conceptually (to social science theories and disciplines).[46]

Eight weeks would not competent analysts make, but it may be all that is possible given State's resources. Unlike the Defense Department, State has never had sufficient staff positions or financial resources to devote to extensive training, beyond that given in languages (where by most opinions FSI does very well indeed) and, more recently, the twenty-six-week course in economics mentioned earlier. Even the limited amount of mid-career extended-term training that is possible—the senior seminar in

[45] See any issue of *State Magazine* published by the Department for a list of upcoming Foreign Service Institute courses which will sustain this point. The innovative professional development program adopted by FSI in 1980-81 gave emphasis to language training and management and analytic/policy skills, but did little by way of area studies enrichment.

[46] Viron P. Vaky, "Training for Latin American Assignments," unpublished, 1972, p. 2.

foreign policy, university years, and, since 1981, the five-month mid-career course for newly tenured FSO's—is dissipated. This training is not properly applied to the areas that need attention, through the chronic inability of the system to make follow-on assignments so that those in training can tailor their study programs to their next assignment. (As of 1981, attempts were being made to correct this situation.) Even worse, managers, as usual anywhere, are reluctant to release the very best officers from operational duties for training.[47]

Thus a major weakness exists in the Foreign Service's central core of skills. Specialists in functional issues, if the need is great, can be obtained from other parts of the government; but truly competent and practical area specialists (as opposed to academics) will only be found by accident outside State, AID, and USIA. This makes it doubly essential that the Foreign Service maintain necessary area expertise, and the language ability which goes hand in hand with it. This may suggest FSO careers which are focused more sharply, at least for political and economic officers, on one area or region.

Yet there is another aspect of area and country familiarity which also must be taken into account. One complaint about the Foreign Service heard throughout its existence is that it is subject to parochialism or to "clientism"; that is, particular officers tend to resist almost instinctively any policy which may cause difficulties with the government to which they are accredited. It is further argued that the narrower the experience and the greater the exposure to one country or area, the more likely this is to occur. This sort of parochialism "distorts the way we make decisions more than it imposes any clear direction on our foreign policy. We may disagree about whether the U.S. should ever intervene . . . but we should be able to agree to make those policy choices with all the logic and clearheadedness we can muster."[48] The fact that FSO's understand Chinese and China, or Arabic and the

---

[47] This problem, of course, is present in almost all organizations, and can be one of the major impediments to serious career and executive development activities.

[48] Roger Morris, "Rooting for the Other Team: Clientism in the Foreign Service," *Washington Monthly* 5 (November 1973), 42.

Arabs, does not automatically mean that they cannot be tough and effective in using that knowledge to further U.S. interests, but it does pose dangers and, unless countered, allows other agencies, out of self-interest, to accuse the FSO's of such clientism.[49] This will pose increasingly greater problems in the future, if the Foreign Service does in fact accept the advocacy role mentioned in Chapter I of ensuring that foreign considerations are not ignored in overall national policy-making.

In 1974, Secretary of State Kissinger became so concerned with parochialism and in-breeding in the regional "sub-clubs" of the Foreign Service that he began the Global Outlook Program (less elegantly, GLOP). It required that 20 percent of all assignments be made to a new geographic area (i.e., from a European post to a Latin American one, or vice versa), rather than within the same area, as had typically been the case.[50] Such a policy would provide a more varied pattern of experience for the average officer but would be likely to exacerbate the problems of developing deep area competence. Whether it is possible to strike the proper balance using the current personnel system is open to serious question.

Executives and Policy Generalists

It has already been argued how critical and difficult it is—and will be—to find top career leadership for staffing foreign affairs. That diagnosis is easier than correction is amply shown by the lucid summary of Ambassador Samuel D. Berger, which dates from the early 1960's:

> The broader the interest of the specialist, the greater his capacity and initiative, the more he can contribute to the op-

[49] Familiarity with China is of course the most obvious example. See E. J. Kahn, Jr., *The China Hands: America's Foreign Service Officers and What Befell Them* (New York: Viking, 1973; Penguin edition, 1976), and John Paton Davies, Jr., *Dragon by the Tail: American, British, Japanese, and Russian Encounters with China and One Another* (New York: W. W. Norton, 1972).

[50] "Secretary Decides on New Assignments Policy," *Department of State News Letter* 154 (March 1974), 4. By 1981, "GLOP" was officially dead, but the philosophy continued to be attended to when possible in assignments.

erations of an embassy and the higher he can aspire in the Foreign Service.

Conversely, the senior generalist who is familiar with all problems but has failed to develop a deep and critical grasp of any of the major fields will lack the self-confidence required to make independent judgments, evaluations, and decisions that he is called on to make week in and week out in a variety of fields. . . .

Stated in another way, the great need in the Foreign Service is for more officers at the top—whether they are generalists or specialists—who have drive and the kind of experience that enables them to relate one field to another.[51]

There are many indications that this ideal type of officer is not widely found. Destler, for example, has pinpointed one particularly difficult problem:

. . . Presidents do not normally have at their disposal analyses explicitly relating foreign policy choices to domestic political realities. To relate them *ad hoc* is to some degree the responsibility of all politically appointed leaders. But foreign policy officials seem to perform this task incompletely, reluctantly, and with a sense that such "low politics" ought not to sully the pursuit of high diplomacy.[52]

Within State there is the same concern about the capability of the senior FSO in policy development, and attempts to correct the problem insofar as training can do the job are an inherent part of the previously mentioned career development program begun in 1980. Whether this will suffice, however, must be viewed with skepticism. The Executive Seminar in Foreign Policy, for example, an intensive course for prospective senior officers of State and other foreign affairs agencies, was designed for the needs of

[51] Samuel D. Berger, "Specialist vs. Generalist in the Foreign Service," Memorandum for Senate Subcommittee on National Security and International Operations, Committee on Government Operations, *Specialist and Generalists: A Selection of Readings* (Washington, D.C.: GPO, 1968), p. 67. See also Chap. IV.

[52] Destler, "National Security Advice to U.S. Presidents," p. 172.

the "policy generalist," but it has been uneven in quality, its impact has never been professionally evaluated, and in any event there is considerable skepticism about whether the most talented individuals have been assigned as students.

One interesting thesis advanced to the Murphy Commission was that the competition for promotion and the relatively small number of demanding positions causes FSO's to avoid risks, in order to ensure their future careers and assignments, and that the resulting failure to be creative and innovative in earlier stages of their careers leaves them ill equipped for senior responsibilities.[53]

The picture is virtually the same with respect to the suitability of FSO's as managers, a question which has received considerably more attention. Concern with the "failure rate" of FSO's in their first significant managerial positions led, a few years back, to the establishment of a course at the Foreign Service Institute for prospective Deputy Chiefs of Mission (DCM's) designed to give them, or at least sensitize them to the need for, some of the "missing" skills. Even with this course, unverified folklore in the Department holds that the failure rate of new DCM's is about 40 percent.[54] As with failures in area expertise and in policy-making, the 1980-81 plan for career development was designed to address this problem intensively.

In spite of numerous studies concluding they were needed, as of late 1982 no effective executive development or "policy generalist" development programs existed in the foreign affairs community, if by those terms one means programs which combine close control of assignments with appropriate training, directed to senior responsibilities rather than to immediate circumstances. This is in spite of the fact that such was intended by the Foreign

[53] Summarized from Jonathan Dean, "Some Remarks on the Foreign Service as a Profession," typescript submitted to the Murphy Commission February 11, 1975, pp.1, 9, 9-10. Dean is a successful senior career officer.

[54] Based on discussions with senior officials at FSI, 1981. The 40% failure rate figure has been used in personnel and training circles since at least the mid-70's, in the author's personal knowledge, but he has been unable, in repeated efforts, to discover documented evidence supporting it. Nevertheless, it continues to receive wide acceptance, suggesting there is considerable validity to the assertion, if not to a precise figure.

Service Act of 1946, and for that matter of 1980. In this lack the foreign affairs agencies are not alone, for in general "Executive Development in the U.S. Federal Service . . . began only in the recent past and its subsequent growth has been less than precocious."[55]

The usual assumption, evidence to the contrary notwithstanding, continues to be that the normal generalist oriented, rotational career pattern will provide enough qualified individuals and that to the extent it does not, it will be possible to obtain help for short periods of time from the "outside." But several recent attempts to establish comprehensive career development programs have produced minimal results, as already noted. There is justifiable skepticism about their utility, at least in the milieu of the Foreign Service and the Department of State.

Most executive development programs in the private sector,[56] as well as some in government, such as that of the Central Intelligence Agency,[57] are based on "star" systems, where "waterwalkers" or "high-flyers" are identified and their careers managed separately from those of other employees as long as they remain among the chosen. These programs, however, usually depend upon secrecy in order to avoid reducing morale among those not included, and as early as 1976 it was concluded that such a procedure would not be acceptable in State. Since the Foreign Service was already an elite, a superelite would be too

---

[55] William T. McDonald, "Executive Development in the Federal Service (with emphasis on foreign affairs executives)," study prepared for the Murphy Commission, Appendix P to the report, "Personnel for Foreign Affairs," Appendix Volume VI, p. 273. In apparent recognition of this, the Civil Service Reform Act of 1978, which created the Senior Executive Service (SES), gave major emphasis to executive development, and Office of Personnel Management (OPM) implementing regulations favored candidates for the SES who were "graduates" of a formal executive development program.

[56] Theodore P. LeVino and William K. Cordier, "Executive Manpower Systems and Overseas Assignment Practices in Multinational Corporations," Apendix P to Murphy Commission Report, Appendix Volume VI, pp. 224-31.

[57] Interview conducted by the author with CIA management officials, August 1977, in conjunction with the work of the Federal Personnel Management Project, which did preparatory work for the Civil Service Reform Act of 1978.

demoralizing.[58] In any event, the Foreign Service needs to develop the "mass" of its personnel to do the "mass" of its jobs, and thus, even if feasible, it is far from clear that "star-systems" provide the appropriate model.[59]

In short, while the deficiencies in competence are admitted, the solutions are tentative and at best in the formative stages. Nowhere is this demonstrated better than in the current failure to gain agreement about which qualities are needed for success in carrying senior responsibilities, be they managerial or policy oriented. A recent example is the disagreement surrounding the results of a 1977 attempt to analyze those special competences which have distinguished superior from average performance in the Foreign Service, in order that they might be recognized and fostered. During interviews with the firm conducting the study, members of the Service chose seventeen competences as particularly relevant. When a validation study using similar methodology was conducted, however, a largely different set of competences was selected—also by members of the Service![60] To compound the problem, there is reason to believe that in each case the choices of what it takes to succeed were based on static conceptions of what had led to superior performance in the past, and did not reflect future needs, which might be considerably different.

A related problem, and one that exists throughout the government, is the assumption that senior managers are and should be essentially interchangeable,[61] and that functional differentiation

---

[58] Carol C. Laise, Director General of the Foreign Service, unpublished memorandum to members of State's Board of Professional Development, December 3, 1976.

[59] Paul Boeker is the source of this point.

[60] The initial study was conducted by McBer Associates, the validation study by Torrey Whitman of State's Bureau of Personnel. Although the differences in opinion were never reconciled, the McBer study was accepted by the Department and became the basis of a number of changes in performance evaluation in following years. For more details, see Chap. V, notes 21 and 22.

[61] This viewpoint, for example, was clearly dominant in the development of the Senior Executive Service concept in the Civil Service Reform Act of 1978, which placed primary emphasis on managerial competence rather than on specific knowledge related to the functions of the executive's organization.

among them, on the basis of the particular activity being managed, counts for much less than general managerial competence.[62]

There *are* changes that could be made in the foreign affairs personnel systems which could substantially ameliorate the problems discussed in this chapter. First, however, it is necessary to probe the causes of these problems more deeply.

---

[62] The extreme version of this point of view was perhaps best exemplified by an Office Director in State's Bureau of Personnel who told the author in 1976 that each of the forty to fifty (on average) Career Ministers in the Foreign Service should be—and were—qualified for *every* position at that level, whether as Assistant Secretary for any of the five geographic bureaus in the Department or any of the functional bureaus; as senior officers in management, personnel, or administration; or as Ambassador to any of the major nations of the world. This is the generalist concept run amok.

CHAPTER THREE

Obstacles to Reform:
Sources of Existing Weaknesses

The failures of foreign affairs personnel systems to meet current needs cannot be laid to a single cause, nor are they simple to correct. They are a combined result of tradition and of the understandable need of system managers to deal with what is, rather than what should be.

In the first place, there is a fundamental ambiguity of roles: What needs to be done, and who should do it?

Second, this is made worse by fragmentation, not only from agency to agency but within them, especially in State. The result is unnecessary complexity in structure and in management, which does not, however, bring the plausible reward of diversity—the ability to adapt. This fragmentation, in turn, results in a form of tribalism, manifested in an internal us-against-them mentality.

Third, although there are exceptions, most of the personnel systems which serve the foreign affairs community have been indifferently and unprofessionally managed.

Fourth, in spite of exceptions allowed the Foreign Service from laws and regulations applying to the competitive Civil Service, it can be as inflexible and unresponsive to new circumstances as the latter, primarily because of a noticeable lack of long-range vision.

Finally, the socialization of the Foreign Service has led to self-serving careerist attitudes which serve neither the interests of the public nor those of its members; in turn, criticism of this situation results in a decline of morale and comradeship, and a less accommodating relationship between the Service as an institution and the individuals within it. And, somewhat paradoxically, it also leads to a misplaced sense of elitism, which has no functional purpose in today's world.

This chapter examines these seriously debilitating problems.

ROLE AMBIGUITY

To the casual observer, the Foreign Service of the United States may appear to be among the best established governmental professions, with its high visibility and extensive traditions.[1] This is a doubtful conclusion. Today there are serious questions about its ability to adapt to changing circumstances, about the degree to which it will be able to establish or retain exclusive functions, and therefore about its future role. Many of the same questions arise with respect to the much larger group of government officials outside the Foreign Service who also devote their careers to foreign affairs.

Such uncertainty is not new. The modern Foreign Service did not come into being until the Rogers Act of 1924, which as has been discussed amalgamated the previously separate Diplomatic and Consular Services and provided the basis for the development of a self-consciously elite corps of generalists. By most accounts, the Service was well equipped to carry out its limited responsibilities until the beginning of World War II. Wartime is never auspicious for diplomats, and by 1945 the Foreign Service faced a pressing need to rebuild (attrition and the suspension of recruitment had considerably reduced its size) and to find an appropriate place in the new world of postwar diplomacy. The chosen instrument of this renewal was the Foreign Service Act of 1946, under which, with some amendments, it operated until 1981.[2]

The Act was designed to provide a *foreign* service equipped to undertake diplomatic responsibilities abroad. It was however, lacking with respect to what occurred at home, and this became a critical flaw as the number of agencies involved in foreign affairs expanded, as the issues became more technical and more closely related to the domestic scene, and as modern communications and

[1] This section is adapted from Bacchus, "Foreign Affairs Officials," pp. 641-50. (See note 1, Chap. II.)

[2] The most useful sources for the early years of the Foreign Service are Warren F. Ilchman, *Professional Diplomacy in the United States 1779-1939: A Study in Administrative History* (Chicago: University of Chicago Press, 1961), and Barnes and Morgen, *The Foreign Service of the United States*. For the history of the Foreign Service Act of 1946, see Stein, "The Foreign Service Act of 1946," introduction, n. 2.

the need for closer coordination inevitably shifted the focal point of policy to Washington and away from the Chief of Mission in the field.

Part of the reason that there was little attention given to headquarters in 1946, as opposed to the overseas missions, was that at that time the State Department was still blessed with a very strong Civil Service component in its staff, who had a major impact as the new design for making and carrying out policy was being developed. At this point, at least, the differences between the Washington and overseas roles were still clear, and the personnel systems reflected it. This distinction, however, has been complicated for the State Department at least since the Wriston program of the mid-1950's, which moved many domestic Civil Service employees of the Department into the FSO corps, partly in order to open positions in Washington for what was then virtually an expatriate Foreign Service, the better to "re-Americanize" them. Since that time, a large majority of the key career positions in State have been filled by FSO's, serving on tours of limited duration. While there have been many outstanding exceptions, FSO's for the most part have never been completely at ease with these responsibilities, especially those whose entire career has been in the Foreign Service.[3] Similarly, many of the former domestic employees who were integrated into the FSO corps did not prove to be particularly suited to the demands of a diplomatic career overseas, and many of them were "selected-out" of the Service.[4]

FSO careers are built upon short assignments with varying functional requirements and rotation among a number of countries abroad, and quite different responsibilities in Washington. Pri-

[3] See Bacchus, *Foreign Policy and the Bureaucratic Process*, pp. 229-30, for a discussion of the possibility that "atypical FSO's" (those whose careers feature experience outside the Foreign Service rather than exclusively within it) may be more likely to succeed in the Washington environment.

[4] However, many others were extremely successful and in later years filled many of the most senior positions in the Department and overseas with distinction. This may suggest that innate quality, rather than career experience, is the most critical attribute for success.

mary emphasis is given to the career as a whole, with less to the expertise necessary for strong performance in any single position. In the best of circumstances, this produces broad-gauged individuals with diverse experiences who are fully equipped as senior officers to deal with many kinds of situations. Such a rotational pattern is also necessary to keep those who represent the nation abroad in touch with their own society, to prevent the development of "clientism" from extended stays at a single foreign post, and, increasingly, to prevent undue hardship for members of the Service and their families, since many posts are not particularly desirable places to live.[5]

In contrast, most of those in the career foreign affairs community (other than FSO's) specialize in one area of related policy issues or occasionally a country or geographic area. Whereas most FSO's enter at the bottom, recruitment for these others can be at any level, and is on the basis of qualifications, including both relevant academic training and job experience for the duties of specific positions. Each change of position is voluntary and is generally made by selection among several qualified candidates. Service is likely to be in the same locale throughout the career (usually Washington) and, more often than not, in the same agency or department. At the same time, there is some movement to and from those parts of the private sector concerned with the same range of policy issues. All this tends to produce experts who have deep familiarity with a relatively narrow set of related problems, but often at the price of inability to accommodate conflicting perspectives. Moreover, they tend to develop a constricted view of national interests. The frame of reference is that of a functional speciality practiced in an international affairs context; in contrast,

[5] Some posts are designated as hardship posts by the Department, and an additional increment of pay, from 10 to 25%, is added during service at such a post. The amount of the differential is determined by a point system which takes into account such factors as climate, isolation, the possibility of terrorism, educational, recreational, and medical services available, and general living conditions. As of September 1982, 128 State posts of a total of 253 were eligible for the differential for hardship (31 at 10%, 24 at 15%, 38 at 20%, and 35 at 25%). The 1980 Act added additional allowances to encourage service at such posts and to account for dangerous circumstances at some. Figures supplied by the Department's Allowances Staff, Bureau of Administration.

for most FSO's that context, or some geographically defined part of it, is the paramount occupational interest. A striking example of the orientation of FSO's comes from their self-chosen institutional affiliation. Rather than saying, "I work for the State Department," as others would mention Treasury or Commerce, their answer is most likely to be, "I'm in the Foreign Service." In short, the overseas career is still the primary focus of the Foreign Service; problems result from the need for FSO's to participate in domestic policy-making as well.

The two quite different kinds of foreign affairs occupations ought not to be in conflict, for both are essential. What has been unfortunate has been the tendency to downplay the differences between the two by trying to force both groups into a common (i.e., Foreign Service) mold, or sometimes to deny the importance of the domestic-based group of functional experts.

> But the functions of diplomacy are quite different from the analytical and conceptual requirements for the staff development (in Washington) of an aggressive, intelligent and forthcoming foreign policy. There is no reason to believe that those who are able diplomats are automatically also good foreign policy-makers or analysts, and vice versa. Yet the system operates in a way which shifts officers from one role to the other with the implicit assumption that the mind-sets, experience and qualities required for each role are about the same. The Foreign Service has been predominantly field oriented. . . . The system tends to reward the DCM [Deputy Chief of Mission] in a minor post more than the special or staff assistant to a critical officer. But the national interest requires absolutely first rate staff work for the principals, whereas we can stand more than one idiot DCM without adverse impact on our world posture. . . . In any case, whatever the emphasis, a conscious awareness of the distinction between the two roles is essential.[6]

The foreign affairs community requires a total personnel system which accommodates and values the different contributions each group can bring to bear on increasingly complicated policy issues.

[6] Vaky, "Training for Latin American Assignments," p. 11.

It should be possible to recognize the need for diversity of function without losing unity of purpose.

Confusion over what two very different groups of professionals should do in two very different locales is made worse by another form of role ambiguity which complicates the development of more effective personnel systems: the ambiguity in organizational responsibilities of the various parts of government. As long as federal personnel systems are for all intents and purposes agency based, with no central mechanism overseeing recruitment, assignment, or other major personnel functions for all, each agency must staff itself with its own needs paramount, since there exists no easy way to shift employees from one agency to another to match skills with requirements.[7]

To take one example, the staffing required for the State Department would be very different under three possible roles often considered in studies of functions of the Department. If the Department is ever to be truly dominant over the whole range of foreign policy, it would obviously have to have a staff with great functional competence to address all the kinds of issues described earlier. If the Department is not to be dominant but nevertheless to have a significant staff role to the President as the only organization below the White House with the overall function of policy synthesis, it would need somewhat less functional competence, since it would be sharing responsibility with other departments and agencies; but it would still need enough to comprehend the product of other departments and to guard against parochialism in other agencies. Finally, if its function is to be primarily in the traditional diplomatic area, it would need relatively little functional expertise, since other agencies can provide it, and should concentrate its staffing on country and area related political and

[7] The Department of State proposed draft language for the new Foreign Service Act which would have mandated greater uniformity among the agencies using the Foreign Service system, but this was fought vociferously by USICA and AID, who wished to preserve as much operational autonomy as possible. Congressman Jim Leach introduced an amendment for a uniform Senior Foreign Service during House "mark-up" of the bill, but was defeated on the basis of a letter from these two agencies, joined by Agriculture and Commerce. The new Act should allow a modest improvement in compatibility among the various agencies, but will not go to the heart of the problem discussed here. (See Chaps. VI and VII.)

economic skills. A similar kind of difference in requirements for staffing can be projected with respect to variations in responsibilities overseas, depending on what proportion and what kinds of staff are to be provided by each agency. But without a firm choice of which role is to be played, it becomes difficult to cast the actors needed.

Unfortunately, there sometimes has been a tendency in State to ignore the neccessity to choose, most often through denying the legitimacy of the expanded range of issues that now raise international questions, and thereby avoiding the problem. Viron P. Vaky points out one common form of denial:

> There is a parochialism in our bureaucracy . . . one quality which characterizes State officers is their tendency to confuse leadership with exclusivity, i.e., to seek to stake out their own operational turf and exclude others from any kind of authority over the subject matter dealt with. This is exemplified by the kinds of comments we hear so often: "We have to protect the President (or the Secretary) from himself; let's not call a meeting (or tell them about this) because DOD will use the occasion to raise points we don't want raised."[8]

And Bayless Manning sees the same theme in another variation: "It seems to be the vision of every old State Department hand that foreign affairs belong to the State Department and that all other U.S. officials, appointed and elected, ought to stay out of such matters because they do not understand them and will simply mush them up."[9]

Even when State's different roles are recognized, conclusions are sometimes misdrawn. For example, after exhorting the Foreign Service to concentrate more on its overseas responsibilities and less on Washington and domestic politics at home, correctly citing the importance of the overseas role and the Service's comparative advantage for playing it, Peter F. Krogh downplays the importance of a major policy-making role for the Department of State, largely because he assumes that the Foreign Service and the Department

---

[8] Vaky, "Training for Latin American Assignments," p. 11.
[9] Manning, "The Congress, the Executive and Intermestic Affairs," p. 314.

are identical.[10] But today's diverse requirements almost certainly mean that different competences, held by different groups of career officials, are needed.

COMPLEXITY AND FRAGMENTATION

Government personnel systems have become so complex that it is almost impossible to identify all their components, or even to track with precision specific groups of people performing the same work across agency lines.[11] The foreign affairs community is, of course, a much smaller group of federal employees, but only marginally different in this respect.

In part because of these difficulties, personnel system structure—the organization, procedures, and mechanisms established to carry out personnel functions—for foreign affairs has been the subject of continuing concern and study throughout the past three decades. The implications of the changes in international relations described in Chapter I have not gone unnoticed, nor have operational personnel problems, but changes in the personnel system devised to meet the new conditions either have not resolved the difficulties or were never placed into effect. For example, the partial amalgamation of the Foreign Service and the State Department's home service following the 1954 Wriston report never achieved the desired results, nor did the effort in the early 1970's to establish a corps of specialists, primarily in support functions, to bridge the overseas-domestic line. And the "family of compatible Foreign Affairs Services" for the several foreign affairs agencies proposed by the Herter Committee in 1962 never materialized.[12]

[10] Peter F. Krogh, "Foreign Service should be more attentive to diplomacy," Speech to the Council on Foreign Relations, date not given. Reprinted in *Department of State News Letter* 195 (November 1977), 9-11.

[11] The author discovered, for example, while working on the Federal Personnel Management Project in 1977, that nowhere did there exist an inclusive list of all personnel systems with statutory or administrative exemption from the competitive service. (See also Chap. IV, note 46.)

[12] The Wriston Report is published as *Toward A Stronger Foreign Service*, Report of the Secretary of State's Public Committee on Personnel, Department of State Publication 5458 (Washington, D.C.: GPO, 1954); that of the Herter

Perhaps nowhere in personnel is there more theological argument than about system structure; defenders of good government and the merit principle (i.e., rank-in-job) are convinced that any system which differs from that norm is illegitimate,[13] while advocates of separate systems such as the Foreign Service take satisfaction at being different from the common (in both meanings) system and are terrified at the prospect of being subject to laws, regulations, and oversight from the Office of Personnel Management, which is not a part of the "family."[14]

An important starting point in reviewing current complexity is a survey of career professionals engaged full time in foreign policy activities (omitting administrative and support functions). While the summary in Table 2 is dated, it is virtually the only comprehensive effort that has been made to gather such data, and it required a major effort on the part of the staff of the Murphy Commission. This figure shows about 18,000 professionals, and another 2,100 executives, exclusive of intelligence agencies, working in foreign affairs. In State, AID, USIA, ACDA (Arms Control and Disarmament Agency), and the Peace Corps, these employees were primarily in the Foreign Service system; elsewhere in government they were in the Civil Service, for the most part, with a few being in other excepted systems.

Committee as *Personnel for the New Diplomacy*, Report of the Committee on Foreign Affairs Personnel (Washington, D.C.: Carnegie Endowment for International Peace, 1962). A fuller listing of postwar reform efforts can be found in William I. Bacchus, "Diplomacy for the 70's: An Afterview and Appraisal," *American Political Science Review* 68 (June 1974), 736-48, and especially note 3, 736-38.

[13] See, for example, the diatribe of O. Glenn Stahl, about the Foreign Service and its rank-in-person system, in "Of Jobs and Men," Address to the Conference on Personnel Administration sponsored by the Indian Institute of Public Administration, March 7, 1968, reprinted in *Public Administration Review* 29 (July/August 1969), 379-84.

[14] This type of argument abounded in late 1975 and early 1976, when Carol Laise and some but not all of her staff were attempting to force the decision for a dual (Foreign and Civil Service) system not dissimilar in concept from that which was eventually legislated in the Foreign Service Act of 1980. This articulate and sometimes impassioned opposition played a significant part in the reluctance of senior managers of the Department to make a final decision on the structure issue in 1976 (see Chap. VI).

TABLE 2
Employment in International Activities (1975 Levels)

Department or Agency	Total Americans			Professionals			Executives		
	U.S.	O/S	Total	U.S.	O/S	Total	U.S.	O/S	Total
A. Foreign affairs agencies									
State Department	6,541	5,581	12,122	4,091	3,794	7,885	562	479	1,041
AID	2,876	1,613	4,489	2,043	1,394	3,437	241	282	523
USIA	3,242	943	4,185	2,170	821	2,991	154	111	265
ACDA	208	—	208	88	—	88	42	—	42
Peace Corps (ACTION)	175	193	368	96	185	281	8	8	16
Subtotal A	13,042	8,330	21,372	8,488	6,194	14,682	1,007	880	1,887
B. Departments and agencies with major international activities									
Agriculture	792	131	923	423	105	528	9	11	20
Commerce	1,023	15	1,038	807	14	821	19	0	19
Defense	211	49	260	109	28	137	19	5	24
Labor	165	—	165	89	—	89	4	—	4
Treasury	337	34	371	165	20	185	42	7	49
Executive Office of the President	254	—	254	175	—	175	49	—	49
• NSC	(70)	—	(70)	(47)	—	(47)	(12)	—	(12)
• Council on International Economic Policy	(31)	—	(31)	(21)	—	(21)	(11)	—	(11)
• Special Representative for Trade Negotiations	(45)	—	(45)	(30)	—	(30)	(11)	—	(11)

	(106)	—	(106)	(76)	—	(76)	(15)	—	(15)
• OMB	(2)	—	(2)	(1)	—	(1)	(—)	—	(—)
• Council of Economic Advisors									
HEW	293	51	344	116	44	160	6	—	6
HUD	24	—	24	14	—	14	2	—	2
Interior	71	62	133	43	56	99	2	1	3
Justice	26	334	360	17	263	280	1	5	6
Transportation	164	—	164	104	—	104	16	—	16
EPA	32	—	32	20	—	20	1	—	1
Export-Import Bank	429	1	430	267	1	268	14	—	14
International Trade Commission									
Inter-American Foundation	380	—	380	237	—	237	12	—	12
FEA/ERDA	74	—	74	45	—	45	3	—	3
Foreign Claims Settlement Commission	99	11	110	56	6	62	13	2	15
NASA									
National Science Foundation	15	18	33	7	17	24	3	—	3
Overseas Private Investment Corporation (OPIC)	25	14	39	15	14	29	3	1	4
Smithsonian Institution	101	3	104	58	3	61	9	—	9
Subtotal B	113	—	113	46	—	46	9	—	9
	11	—	11	7	—	7			
GRAND TOTAL	4,639	723	5,362	2,820	571	3,391	236	32	268
	17,681	9,053	26,734	11,308	6,765	18,073	1,243	912	2,155

SOURCE: James W. Clark, "Foreign Affairs Personnel Management," Appendix P to the *Report of the Commission on the Organization of the Government for the Conduct of Foreign Policy* (Murphy Commission), Appendix Volume VI (Washington, D.C.: U.S. Government

Even these figures understate the numbers involved in foreign affairs, for they exclude support personnel whose activities are not per se in international affairs but whose efforts make it possible for the others to perform. (For the foreign affairs agencies, many or most of these supporting personnel are included in the Foreign Service system, thereby adding to the complexity.) Nor do the figures include individuals who are the most difficult of all to identify but who will be increasingly critical: those whose areas of responsibility by all traditional measures are domestic but whose actions may nevertheless have major import for international relations, in a world of increasing interdependence.

In response to the question "Who is exercising overall management for this employee population?" the honest answer is, no one. The fragmentation that exists today has resulted from the perceived needs of individual agencies and the incremental actions of the Congress, rather than from any rational design. Even those few agencies which used the Foreign Service Act of 1946 as their basic personnel authority did not employ anything resembling a common personnel approach. The 1980 Act was expressly intended as a partial remedy to this problem.

Even within agencies, there is unnecessary fragmentation. State has been fortunate in having both the Foreign and Civil Service authorities available to it, so in theory could use each system for what it could best accomplish. Instead, State by the 1970's was in limbo, with a dizzying array of systems and subsystems, distinguished not by purpose but by the convenience of the moment. Consider the personnel categories used until 1981 by the foreign affairs agencies, which also show subsequent changes (Table 3). With the possible exception of the FSO/FSIO group, none of these categories was clear-cut, nor used for an exclusive purpose. It was common, for example, for certain functional categories, such as Washington budget and fiscal positions, to be filled by members of a number of different pay plans: FSO, FSRU, FSR, FSS, and GS; and for the FSRU's and FSR's to be further divided among those who were available for assignment overseas, those who in theory were available but usually were not, and those who had been given a specific promise that they would serve only at home. The resulting confusion plagued almost all personnel operations.

TABLE 3

Personnel Categories: Before and After Foreign Service Act of 1980

Career Categories to 1980	Career Categories after 1980	
Worldwide service Foreign Service Officer(FSO)— State Foreign Service Information Officer(FSIO)—USIA	FSO—State, Commerce Agriculture, AID FSIO—USIA	Senior Foreign Service (SFS)— All 5 agencies
Foreign Service Staff(FSS)— State, AID, USIA Foreign Service Reserve Unlimited(FSRU)—State, USIA Foreign Service Reserve (Excepted Service)—AID General Schedule (Excepted Service)— Overseas Assignments—Agriculture	Foreign Service Specialists(FS or FP)— All 5 agencies	
Domestic service General Schedule(GS) —All 5 agencies FSS—limited worldwide available—State FSS—domestic service only —State, USIA FSRU—limited worldwide available—State FSRU—domestic service only —State, USIA FSR(Excepted Service)— domestic service only—AID	GS—All 5 agencies	Senior Executive Service (SES)— All 5 agencies

NOTES: In addition to the career categories listed, both the old and new Foreign Service Acts contained provisions for noncareer, time-limited appointments. In the old system, there were limited FSR and FSS appointments; under the new, limited SFS and FS (FP) appointments. In both cases, such appointments, with a few exceptions, were limited to no more than five consecutive years.

The Foreign Service Act of 1980 has two main categories below the SFS level: FSO's (FSIO's for USIA), and "Members of the Foreign Service," for all other appointments. FSO's are to be generalists, others normally specialists. The name "Foreign Service Specialists" has come into informal use for the statutory "Members of the Service" category and is designated in shorthand as either FS (Foreign Service) or FP (Foreign Service Personnel), depending on the purpose at hand and the agency involved.

For example, in what categories should new employees be hired? How should promotion be managed, since some in a given occupational group were in a rank-in-person system, and some in a rank-in-job? How could effective human resources planning be accomplished? How could equity of treatment for all employees be ensured, since the FS and GS salary scales differed, since there were different sets of regulations on employees' rights to organize and to appeal, and since some FS employees were subject to selection-out while other FS employees and all GS employees were not?

State began a major but initially unsuccessful effort in 1975 to simplify this system, goaded by a loss of patience in Congress,[15] and this program finally came to fruition in late 1980 (see Chapter VI). Meanwhile, USIA, faced with a similar situation, in 1977 began to simplify its personnel structure, deciding to rely, after a period of transition, on the FSIO and FSR/RU groupings for generalists and specialists respectively who serve both at home and abroad, and GS for its domestic employees.[16]

AID's situation was even worse than that of State, since as a temporary agency it lacked the means to establish a true career system for its employees serving overseas. Rather, it was forced to use a variation of the FSR authority, which was intended to be a noncareer, short-term employment category; yet AID employees had served as FSR's for decades.[17] ACDA and the Peace

[15] Senator Claiborne Pell initially proposed an amendment to the FY 1976 Foreign Affairs Authorization bill which would have limited use of the Foreign Service Reserve Unlimited authority (FSRU) in State and USIA, especially for domestic-only employees, but he settled, after subsequent negotiations with the Department of State, for a requirement for a report within 120 days on steps taken to improve and simplify the Foreign Service personnel system. Unhappy with the tentative nature of the report he received, Pell inserted a formal reporting requirement in the FY 1977 authorization bill. See Chapter VI for fuller details and the subsequent history.

[16] USIA Circular #487D and 486F, December 19, 1977, "Revised Personnel System." (USIA became USICA, United States International Communication Agency, in 1979, but reverted to the older name in August 1982.)

[17] Through the previously mentioned foreign assistance reorganization, AID did become a permanent agency; and through the new Foreign Service Act it subsequently obtained statutory authority to use the full range of career and noncareer Foreign Service appointment authorities.

Corps are both small organizations, and each had its own ways
of using Civil Service and FSR authorities.[18]

The results of this excessively complicated pattern were, un-
surprisingly, negative. One outcome was tribalism, the development of an us-them mentality among the various subgroups of
employees. To the outsider, it sometimes appeared that almost
everyone felt part of a beleaguered minority, contending with
others for a share of the limited rewards the system could offer.
Some argued that the solution was a single system, so that there
would be less obvious distinctions among employees, while others
thought this would only compound the problem, adding an element
of hypocrisy to a system that the employees already did not trust.

MANAGERIAL SHORTCOMINGS

Another source of inadequacy in foreign affairs personnel systems is that their management is ill suited to the tasks at hand,
and poorly equipped to force necessary changes.

The management of foreign affairs, like the community itself,
has become highly fragmented. Nominally, personnel authority
belongs to the heads of the agencies and departments, but especially for the GS system, agencies are also subject to regulation
and oversight from the Office of Personnel Management. In the
government generally, improving personnel management is rarely
high on the priority list of senior officials, in part because of their
own short time-horizons compared with the extended period it
takes the effects of changes in personnel systems to be felt.[19] For
their part, agency personnel directors, who do feel responsible,
do not usually have the necessary authority, find themselves too

[18] The Peace Corps, which under the Peace Corps Act of 1965 cannot have
career personnel, uses Foreign Service limited appointments for periods of no
longer than five years. ACDA, while it could appoint its own noncareer members
of the Foreign Service, instead works through State, which appoints ACDA's
choices and then details them to ACDA. The purpose is economy, since ACDA
is too small an agency to warrant a full-fledged personnel office.

[19] For discussions of this problem, see Arch Patton, "Government's revolving
door: Turnover among key executives hits a rate no corporation could stand,"
Business Week 2298 (September 22, 1973), 12-13, and Heclo, *Government of
Strangers*. There has been little change since they wrote.

remote from the rest of agency management, and often, as they attempt to keep a highly complicated and overregulated system "legal," find themselves viewed as obstructionists or even enemies by transitory political leaders (especially at the time of turnover from one administration to another).

For the Foreign Service the situation has been, if anything, more unsatisfactory. Since the Foreign Service Act of 1946, the Director General of the Foreign Service has been charged with administering the Foreign Service, and as such has by law and practice been required to be a Foreign Service Officer of senior rank. Originally, the "Department's organizational structure reflected a clear line between the administration of the Foreign Service and the administration of the Departmental Service," but through the years both the Foreign Service and Civil Service components have come under the Director General.[20] This process culminated in 1975 with the formal establishment of a Bureau of Personnel, with the Director General as a de facto Assistant Secretary for Personnel in the Department's hierarchy[21] (although operationally this had happened earlier). Meanwhile, the almost inevitable result was that the Foreign Service ceased to function as a corps serving all the foreign affairs agencies. The 1946 Act also created a Board of the Foreign Service as an interagency, servicewide policy and governing mechanism, but it has only intermittently fulfilled such a role, and its senior members have often shown little interest.[22]

Even within the Department, the Director General has normally been unable to function as a forceful head of the personnel system. Administratively, he or she is subordinate to the Under Secretary

---

[20] "The Historical Role of the Director General in the Department of State," internal memorandum, Office of Personnel, Department of State, February 27, 1975, p. 2. This memorandum is also the source for some of the other details in this paragraph.

[21] This change was announced in a Departmental notice of November 21, 1975, effective November 23.

[22] The Board later became nonstatutory, with its functions transferred to the President in 1965, and a reconstituted Board established under E. O. 11264. It was again made statutory by the Foreign Service Act of 1980, and an effort made to clarify its role. Under the new Act, Section 210, it was to be purely a policy advisory body.

of State for Management,[23] and has not always found a sympathetic ear at that level for necessary changes, given the primarily political orientation of "M."

Other circumstances have also had a negative impact on the DG's ability to manage the personnel system effectively. First, although a number of innovative officers have been named as Director General through the years, there has been such a siege mentality that incumbents tend to become "Protector General," attempting to shield the Service they know and love from the buffeting of outside forces. Unfortunately, this has often carried over into excessive resistance to necessary change.

Second, the ceremonial and operational responsibilities of the Director General inhibit sustained attention to longer-term management requirements. Every U.S. Ambassador feels it is his right to deal directly with the DG on what he perceives as his major personnel requirements, even if all the work on personnel assignments is done elsewhere; and there is a constant round of swearings-in, retirements, and other ceremonial occasions, not to mention extended field travel to "show the flag" to the troops overseas. And if the DG has further career aspirations, he or she must spend more time maintaining contacts with senior officials on the policy side of the Department.

Third, by law, the Director General must be a member of the Senior Foreign Service. Reflecting both custom and the balance of power in the Service, he or she will almost inevitably have made a mark by substantive work in the political and/or economic fields rather than as a manager. Yet the complication of staffing 253 foreign posts (as of May 1, 1982) and some 9,000 Foreign Service positions in Washington and overseas as well as dealing with a home Civil Service cadre that numbers about 4,000, and approximately 10,000 foreign nationals abroad,[24] is a major man-

---

[23] Prior to 1978, the Deputy Under Secretary for Management. The change was made by the Congress in the Department's FY 1979 Authorization Act.

[24] Number of posts provided by the Bureau of Personnel; figures on Foreign and Civil Service positions derived from Departmental personnel data as of September 1, 1981. Joan M. Clark, DG beginning in 1981 and a senior administrative officer, is a lone exception to the generalization about DG's being political or economic officers.

agerial undertaking, especially in a system which must devote major resources to moving large numbers of people quite frequently, unlike the more static GS system. Add to this the now inevitable imperatives for change, and one is forced to the conclusion that Directors General are ill equipped and poorly supported for the responsibilities they face.

This could be partially overcome were it not for the fourth impediment, rapid managerial turnover. Since 1946, when the system came into effect, sixteen individuals have held the position of Director General (as of early 1983), for an average tenure of little more than two years. By the time a conscientious officer is on top of the job, it is time to move on. There is no greater continuity at the next levels. Of the twenty key personnel managerial positions in the Bureau of Personnel as of the fall of 1982, fourteen were filled by rotational FSO's, including all but two of the key policy jobs—and only five of these had been in the Bureau for as long as two years. Four of these five, however, were in new jobs, and the fifth was still there only because he had agreed to a one-year extension of his tour. All six of the key "continuity" officials were new within five years,[25] and this pattern would be essentially the same for any period in the last fifteen years. Thus, in a very complicated managerial situation, most critical positions are filled by inexperienced officers who will not remain long enough to achieve full effectiveness.

The same problems plague Personnel Directors of the other foreign affairs agencies. These officials also tend not to be personnel experts; like the Director General, they tend to come from the mainstream of their agencies. As such, they serve short tours and then move on to other assignments.

At the operating levels, there is also a shortage of trained personnel specialists. For example, during a typical period, 21 of 204 officer/professional positions in State's Bureau of Personnel were vacant as of October 31, 1977, or 10 percent of the total. Of the remaining 183, only 100 were filled with individuals whose personal "skill" codes indicated that they were personnel specialists, 26 more with those who had plausibly related administrative skill codes, and 57 with persons having basically unrelated

[25] Author's figures, based on analysis of Bureau of Personnel staffing patterns.

skill codes.[26] The bulk of the professional personnelists, moreover, were GS employees concentrated in the lower-graded and more routine operational positions. Some nonpersonnelists were performing functions where their own skills were partially relevant—for example, economic officers counseling and assigning other economic officers—but even when this is taken into account, the competence level of the Bureau was simply not adequate for the tasks at hand. For example, a 1976 internal review concluded that at least twenty-five of the positions filled by rotational members of the Foreign Service should be filled by GS personnel experts, including more of the senior positions, if the Bureau was to have adequate managerial continuity.[27]

Against this background, it should come as no surprise that there has been little success in developing a coherent and explicit personnel management philosophy, in spite of some notable attempts.

In 1962, the Herter Committee concluded that "there is no central machinery or procedure in the State Department either to coordinate foreign affairs program planning or to use program plans as a basis for estimates of immediate and longer-range personnel needs."[28]

Four years later, a staff analysis for the Heineman Task Force, commenting on this assessment, found that "if there has been any operational change in this situation since 1962, it has been in the direction of further fragmentation of decision-making and increasing chaos, particularly in the assignment process. There is no systematic career development program for State Department personnel."[29]

The American Foreign Service Association (AFSA) in its 1968

[26] Author's figures, developed from the Bureau staffing pattern. Skill codes are indicators which describe each individual's qualifications. Similar codes are attached to each position. Thus these figures reflect the degree of "fit" between individuals and positions.

[27] This was the result of an exercise designed to discover the proper balance of "continuity" and "rotational" incumbents, throughout the Department. The figures cited for change were approved by the then Director General and her deputy.

[28] Herter Committee Report, p. 14.

[29] "Major Problems of Personnel Management in the Department of State," unpublished Staff Paper prepared for the President's Task Force on Reorganization (The Heineman Commission) by the White House Staff, April 11, 1967, p. 1.

report, Macomber's "Diplomacy for the 70's" report, a 1974/75
internal Inspection Report, and the Murphy Commission all made
essentially the same point.[30] In May 1975, the new Director General, Carol C. Laise, argued for a substantial reform program in
a memorandum to Secretary of State Kissinger which concluded
that *"the central and overriding fact is that to have a coherent
organization and personnel system requires a centralized management strategy responsive to the foreign policy priorities established by the President and you."*[31]

The Laise program addressed a number of management problems. Its lead element was creation of a Priorities Policy Group
(PPG) of senior managers which was to be a "mechanism for
linking decisions on resource allocation to the broader considerations of foreign policy," whether the resources in question were
people or budget.[32] It was argued that establishment of this group
would permit major improvements in six key areas: development
of an *"integrated" service*, using a common management for
Foreign and Civil Service components; drastic *overhaul of recruitment* for the Foreign Service Reserve and Civil Service categories, in particular, for which there were few standards and
little real competition; development of mechanisms to ensure the
rise of *"The Best to the Top,"* regardless of how individuals first
entered the Department; opening up and making more equitable

---

[30] *Toward A Modern Diplomacy*, A Report to the American Foreign Service
Association by its Committee on Career Principles (Washington, D.C.: American
Foreign Service Association, 1968); *Diplomacy for the 70's: A Program of Management Reform for the Department of State*, Department of State Publication
8593, Department and Foreign Service Series 1430 (Washington, D.C.: GPO,
1970); Murphy Report (see Chap. I, note 2); and Office of the Inspector General,
Department of State, Inspection Report: "Strengthening the Department of State
Personnel System," Department of State, December 1974, multilith.

[31] Laise to Kissinger memorandum, "The Professional Service of the Department of State, unpublished, May 17, 1975, p. 1. Emphasis in original. (See Chap.
VI for more details.)

[32] Henry A. Kissinger, speech at swearing-in of 119th Foreign Service Officer
Class, June 27, 1975. Text distributed in Department of State Press Release No.
349, June 27, 1975. The "PPG" was established, and remained as of 1982 the
Department's primary internal budget and resource allocation mechanism, although it was heavily and increasingly criticized as time passed and underwent a
number of operational modifications.

the *assignment process* for Foreign Service employees; establishment of a *professional development program* for all categories of employees; and development of necessary *manpower information systems* to guide all the personnel functions, particularly resource allocation.[33]

Kissinger accepted this program essentially intact (with the important exception of the "integrated service," which was deferred for further study) as announced in his June 27, 1975, speech previously noted.

Major efforts were made on all of these problems in the next two and one-half years, but except for making the PPG operational (if not effective) as of early 1983, only limited progress could fairly have been said to have been made. Partly, this is because senior officials of the Department had not been able to provide what Laise's memorandum had foreseen would be needed: "Strong central direction and your personal authority will be required to pull together our long-fractured system because it is split by numerous vested interests which will see changes as jeopardizing their territorial imperatives."[34]

Transition papers prepared in the Bureau of Personnel for the incoming Carter Administration focused on many of the same problems: a need to enlist top leadership participation in ordering priorities; rationalizing career structures (i.e., the "integrated system"); developing manpower information systems; harnessing recruitment, assignment, training and promotion systems to priorities established by top management; enhancing professionalism and competence; and attending to implementation problems.[35] Eight months into the new Administration, however, there was little motion, in part because of a vacancy in the office of the Deputy Under Secretary for Management; and once one was appointed, there was only a cautious approach to change. In an early draft of a memo to the new Deputy Under Secretary and the Secretary, Director General Laise and Director of the Office of Management Operations Joan M. Clark (later Director General

---

[33] Summarized from Laise to Kissinger memorandum, note 31 above.

[34] Ibid., p. 11.

[35] Bureau of Personnel Transition Papers, "Overview: Our Approach to Personnel Management," unpublished, November 1976.

herself) found it necessary initially to use the title of "Change and Crisis in the Department and Foreign Service" to convey their sense both of the pressures which were present and the managerial problems which hindered dealing with them. But the urgently needed management reform was not yet forthcoming, in part because a governmentwide personnel reform was in the wings and there was much uncertainty.[36]

These managerial inadequacies are particularly harmful to personnel systems which, like the Foreign Service, are free from some of the outside controls of the competitive Civil Service. Such independent systems are much more dependent upon their own managers for the development of high effectiveness than is true elsewhere in government. Managerial freedom and flexibility can result in a system that is closely tailored to the organization's needs and unencumbered by arbitrary procedures, or it can lead to a system devoid of guiding standards, without equity for employees, and plagued by ad hoc reactions to immediate problems without regard to long-run needs. When there is no policeman, behavior must be self-regulated.

For example, excepted services, usually free from requirements for competitive hiring and/or exempted from the requirements of the classification act, are free to set their own hiring procedures and, within guidelines, to classify positions at levels they find appropriate. Sometimes, as with the FSO system, this can lead to very rigorous recruitment and hiring which is fully competitive without being bound by aberrations such as the "rule of three" or veteran's preference; but equally it can result in the absence of objective standards against which to weigh an individual's qualifications and the absence of competition among a number of qualified individuals to ensure that the best available are hired, which was a major failing of State's FSR system through the years. Such freedom also makes a personnel system more susceptible to political abuse, as State has learned to its sorrow from time to time, since it is difficult to argue that self-devised rules

[36] Laise and Joan M. Clark memorandum, via Under Secretary for Political Affairs Philip C. Habib, to Secretary of State Vance, August 1977. The final title was softened to "Managing Change in the Department and Foreign Service."

preventing the appointment of favorites cannot be waived or changed.

It must be concluded that because of insufficient attention to the need for sustained and effective management, the Department of State and other agencies using the Foreign Service system have not used their freedom of action wisely, and that without major changes the Foreign Service will not be able to function at the levels required in the future. The Department of State and other foreign affairs agencies must gain better control of the essential personnel functions of classification, recruitment, promotion, assignment, separation, and retirement if they are to succeed in providing the competences required.

INFLEXIBILITY AND UNRESPONSIVENESS

A major irony is that the freedom granted managers of the Foreign Service system has not led to effective personnel management.

Perhaps the fundamental point is that *any* personnel system which relies heavily on entry at the junior ranks and orderly progression throughout a career works best when demands placed on the system remain constant or evolve slowly, and worst at times when the working environment the system serves is evolving rapidly. A career service provides stability, but limits the possibilities of radical change to meet new circumstances. Most of the senior FSO's now on duty entered the Service no later than 1960; the new FSO classes of the early 1980's will not assume senior responsibility as a group until after the year 2000. There is thus likely to be a mismatch between the skills and talents of people who are hired and the demands of jobs decades hence, even if initial recruitment were perfectly matched with needs of the time. Only if a system can renew itself through systematic infusion of people with the required new competences, or can give members of its existing workforce those competences, can the gulf between skills and demands be closed.

This problem exists for both the Foreign and Civil Service career systems. Either service can obtain outside employees at the mid-career or even senior levels, but in practice this has been difficult, because of pressure not to bring in outsiders, thus depriving those already in the system of promotion opportunities.[37] Although about 20 percent of the current FSO corps entered in ways other than the standard examination route, after 1971 there was no possibility of unrestricted "lateral entry" to the FSO corps from outside the government, until 1981.[38] From 1973 to 1978, there was little significant Civil Service hiring in professional categories in State, because of the decision to use the Foreign Service Reserve system whenever possible for both short-term and career employment. Reserve appointments, originally intended to provide specialized and technical competence, have worked best when used for support and administrative activities. Disputes have arisen whenever a senior manager has attempted to use these appointing authorities to obtain the services of individuals with substantive policy expertise; for example, in politico-military or scientific areas, concern has been expressed that these individuals are taking jobs away from FSO's. This reflects both the lack of importance attached to specialized competence and a predilection to place the ambitions of the career service above the needs of the agency in which it serves.

From top to bottom, the rank-in-person Foreign Service system is not now open enough to allow for the self-renewal which is almost certain to be necessary. The FSO corps has often had a surplus of senior officers or, put another way, a shortage of positions to which they could be assigned.[39] This was exacerbated

[37] A study done by the Bureau of Personnel dated August 31, 1979, showed that only 20 of 3,281 FSO's had entered (other than at the bottom) from completely outside the government, and that 79.3% of all FSO's as of that date had entered by the examination route (the remainder had been in government in some other capacity). This data essentially confirmed a study done by the author from a somewhat different perspective in 1976.

[38] Outside lateral entry was stopped in 1971 during a governmentwide hiring freeze, and resumed (in theory) only in 1981. During the interim, the only lateral entry programs used have either converted State employees in other categories to FSO, which may be sensible but does not bring new competences into the system, or have brought women and minority group members into the service in order to increase its representiveness and diversity (see Chap. IV).

[39] This problem was noticed as early as 1967, by the Heineman Commission. For reasons discussed later in this paragraph, the problem reached its worst stage in the summer of 1977, when there was a surplus of senior officers seeking assignment over senior positions available to them in the ratio of 3:2 (Bureau of

by a 1977 District Court decision (*Bradley* v. *Vance*) which de-
clared mandatory retirement unconstitutional (although it was re-
stored in early 1979 on appeal to the Supreme Court) and by a
significant senior-level pay increase, both of which reduced attrition, since many senior officers opted not to retire.[40] This in
turn reduced promotion opportunities, causing some of those who
are most needed to seek careers elsewhere. Meanwhile, because
of a shifting workload, particularly toward the consular area,[41]
there was a major shortage of junior officers—but a reluctance
either to increase the number of junior officers, owing to well-
founded fears that they could not be accommodated at later stages
of their careers because of the lower grading of the consular cone
positions compared with other cones, *or* to consider using non-
FSO's for such work, with frank acceptance of their careers top-
ping out at somewhat lower levels.[42]

Personnel figures). It is important to remember, however, that the problem is not
one of absolute numbers—in fact, there are always fewer senior officers than the
total number of senior positions—but of "matches." That is, for some senior
officers there are no appropriate jobs, either because they do not have needed
skills and experience, because jobs are filled from the outside, or because they
are filled by more junior officers on "stretch" assignments. (See Chap. VI for
the centrality of this problem in development of the Foreign Service Act of 1980.)

[40] Government retirement computations, including the Foreign Service, are based
on an average of the "highest three years" salary, multiplied by the years of
service times a percentage. For the Foreign Service, this percentage is 2% of the
"high three" average, for each year of service. Thus the salary-limit increase in
early 1977, which raised the maximum salary from $39,600 to $47,500 (19.9%)
was very significant for retirement annuities and encouraged a large number of
officers to remain in the Service until they had three years at $47,500. In short,
the pay increase, combined with the temporary loss of mandatory retirement at
age sixty, caused many officers to remain on active duty who would have otherwise
retired, and the system was thus clogged. Much the same thing happened as a
result of similar pay increases from $50,112.50 to $58,500 on January 1, 1982,
and to $67,200 on December 18, 1982, and with the permanent lifting of the
mandatory retirement age for the Foreign Service from sixty to sixty-five in the
fall of 1980, as mandated by the new Foreign Service Act.

[41] Between 1970 and 1980, the total number of positions devoted to consular
work in the Department and overseas increased by 358, while those devoted to
crucial political functions declined by 205. As noted elsewhere, the decline in the
latter caused other problems. State Office of Management Operations data, October
27, 1980.

[42] This opinion was expressed to the author in strong terms on a number of
occasions by several senior officers in the Bureau of Consular Affairs, from 1975

Even the attempts which *are* made to provide the necessary kinds of people are often thwarted. After several years of planning and negotiation with the American Foreign Service Association (AFSA), the Department in 1978 began its career candidate program, under which new FSO candidates would serve a three-to-four-year probationary period as FSR's rather than being appointed directly as FSO's. The original concept was that during this period each new officer would serve one year in three of the four basic cones (including consular), at two different posts, and receive frequent evaluations from a number of supervisors. The purpose would be to identify each officer's strongest points and to provide better information for the "junior threshold" boards which would decide whether an officer had career potential.[43] Similarly, in 1976-77 investigation was begun into the possibility of using assessment center techniques to allow a more thorough evaluation than the existing one-hour oral examination provided. Given favorable conclusions to this study, in January 1978 State adopted a day-long assessment process, consisting of group and individual exercises intended to test individuals in approximations of the work environment they would face in the Service, to replace the traditional oral exam.[44]

Before the career candidate program had taken its first class of new officers, however, operating pressures mortgaged the future. The greatly increased need for junior consular officers already cited, combined with reduced junior officer intake compared with previous years, led to a modification of the "1-1-1" assignment pattern in three cones. Instead, new officers were to spend eighteen months in consular affairs and eighteen months in one of the other three cones—an ad hoc modification for expediency's sake which

---

to late 1979. By 1980 there were some indications that the difficulty of staffing all necessary positions through traditional means might be causing reassessment of the absolutist position of "only FSO's," although as of late 1982 there was not yet firm acceptance of a more realistic approach.

[43] For a discussion of the career candidate program, which was approved by Congress and begun in January 1978, see "State's proposal to Congress: Junior Officers could get 48-month provisional status,"*Department of State News Letter* 190 (May 1977), 19.

[44] Announced in *Periscope*, the Bureau of Personnel's internal newsletter, February 18, 1977, p. 1. (See Chap. V for more discussion of the assessment idea.)

damaged considerably the underlying rationale of the program. Still later, consular needs more often than not led to a full two-year consular tour.[45]

The chronic inability of the Foreign Service adequately to renew itself was demonstrated in another area as well. A basic tenet of the Foreign Service system, a feature that has been a source of pride for its members as well as one rationale for earlier retirement and better benefits (and some would say, a disproportionately high grade structure) is its selection-out, or "up-or-out," feature: "The Foreign Service system is more generous because of the higher average salaries of people in it, and because of a number of unique factors, not the least of which is often brutal selection-out process (like the military's promotion-or-perish deal), which can cut short a promising career."[46] Unlike the Civil Service system, in which a career employee can be fired only for documented cause, selection-out provides for involuntary separation either for excessive time in (one) class (TIC) without promotion or for being ranked at the bottom of the comparable group of officers even if performing at acceptable levels.[47] The intent is to ensure that those who remain in the Service are up to the demands they face, to provide reasonable promotion opportunities for those who are

[45] Comment based on author's discussions with Bureau of Personnel officers responsible for the junior officer program, throughout the 1978-1981 period. The most recent applicable regulations (3 FAM, 592.1), renegotiated in 1982, call for service in two and preferably three cones, at least one year in the candidate's own functional field, a minimum of one year in consular work for all, and for consular officer candidates at least one year outside the consular area, unless the individual does not wish so to serve.

[46] Mike Causey, "The Federal Diary: Foreign Service Pensions Highest," *Washington Star*, January 26, 1976. Many in the Service who favor selection-out do not see it as "brutal" in view of the limited number selected out, the adoption of careful due process provisions in recent years, and the possibility of immediate retirement annuity in some cases and substantial severance pay in all others.

[47] The time-in-class allowed and the low-ranking rules have varied from time to time. Currently, for example, the time allowed for FSO's to make the Senior Foreign Service after receiving career tenure at class 4 is twenty-two years, with no more than fifteen years in any one class. Identification for possible selection-out occurs when a selection board identifies an individual as significantly inferior to contemporaries in performance. At this time, there is no automatic triggering percentage, such as being in the low 10%.

performing at outstanding levels, and to loosen up a system which would otherwise stagnate.

Recently, however, the selection-out process has deteriorated. The appeals process has become cumbersome, and "low-ranking" selection-out for FSO's virtually disappeared in the early 1970's, as Table 4 indicates, although the Department is hopeful that it can be revitalized through improvements in standards and protections.

Attempts to restore the role of selection-out were begun in 1977, but long-term success was uncertain. A number of knowledgeable individuals, familiar with the Foreign Service and aware of the trends toward greater due process and employee protection in the courts, are skeptical that the Foreign Service will ever again be able to use selection-out in any meaningful way.[48] However, the concept received strong congressional reaffirmation with passage of the Foreign Service Act of 1980, which not only endorsed selection-out but extended it to the entire Foreign Service, including support staff who had previously been excluded.

In addition to its problems in selecting-out the people who are not strong performers, the Foreign Service has increasing difficulty using the employees it has to best advantage. Mention has already been made of the reluctance of FSO's to follow specialties too intensively, for fear of hurting their career prospects in a generalist system. There are also additional impediments regarding assignments, which have become a major concern for personnel system managers. The previously cited 1977 memorandum to the Secretary is worth quoting at some length because it conveys the difficulties involved:

—The changing social mood of the nation over the past decade has created a population far less inclined to accept arguments

[48] For example, this was the consensus opinion of a distinguished panel of experts, including several former senior management officials of the Department of State, assembled by the Murphy Commission in April 1975 to review the Commission's personnel recommendations. The Department by 1982 was more sanguine, believing that new procedures featuring appeal rights which meet due process standards would make it possible to employ selection-out with more regularity. Selection-out procedures are contained in Sections 607 and 608 of the new Act.

TABLE 4 Selection-out in the Foreign Service (Department of State)

Fiscal Year	Number of Employees Subject to Selection-out*	Total Selected-out and Separated for Cause	Selected-out for Time-in-Class	Selected-out for Substandard Performance	Resigned/Retired Voluntarily after being Identified for Selection-Out or TIC	Separated for Cause
1981	3,516**	25	21	4	—	—
1980	3,516	21	20	0	5	1
1979	3,485	23	20	2	8	1
1978	3,606	21	18	2	9	1
1977	3,578	16	13	0	7	3
1976	3,478	10	10	0	0	0
1975	3,453	6	2	4		
1974	3,375	29	20	9		
1973	3,037	12	7	5		
1972	3,082	19	8	11		
1971	3,080	34	23	11		
1970	3,275	102	82	20		
1969	3,489	104	66	38		
1968	3,566	74	30	44		
1967	3,541	57	5	52		
1966	3,631	96	3	93		
1965	3,733	108	0	108		
1964	3,718	57	0	57		

* Some members of the former Foreign Service Reserve Unlimited (FSRU) category were made subject to selection-out for substandard performance after 1976, and everyone in the Foreign Service, after a transaction period, will be subject to both types of selection-out under the Foreign Service Act of 1980. As a practical matter, however, neither of these changes has as yet had an impact, so the figures above reflect only State's Foreign Service Officer (FSO) population for the years listed. ** Estimate.

of "service needs" or "national interest" as overriding individual or family preferences and needs. As a result it is harder to find people willing to serve in hardship posts where economic and human pressures can be considerable.

—This is paralleled by social change affecting the family— long the fundamental unit of our public diplomacy overseas. More FSO's are married to each other and want to be assigned to the same post. At times this can only be done at some cost to meeting real needs. More serious is the increasing number of women, married to FSO's who have careers of their own and want to stay in Washington where their work is. Or, they want good jobs overseas where their husband is assigned. Such jobs predominantly are available in the industrially advanced nations, thus decreasing the number of FSO's willing to serve in difficult locations. In the long term, the issue is whether the Foreign Service with its high mobility and heavy demands on one family member, can accommodate the modern, highly educated American family.

— . . . a situation could result in which it would be predominantly young, single people who would be fully able, if not willing, to serve in hardship posts.

—With the glamor and rewards of overseas service declining, strong inducements are needed. But such financial incentives as we have been able to provide are now under serious attack.[49]

Service discipline, in terms of an increasing reluctance by individuals to accept assignments offered, is increasingly compromised. In an effort to provide more choices to individuals to mitigate this problem, in 1976 a "Centralized Open Assignments" policy was adopted, with greater information being made available about positions which will be open and more opportunities for employees to make their preferences known, but with greater central (as opposed to regional bureau) control. The assignment

---

[49] Laise/Clark to Vance memorandum, pp. 5-6 (see note 36). New allowance authorities in the 1980 Foreign Service Act were directed to correcting problems cited in the last paragraph.

system is inherently fraught with conflicting pressures, and the problem of balancing trade-offs is at times severe. Individual desires versus Service needs; an equal chance for good assignments for all versus the preference of senior officers to have particular individuals assigned; career development for individuals versus immediate bureau requirements; and tours of duty long enough to develop expertise in a country versus the equal sharing of hardship posts—all are legitimate considerations which must be reconciled. The current system, in attempting to accommodate all the forces brought to bear on it, is nothing if not flexible; but in being so it runs the risk of becoming responsive to whoever is strongest and most insistent, and not necessarily to what will improve the total effectiveness of the Service.

There are other problems. Any system, if it is to keep its good people, must provide incentives and rewards in the form of reasonable rates of promotion, increases in responsibility, and pay raises. But for the Foreign Service, the previous mentioned decline in retirements and past overpromotion had combined by the mid-1970's to slow promotion rates drastically. In the worst case, by a 1977 estimate, "promotion opportunities may become so bad that many mid-career officers will be tempted to resign, and many able junior officers could be selected out for excessive time-in-grade."[50] A bottom-entry career system which cannot keep its best officers and use them to good effect is in serious trouble.

It might still be possible to respond to new circumstances through training or "reprogramming": the alternative to obtaining different people with the requisite skills could be to equip those already in the system with the needed skills. This has not occurred to any significant degree, except in language instruction and perhaps in the area of general-purpose economics. The Department of State has had a limited training and instruction budget, and a large

[50] Ibid., p. 3. However, projections for the early 1980's, prepared in 1979, were considerably more sanguine. This of course reinforces the point made earlier about the inadequacies of the current data and manpower planning systems. The 1980 Foreign Service Act, which requires a "regular, predictable flow" into the senior ranks, was designed with this problem in mind, as was the accompanying adjustment in Foreign Service pay.

proportion must be devoted to the basic diplomatic and job tools (language instruction, basic officers' course, consular course) or to the preparation of senior generalists. Very few resources are available to give employees additional skills in substantive policy areas. There is only a limited amount of outside, extended-term education offered at universities or elsewhere, and what little there is may be misdirected. Such instruction has been heavily concentrated in the management field in recent years, or at public affairs schools, rather than in functional competences (e.g., science, economics), and its effect has been weakened by the inability to control assignments after the training period with any degree of consistency, which would allow the course of instruction to be tailored to specific job requirements.[51] Thus, training and educational programs in the State Department do not appreciably reduce the shortage of needed competences.

This lack of training is paralleled by the absence of any coherent career development planning, particularly from the point of view of the individual. Numerous attempts have been made to correct this, but all, as of early 1983, had foundered on the resistance of the Service, lack of resources, or simple uncertainty about what should be done.

The circle is now complete. The personnel systems of the Department of State and the other foreign affairs agencies are simply not equipped to respond to changing requirements.

ELITISM, MORALE, AND LABOR RELATIONS

Americans are normally uncomfortable with real or perceived elites (unless they see themselves as members); this is especially true if they believe that an elite group benefits undeservedly from such status. It is clear that for many the Foreign Service Officer corps belongs in this category. It is often the butt of sarcastic humor which reflects a resentment of its supposed privileges, doubts about its competence, or disgust with the frivolousness of its activities. Jules Feiffer's 1974 cartoon of two Foreign Service officers, "Bromley Hodgkins" and "Hadley Wainwright," is a

---

[51] See Chapter II for further elaboration of this situation.

case in point.[52] They are shown discussing, exhaustively and smugly, the tactics and cheap tricks of an unnamed negotiation, without ever mentioning its substance, and then concluding that the talks should be broken off on ground of the *other side's* bad faith. Both the choice of names and the scenario leave the impression that the Foreign Service is unprofessional and is not serious about conducting the nation's business. By image, word, and implication, the cartoon represents a common and damaging stereotype of the Foreign Service.

In related vein, former Senator Eugene J. McCarthy, noting a lack of progress in late 1977 on a new SALT agreement and a peace settlement in the Middle East, continues to say, "Now for the good news: Despite discouraging reports about the secretary's efforts around the world, under Secretary Vance the morale in the State Department is good and also improving. . . ." After commenting that no one ever seems to worry about morale elsewhere in government, McCarthy concludes,

> Because it is so important, it would be good to establish objective standards for measuring State Department morale. Or, failing in that, we could designate someone to make subjective judgments about the level and quality of department morale. Each day, following the weather report, the baseball scores, and the Dow Jones averages, Walter Cronkite, just before he says, "That's the way it is," could give us the morale index for the State Department. We might sleep better, knowing that, despite the headlines and stories about a troubled world and failures in American foreign policy, morale at the State Department is stable, high, or rising.[53]

Sometimes, gratuitous put-downs appear in discussions of matters entirely unrelated to the Service, as in the following, taken from a treatment of the pros and cons of political versus merit selection of U.S. Attorneys: "Even an exalted group like law school deans

[52] Jules Feiffer, "Endpaper: The New York Times Comics: Jules Feiffer's version of Comic Strips The New York Times might print if the New York Times printed Comics," *New York Times Magazine*, December 15, 1974, 110.

[53] Eugene McCarthy, "State is happy. And that's the good news!" *Washington Star*, October 9, 1977, Op Ed Column.

and judges is neither a representative nor a disinterested one, and its errors in merit selection would be on the side of kid-glove treatment of the establishment and lack of fresh ideas. In rough analogy, we'd have Foreign Service Officers for United States Attorneys."[54]

Much of the skepticism about the Foreign Service is not of its own making. The Service has often been blamed for policy outcomes not within it control, most notably perhaps the "loss of China," and has paid a heavy price for it.[55] Some of the doubt comes from its lack of a direct constituency relationship with any significant part of the domestic population, which is accompanied by the public's lack of understanding of the diplomatic function. This contributes to an image, sometimes furthered by politicians, of high living at glamorous locations overseas at the expense of the taxpayer.

Some of the damage, however, is self-inflicted. The Service is extremely vocal in defending its perquisites as, for example, in the argument of Ellis O. Briggs, who served as an Ambassador in seven different countries: "In diplomacy, the prerogatives of official position—the prestige of the office, the immunities while abroad, the diplomatic passport while traveling—are legitimate attractions."[56] Such an attitude, even if justified by the less pleasant aspects of modern diplomacy, can hardly improve the ability of the Service to convince others that it should play the major role in developing and executing policy, a role which, it has been argued, will be required of it in the future. As Kennan has noted,

> . . . the diplomat comes only too easily to be viewed as a species of snobbish and conceited elitist, *depayse*, estranged from his own country and countrymen, giving himself airs, looking down upon his fellow citizens, fancying himself su-

[54] Nicholas Leman, "The Case for Political Patronage," *Washington Monthly* 9 (December 1977), 17.

[55] See note 49, Chap. II. A case could be made, however, that the Foreign Service *should* bear some blame for the Vietnam outcome, in that it was very short of officers with a developed competence in Southeast Asian languages and area experience in the late 1950's and early 1960's and did not really overcome this problem until it was much too late to affect the course of policy.

[56] Ellis Briggs, quoted in an unpublished staff paper for Heineman Commission.

perior to them by virtue of his claim to an esoteric knowledge and expertise in which they cannot share and which by the very fact of its foreign origin challenges the soundness and adequacy of their world of thought.[57]

He regards this as a false sterotype which never had much substance and for which any justification has long since disappeared, but he nevertheless subscribes to the need for an elite based on merit and accepts the fact that the qualities required—most notably a worldview which is sophisticated and features a "deliberate self-distancing" from the great currents of mass reaction in American society—are likely to reinforce the stereotype.

The elitist stereotype has other costs. It has been the author's experience, over a number of years of observing FSO's close at hand, that subconsciously, at least, most believe that non-FSO's cannot be as well qualified as themselves in foreign affairs matters. Therefore, they usually prefer FSO's to be appointed to almost any position if a choice is possible—even if the position in question requires policy analysis or specialized duties in Washington, rather than diplomatic work overseas. This in turn impedes the ability of the Service to be integrated into the much larger foreign affairs community. The result, these days, is more likely to be isolation for the FSO corps, rather than exclusion of others from "the Foreign Service's business."

Another cost is an us-against-them mentality in the Department of State, with non-FSO's often finding their contributions downgraded, and the reverse elsewhere, in those parts of the government where civil servants predominate. Much of the difficulty the Department has had in developing a rational personnel structure springs from this source. Some argue for a single service, with all in the same Foreign Service system, but it is telling that most would not go so far as to make everyone an FSO. From an operational point of view it is far from clear that a single system—because it would almost inevitably be rank-in-person and generalist oriented and dominated—could even come close to meeting the current diverse needs, particularly for specialized competence.

[57] Kennan, "Reflections," p. 152 (see Chap. I, note 19). This article is also the source for ideas summarized in the following paragraph.

But because the obvious need for change has not overcome the reluctance to end the special status of FSO's, the result has been a failure to correct those managerial problems which are the inevitable consequence of not establishing personnel categories that make sense operationally.[58]

The FSO corps *is* gradually becoming more diverse, although in a bottom-entry system any change in the type of people being recruited takes a number of years to work its way through, and considerable difficulty has been encountered in persuading women and members of minority groups who have the requisite qualifications to survive the competitive entry process that they will not be discriminated against in their careers.

Defenders of the Foreign Service system have generally held that the feeling of being unusual individuals called upon to carry unusual and demanding responsibilities is necessary in order to build the morale and discipline necessary for the Service to function effectively. Yet there are many signs that the combination of role uncertainty, changes in American society, and a reluctance to accept hardship duty, among other problems, have reduced the attractiveness of a Foreign Service career and produced circumstances in which much of the Service is restive.[59] Some members are hostile to any major change, as the history of the new Foreign

[58] The 1980 Foreign Service Act does take a step in the right direction by having a single Senior Foreign Service composed of both specialists and generalists, and by having only two categories below the senior levels. Some thought was given to a merger into one category below the senior level as well, but it was decided that this was unnecessary and, more importantly, could cause major political problems within the FSO corps, and perhaps with the Congress.

[59] Taking of hostages, attacks on American diplomatic posts, and murders of American Ambassadors are only the most obvious elements in this. The cost of living abroad increased everywhere, and during the 1970's the dollar declined in value. Allowances for hardship duty and cost of living adjustments are, in the eyes of reasonably objective analysts, increasingly inadequate, in spite of some improvements in the Foreign Service Act of 1980. The rise of the dollar in 1981 and 1982, largely due to excessively high U.S. interest rates which attracted foreign investments, are only a temporary variation in this long-term trend. An increasing number of posts are becoming undesirable, more spouses are becoming frustrated because they cannot maintain their own careers while abroad, and many recent episodes have driven home the all-too-real threats to personal safety.

Service Act amply shows (Chapter VI), while others are scathing in their contempt for the status quo.

It is clear that the morale and comradeship which have held the Foreign Service together are in jeopardy. A major change has occurred in perceptions of what constitutes an appropriate relationship between individuals, the leadership of the Service, and the Department of State. Officers are more assertive about their careers, less willing to accept any assignment offered, and more inclined to enter into formal actions such as grievances to obtain redress for personally disadvantageous management actions. For their part, managers lament the loss of discipline in the Service. Contentiousness and mutual suspicion have become the norm. One internal management memorandum, prepared by an officer with direct experience in the grievance process, may help capture the flavor:[60]

> From the perspective of the Grievance Staff, it appears that the Department and Bureau face two rather new challenges. One is the individual challenge, exemplified by the grievance procedures, which carries with it the ability of individual officers and employees of the Department and the Foreign Service to have a much greater say than ever before in matters affecting their work and career expectations. The individual challenge manifests itself in the new and potent grievance procedures, the open assignment policy, the dissent channel and Open Forum, the expectation that assignments can be negotiated, the urgency of the spouse problem, the capacity to resist discipline, the ability to prevent anticipated Departmental actions, and so forth. The institutional challenge is that produced by the requirement that AFSA, as the exclusive employee representative, pursuant to Executive Order 11636, be consulted about matters which formerly were Management prerogatives. Both of these challenges vastly complicate the problems of Management, and the greatest burden of dealing with them falls upon the Personnel Bureau.

[60] Memorandum for the Director of the Department's Grievance Staff to Bureau of Personnel Managers, October 4, 1976. Viewed from late 1982, this discussion substantially understated the problem.

Under these circumstances, AFSA has been evolving from a professional association into an often aggressive employees' union. In 1973, it became the exclusive representative for Foreign Service employees of the State Department, AID, and USIA. Since that time, many issues which in earlier years would have been settled informally among colleagues have become subject to formal employee-management consultation or negotiation.

AFSA, however, has not always succeeded in convincing many Foreign Service professionals, particularly those who are not FSO's, that it is able to represent their interests. In 1976, the American Federation of Government Employees (AFGE), a more established government employees' union, succeeded in displacing AFSA as exclusive representative for USIA employees. Moreover, AFSA's internal politics have sometimes been worthy of the Borgias, with factionalism making it very difficult in some cases to arrive at a unified position, let alone be effective in negotiations with management.[61]

The trend toward organization of public employees seems well established. Some argue however, that AFSA ultimately may have to revert to its earlier form as strictly a professional association, leaving employee representation to another organization, or alternatively it may have to become a true union, because it cannot effectively do both.

Whatever the future of employee representation, a more formal and less accommodating relationship between Foreign Service managers and employees seems almost inevitable. Careerism in its negative sense is a clear danger. New grievance procedures have been legislated, and there is little reluctance to use them. It seems possible that all this activity, which is highly focused upon individual concerns and bread-and-butter issues rather than the service ethic which has so long been characteristic of the Foreign

---

[61] For an example of this, see the "Special Elections Section," *Foreign Service Journal* 54 (May 1977), 17-39, which contains candidates' statements for a regularly scheduled AFSA election of officers and board members, in which a former President who had been recalled in a membership vote was running again for the office, against some of those who had led the recall campaign. A somewhat similar, if less heated example, can be found in the May 1979 issue of the magazine, for the next regular election.

Service, may undercut the image of the FSO corps as an elite professional group of dedicated servants. Like the rest of the foreign affairs community, they risk becoming more an occupational group and less a profession.

The weaknesses of foreign affairs personnel systems leave one obvious question: What must be done, if the system is to have any chance of meeting its responsibilities in the future? This is perhaps the basic issue of this book. To the end of attempting to confront it, it is necessary at this point to consider specific choices which must be made, and dilemmas which must be resolved in making decisions about the best future personnel system for the conduct of American foreign policy.

CHAPTER FOUR

No Perfect Schemes:
Dilemmas of Personnel System Design

No personnel system can do everything needed. Because the purposes to be served are diverse and conflicting, each possible system has serious faults. Something must always be sacrificed. Many of the choices which must be made in designing and running a personnel apparatus can be couched as dilemmas, often not in either-or terms but rather as questions of balance between desirable but conflicting principles.

This chapter examines these dilemmas in order to address the question of how personnel systems can be improved. The most important choices are listed below.

—Should the foreign affairs personnel system of the future be closed, based on bottom entry, which in theory can help to sustain high standards, enforce discipline, and build esprit; or is it more desirable to have an open system with recruitment at all levels, which brings greater flexibility for responding quickly to unforeseen needs, less isolation from the rest of society, and perhaps, therefore, greater representativeness? Or is some combination of the two required?

—What balance should be sought between a high quality foreign affairs service which operates strictly on ability and competence, and a service which is representative of all the elements of American society, if the two principles conflict?

—What are the relative virtues and drawbacks of rank-in-person systems, with their ability to facilitate the frequent movement of individuals and to assign them to varied kinds of positions over time, compared with rank-in-position systems, with their greater emphasis on continuity, closer linkage of ranks and promotions to job requirements, and more refined ability, at least in theory, to hire individuals with special competence for specific positions?

—Is it possible to achieve balance between the broad skills and experiences necessary for senior managerial and policy determining responsibilities, and the specialized competence needed for dealing with the complex issues that are coming to dominate international relations? Should generalists and specialists be in separate career tracks, and if so, what provisions should be made for crossing over? Should foreign affairs officials begin as specialists, becoming generalists at later stages of their careers, or be recruited from the outset by separate procedures?

—Should the foreign affairs personnel system(s) of the future be centralized, providing standardization, consistency, and a more economical use of scarce resources, or do circumstances require a system which is decentralized and therefore more attuned to unique problems and to the perspectives of the "users" of people rather than of the "suppliers"? Whatever this choice, should the system(s) be part of the larger Civil Service, or separate entities operating under their own statutory authorities?

—Whether centralized or not, is it more desirable to have a single personnel system in each unit of the government, for ease of administration and to encourage a sense of unity, or is it preferable to have multiple systems tailored to different conditions, and perhaps therefore more equitable and responsive to individuals?

—Should foreign affairs personnel, in view of their responsibility for carrying out the nation's foreign policies and programs, have a substantially different form of organization for collective bargaining than do other government employees?

—How can the foreign affairs organizations of government accommodate and put to best use the very different experiences and perspectives of political appointees on one hand, and career professionals on the other?

—Is it preferable to have foreign affairs personnel system(s) that are managed by professional personnelists, or systems(s) in which these managerial functions are carried out by members of the "profession" themselves?

—To what extent must the Foreign Service accommodate the special needs of family members, if they conflict with needs and wants of members of the Service itself or with managerial requirements?

Answers to these dilemmas are not self-evident; each has been ferociously fought over in the past. But it is necessary to make some conscious choices for the future.

OPEN VS. CLOSED SYSTEMS

A closed career system is based on the twin principles of entrance at the bottom and promotion from within. In contrast, an open system hires new members or employees at all levels, usually through competition in which both current members and outsiders can participate.[1] Both systems can also use short-term employees, who may or may not eventually become career members. The Foreign Service corps and the uniformed military services are the most obvious American examples of closed systems, while the competitive federal Civil Service is the best-known open system. However, caveats are in order. The Foreign Service has always had, at least since World War II, significant numbers of lateral entrants, who entered the Service by other than the standard examination process or at mid-levels, or both. In late 1979, some 21 percent (677 of 3,281) of the FSO corps in State had entered in "nonstandard" ways, including 8 of 28 at the most senior rank of Career Minister.[2] Conversely, the Civil Service in practice has a strong proclivity for promotion from within, for limited mobility across departmental lines, for extended periods of service within the same agency, and for limited outside hiring at the top. In

[1] See O. Glenn Stahl, *Public Personnel Administration*, 7th ed. (New York: Harper and Row, 1976), pp. 61-63, for one view of these two kinds of systems.

[2] Data as of August 31, 1979, provided by State's Bureau of Personnel. Reflecting the gradual retirement of the former civil servants who entered the Foreign Service in a massive influx under the Wriston program in the mid-fifties, this overall percentage was down from about 26% in early 1976 (author's study at that time).

short, changing circumstances make closed systems more open than might appear; and the principle of "taking care of one's own" leads open systems to be less accessible from the outside than might be assumed.

For the future, the issue of open versus closed systems is probably more important in a different sense. Government *career* systems, whether nominally open or closed, suffer from many of the infirmities of the academic tenure system:[3] career status is awarded after a relatively short time (compared with the total period of employment), after which neither mediocre nor even poor performance, nor changing missions or requirements, can result in employee termination except through elaborate and time-consuming procedures originally designed to protect the employee against caprice. With the recent societal and judicial emphasis on due process, this necessary protection has limited the ability of government managers to adapt their workforce in ways that are normal elsewhere.[4] In the Civil Service an employee can be "fired" only for cause;[5] the only other available mechanism is the "meat-axe" reduction-in-force (RIF) approach, which places primary emphasis on retaining those employees who have the most seniority (and/or are covered by the protection of veteran's preference) and is intended (as the name indicates) for reducing the total workforce, not for replacing some individuals with others.[6] In theory, closed systems with their "up-or-out" features are

[3] See Mark Nadel, "The Trouble with Tenure," *Washington Monthly* 9 (January 1978), 28-33.

[4] For an extensive review article on this topic, see Charles H. Levine and Lloyd G. Nigro, "The Public Personnel System: Can Juridical Administration and Manpower Management Coexist?" *Public Administration Review* 35 (January/February 1975), 98-107. See also David H. Rosenbloom, "Public Personnel Administration and the Constitution: An Emergent Approach," *PAR* 35 (January/February 1975), 52-59, and in particular, Jay M. Shafritz et al., *Personnel Management in Government: Politics and Process* (New York and Basel: Marcel Dekker, 1978), pp. 168-87.

[5] 22 U.S.C. 1007 provides for separation for unsatisfactory performance, "or for such other cause as will promote the efficiency of the service." This applies to the Foreign Service as well.

[6] See *Congressional Quarterly* 36 (1978), 2945-2948, for a summary of current employee conduct and appeal provisions, enacted in the Civil Service Reform Act of 1978.

better equipped to make such adjustments (selection-out is a substitute for RIF), in that they can at least separate those who are rated lowest in a given category of employees; but in practice such mechanisms are as difficult to use and as rigid as the cause/RIF systems.[7]

Thus, unless changes in legislation or judicial interpretation allow government managers to adjust their career workforces to meet changing requirements,[8] the distinction between "career" and "pass-through" systems may be more important than the more traditional one between closed and open systems. It may be increasingly desirable or necessary to hire a significant proportion of the workforce, especially in the new professional fields, for limited terms, in order to avoid becoming locked into commitments to a permanent staff before longer-term needs are known.[9] This could also help to correct two other problems of the Foreign Service: the great difficulty in keeping members of the Service in close contact with the whole nation and the increasing drawbacks of sustained service abroad, especially for family members. Pass-through, like lateral entry, would bring fresh perspectives and talents into the Service, thus guarding against insularity, and would result in more people serving abroad, for shorter portions of their careers, than is now the case.

[7] See notes 47 and 48, Chap. III.

[8] Some of the early work of the Federal Personnel Management Project was concerned with finding ways to make separation for cause easier when warranted, by shifting the burden of proof to the employee, but federal employees' unions protested strongly and the CSRA as passed differed little from previous statutes in its likely results. In spite of a tougher stance toward employees' organizations, the Reagan administration, as of late 1982, had not taken a notably stronger approach on separations.

[9] In a closely related argument, Robert Wesson has advocated that federal employees should be hired for definite periods, perhaps six to twelve years, rather than for indefinite ones, with reappointment possible if needs and performance warrant. Wesson's article, appearing originally in the *Baltimore Sun*, can be most easily found in the *Congressional Record*, October 27, 1979, pp. S13599-S13600. The new Foreign Service Act contains a provision for senior officers to be reviewed periodically, with their career tenure extended only if selection boards finds a need for their services and a continuing high level of performance. See also Lloyd Nigro and Kenneth J. Meier, "Executive Mobility in the Federal Service: A Career Perspective," *PAR* 35 (May/June 1975), 291-95.

There are of course other considerations. Closed systems are more likely to result in individual identification with the system as an institution, and less with the particular agency in which one is employed or with a particular line of work. Especially when conditions of service are stressful, as is often the case for those serving short tours at one post, followed by relocation and uprooting of families, and adjustment to new work conditions and personalities at a new one, the feeling of commonality with a group serving under comparable conditions can be very important.[10] This is one reason members of such systems so strongly resist the mid- or high-level entry by outsiders, who are seen as depriving them of their promotion opportunities and who have not "paid their dues" in the demanding, yet often professionally boring, work at junior levels in the system. The result can be a highly motivated and disciplined workforce which takes pride in the rigors of its profession and in the valuable service it performs for the nation (an attitude which, it seems fair to say, has by and large characterized the Foreign Service). But it can also lead to a sense of isolation and the development of a subculture which feels beleaguered and verges upon paranoia whenever its capabilities or adaptability are called into question or appear to be taken for granted. At a time when the rest of the federal workforce—and society at large—is ever more demanding of employee protection and improved conditions of employment, it is questionable whether the positive attributes of a closed system based on higher individual risks can survive, however much they may be needed.

In contrast, the open system has fewer peaks—and fewer valleys. It tends to be viewed by its "members," or better, perhaps, employees, in a more workaday fashion, with much more concentration, at officer levels, on professional concerns, and much less on institutional loyalty.

One conclusion is that closed systems are still needed, contrary

[10] Military pilots and submariners are two other examples of the same kind of group identification. The classic case may have been the Indian Civil Service during colonial times. See Philip Woodruff, *The Men Who Ruled India* (London: Jonathan Cape, 1953, 1954).

to Stahl's assertion that they are "anachronisms,"[11] but they will be increasingly difficult to sustain with any degree of employee morale unless, perhaps, managed in a more participatory way. This suggests that their use should be limited to those areas where no other approach will suffice.

QUALITY VS. REPRESENTATIVENESS

There is no sadder commentary on our national past than the necessity, if candor is to prevail, of acknowledging that in staffing for foreign affairs, the desires for superior competence and also for a Service representative of the Society at large have probably been in conflict, at least in the past.

For example: the then Director General of the Foreign Service, Ambassador Carol Laise, became distressed at the results of the 1975 Foreign Service written examination, the first hurdle in the extremely competitive process by which new officers enter the FSO corps. Only 4 percent of the women taking the examination passed, compared with 14 percent of the men. Investigation showed that only about 300 of the 3,861 women who took the examination had college majors in the "core" Foreign Service areas of economics, history, political science, and international relations, compared with a much larger percentage of the men. Moreover, 30 percent of the women examined had clerical rather than professional work experience. Thus, they began at a disadvantage, in view of Educational Testing Service (ETS) findings that the rate at which people pass such examinations rises in proportion to work experience as well as level and type of education.[12]

How should the Foreign Service respond to this problem? Should it insist on an examination process loaded in favor of the most appropriate educational background, given its tasks, or should it decide in favor of representativeness, at the expense of educational content most germane to its mission? Similarly, with respect to minorities, should the Department and Foreign Service downplay

---

[11] Stahl, *Public Personnel Administration*, p. 63.

[12] Internal Bureau of Personnel Analysis, March 30, 1977. The Educational Testing Service, a private corporation, administers the Foreign Service Entrance Exam for State and the other Foreign Affairs agencies.

academic achievement, or should they take into account educational deprivation? Both questions are exacerbated by the long lead-time between taking the oral examination and actually entering the Service, which in recent years has averaged twelve months, mostly due to the time required for security clearances. This has meant that superior women and minority candidates, much sought after elsewhere, have had the luxury of choosing among many desirable offers and have frequently been unwilling to wait for State.[13]

In 1977, the Executive Level Task Force on Affirmative Action, composed primarily of officials at the Assistant Secretary level, concluded in strong terms that State must be more aggressive in its efforts to employ minorities and women. In justifying a recommendation that affirmitive-action hiring be expanded substantially (dismissing at the same time the objections of the Director General that this would inevitably reduce the role of normal entry and have a negative impact on efforts to recruit women and minorities through the regular Foreign Service examination process), the Task Force chairman wrote:

> We cannot accept the present state of affairs. It is an unfortunate reality that minority members, women and handicapped persons generally do not regard the foreign affairs agencies of the Government as offering equal employment opportunities. Many members of these groups already employed in these agencies do not feel that they have been fairly treated. We believe that the Department, given its world-wide role and exposure, simply must do better and must be more agressive in pursuing affirmative action.[14]

The Task Force thus indicated that, at least for the short run, it would accept some diminution in the background and competence

---

[13] This problem was first detailed to the author by the then head of State's EEO office, himself a minority group member. Steps have since been taken to speed appointments and make the Service more attractive financially, but the problem still exists and the competition for the most attractive candidates in every category remains severe.

[14] Internal State Department memorandum from the Task Force Chairman, Richard M. Moose, to the Secretary of State, November 7, 1977, p. 3.

of its new employees in order to improve the representativeness of the Service.[15] By the summer of 1979, State was still far behind its own goals, and Secretary Vance made it clear that he expected better, setting off a wild scramble to bring as many affirmative-action candidates on board as possible before the end of the fiscal year on September 30.[16]

In the immediate future there may be no alternative to special programs, but in the longer term they seem likely to be counter-productive. If quality suffers at entrance, at the next step of promotion, when the new employees compete against peers who have entered through the examination process, the results may be very unfortunate. Moreover, there is a danger of stigmatizing women and minority group members, however they enter the Foreign Service. The Service could bypass the problem of promotion by hiring some at higher levels, but many FSO's are convinced that entry of women and minority-group members at mid-levels, through special programs, can only result in fewer promotion opportunities for themselves, and therefore have strongly resisted such changes.[17] And even with entry at the bottom, many fear that the quality of the Service will be diluted if affirmative-action programs are used, as the president of AFSA told members of the Carter Administration to their faces during a December 1977 awards ceremony.[18]

As previously discussed, the FSO corps still retains a sense of being an elite, which has both negative and positive aspects. On one side, it is easy for a sincere and deeply felt belief in the importance of having a highly qualified Service to drive out the

[15] Ibid. The recommendation in question (#29) was intended in part to catch up with prior shortfalls in meeting the Department's goals for the special minority and female hiring programs. However, all recruitment was severely constricted at this time, thus eliciting the Director General's opposition.

[16] Internal Bureau of Personnel memorandum for the record (prepared in Office of Program Coordination), September 7, 1979.

[17] For example, in February 1978, an unsigned "Action Program" written by a number of FSO's received wide circulation in the Department, making essentially this argument.

[18] Lars Hydle—whose remarks were delivered with the approval of the AFSA governing board and later reprinted in a flyer, "AFSA News," No. 78-1, January 29, 1978, which was widely distributed in the Service. Subsequently, AFSA was to become much more supportive on affirmative action issues.

legitimacy of any other consideration, as the following comments by George Kennan, one of the most literate and thoughtful Foreign Service "elitists," suggest:

> We live, as we all know, in an age when egalitarianism is the prevailing passion, at least in many intellectual and political circles. We seem to stand in the face of a widespread belief that there is no function of public life that could not best be performed by a random assemblage of gray mediocrity. For people who see things this way, the idea of selecting people on the basis of their natural suitability for that sort of work must be rejected; because to admit that some people might be more suitable than others would be an elitist thought—hence inadmissible.[19]

The other side of this coin (against which Kennan is probably reacting), a position rarely taken outright but sometimes implied by politicians and Washington outsiders, can be stated almost as a syllogism.

—Federal employees, including the Foreign Service, don't do much, and what they do isn't demanding;
—therefore almost anybody can work for the government without making much difference in efficiency or effectiveness;
—thus those whom we favor—our supporters, the disadvantaged, or whomever—should be hired, even if less qualified than others.

This is not a helpful approach to a complex problem—nor is the attitude of a distressingly large number of FSO's (not much different on close analysis) that survival of the "rites of passage" of the examination process should guarantee retention in the corps and periodic advancement throughout an entire career.

There can, of course, be a positive side to elitism, if it is built upon superior talent and upon continued testing against peers and against objective requirements. There are also signs that a revival of these conditions is possible. In a letter to Secretary Vance

[19] Kennan, "Reflections," p. 152.

delivered in late 1977, more than 500 FSO's subscribed to the following:

> Mr. Secretary, we ask for a renewed commitment to the principles of the Foreign Service Act, which sought to create a Service based on merit, devoted to excellence, and dedicated to the effective conduct of the foreign policy of the United States. We believe that revitalization of these precepts is the indispensable first step in restoring a sense of purpose and forward movement to our institution—and in furthering positive, long-term change.[20]

The earlier, unquoted parts of this letter cast some doubt on this commitment, since they raise alarms about social change and its pressures upon the Service, but the sentiment, if truly held, is not inimical to meeting future demands.

Part of the Foreign Service's dilemma in choosing between representativeness and quality is a result of its generalist mentality (to be discussed below). The guiding generalist assumption, that broad competences and perspectives are the most important qualities, makes the development of objective measures of competence much more difficult than is the case when specific skills and experience are most valued. In turn, this leads to a selection process emphasizing the candidates' general background, which may have little direct relationship to the jobs to be performed. Such a process is very difficult to defend against charges of discrimination, as the Department of State learned to its discomfort many times during House hearings on the proposed new Foreign Service Act in the summer of 1979, as well as from subsequent pressure applied by the Congressional Caucus for Women's Issues.[21]

[20] Letter of the "Group of Forty-Six" to Secretary of State Vance, December 28, 1977, later signed by about 500 other officers. Members of this core group, after organizing as an election slate, all but swept the 1979 AFSA election.

[21] Such comments appear throughout the hearings, but their thrust can be gained from Representatives Patricia Schroeder's initial comments at the very beginning of the first hearing on the bill, on June 21, 1979. See "The Foreign Service Act," Hearings before the Subcommittee on International Operations of the Committee on Foreign Affairs and the Subcommittee on Civil Service of the Committee on

Unlike some of the other dilemmas discussed in this chapter, however, the answer in this case ought to be that both goals are attainable. A choice between representativeness and quality is not admissible in today's world. But to choose both, it will first be necessary for the Foreign Service to be much more precise about the skills, attributes, and backgrounds needed, as earlier chapters have suggested. Next, a true commitment to excellence must be forthcoming. It becomes very difficult to deny entrance to the unqualified underprivileged when the unqualified overprivileged are so easily accommodated. In effect, the values of the system at present lead one automatically to assume that the latter belong and the former do not, without comparing their attributes to the needs and tasks at hand.

Once such a commitment to both representativeness and excellence exists or is imposed,[22] the difficulty is obvious. the Foreign Service must recruit individuals who collectively have the necessary skills and experience, and still satisfy criteria of representativeness. This can only be accomplished by a recruitment program designed to convince the talented individuals of both sexes and all races that the foreign affairs community needs them, and can offer challenging opportunities.[23]

This may seem a simplistic solution to a complex problem, but it is irrefutable that State Department recruitment efforts were

---

Post Office and Civil Service, U.S. House of Representatives, 96th Congress, 1st session (Washington, D.C.: GPO, 1980), p. 2. See below, note 25, concerning the activities of the Congressional Caucus for Women's Issues.

[22] It was clearly imposed as a direct reflection of Secretary Vance's personal attitude in the 1977-1980 period in State.

[23] For an eloquent argument on this point as it affects the ability to recruit women and minority group members, see the so-called Clark Report, prepared by Dr. Kenneth Clark and his associates: Clark, Phipps, Clark and Harris, Inc., *Department of State Foreign Service Special Minority Junior Officer Hiring Program* (Interim Report), January 1977, p. 77 and passim. Much the same point was made in a report commissioned in 1979 by Secretary of State Cyrus Vance. Strongly supportive of affirmative action in general, it concluded, after arguing that the Department's mid-level program must be continued for a few years, that the goal should be "ultimate phase-out of the program," as more women and minorities moved up through the ranks. See "The Report of the Committee to Review Recruitment and Examination for the Foreign Service (Habib Committee), multilith, U.S. Department of State, October 10, 1979. Quote from p. 22.

until recently haphazard, unprofessional, and ill planned.[24] Aggressive recruitment has not appeared to be necessary when upwards of 20,000 individuals in recent years have been competing for some 200 places. But getting the *right* 200 new officers is a more complicated problem. The Foreign Service must exert itself to convince the nation's most talented young people that it can meet their desires for productive and demanding careers.

In spite of the opinions of some vested interests, such as the Congressional Caucus for Women's Issues (or at least its staff) to the contrary,[25] State has in fact made considerable progress toward greater representativeness in recent years, as Table 5 shows. Although pressure to improve female and minority representation at the middle and top continues to be exerted, in a career system such as the Foreign Service, in which entry at the bottom is standard, real progress in the numbers of minorities and women at senior ranks will take time. As discussed earlier, special programs designated to speed up the process in the short term can carry severe long-term costs. By 1981, however, there was significant change for women even at middle levels, as shown by Table 6.

The situation for minorities is not quite as positive, but still on the upturn.

With enough patience by all concerned, there seems a good chance that the Foreign Service can resolve this dilemma. But a philosophical swing—whether toward a reinforcement of the generalist mentality at the expense of actual job requirements, toward affirmative action and representativeness as a goal overwhelming other considerations, or toward the contrary position of ignoring such considerations—could undo the progress which has been

[24] There is general agreement that this was true at least until efforts at reform were begun in 1979, as confirmed by an informal survey of college placement officers (1976), by reports of State's inspection corps, and by the various groups investigating the Department's affirmative action efforts.

[25] In 1981 and 1982, there was a shrill exchange of letters between State and the Co-chairs of the Caucus, Representatives Margaret M. Heckler and Patricia Schroeder, with the latter asking for information and statistics in a clearly accusatory vein, notwithstanding the progress already noted. See on this general topic, Francis X. Clines, "Female Diplomats take Stock of Gains," *New York Times*, January 18, 1981.

TABLE 5
Minority and Women FSO's and FSO Candidates, 1976-1981 (Department of State)

MINORITY GROUP MEMBERS	12/31/76			1/20/81 (Estimated)			Change		
	Total Population	Total Minorities	%	Total Population	Total Minorities	%	Total Population	Total Minorities	%
Senior level	657	17	2.6	653	22	3.4	-4	+5	+0.8
Middle level	2,107	123	5.9	2,095	158	7.5	-12	+35	+1.6
Junior level	764	77	10.8	900	204	22.7	+136	+127	+11.9
TOTAL	3,528	217	6.3	3,648	384	10.5	+120	+167	+4.2

WOMEN	12/31/76			1/20/81 (Estimated)			Change		
	Total Population	Total Women	%	Total Population	Total Women	%	Total Population	Total Women	%
Senior level	657	19	2.9	653	19	2.9	-4	0	0
Middle level	2,107	181	8.5	2,095	261	12.5	-12	+80	+4.0
Junior level	764	149	19.5	900	232	25.8	+136	+83	+6.3
TOTAL	3,528	349	9.9	3,648	512	14.0	+120	+163	+4.1

NOTE: Starting January 1978, all junior officers have been appointed as Career Candidates (as Foreign Service Reserve Officers until February 1981 and as "Members of the Foreign Service" since that time). Prior to 1978, minority and women affirmative action junior officer program entrants were appointed as FSR's, and others as FSO's. Under the career candidate program, those who are awarded tenure become FSO's at that time, usually in their fourth year with the Department.

TABLE 6
Women as a Percentage of FSO's and FSO Candidates, 1971-1980 (*Department of State*)

	1971	1972	1973	1974	1975	1976	1977	1978	1979	1980	1981
Class 4 (now 2)	5.3	4.4	5.7	5.3	5.9	7.3	6.3	6.8	7.2	9.1	10.7
Class 5 (now 3)	4.7	6.4	10.4	10.8	14.4	13.5	14.4	14.9	16.1	19.8	21.7
Class 6 (now 4)	9.5	8.3	11.5	13.5	13.9	19.5	19.7	20.0	20.4	20.0	19.9
Classes 7 and 8 (now 5 and 6)	9.4	9.3	16.3	18.8	22.3	19.5	19.0	18.0	19.7	25.1	30.1

Data provided by State's Bureau of Personnel, Office of Management, 1981/2.

made. To lose the chance at diversity would be a tragedy for the Foreign Service as a whole, which clearly needs the infusion of talented individuals with different experiences; and it would be a tragedy as well for those individuals who might be denied a Foreign Service career.

RANK-IN-PERSON VS. RANK-IN-JOB

No single structural attribute of personnel systems has received as much attention as whether rank rests with the individual or with the job he or she holds. The distinction between the Foreign Service and others who work in foreign affairs arises primarily because the former is a rank-in-person system, or as Glenn Stahl would have it, "rank-in-corps," to capture the feature that this kind of system is "so heavily weighted with the idea of 'membership' in a clearly defined and closely-knit group with common backgrounds and ideas."[26] The principle is equal pay for equal rank, rather than the more common (in the U.S.) equal pay for equal work.

In theory the two systems are sharply different, both in philosophy and in operation. Table 7 outlines the important differences.

The rank-in-person/rank-in-job difference parallels other dilemmas. The rank-in-person system, all other things being equal, is more likely to be closed, while rank-in-job arrangements work better with more open systems. Similarly, the rank-in-job system is more likely to have a specialist orientation, while the rank-in-person approach, which does not match job requirements to individual skills as directly, is more likely to produce generalists at best, or dilettantes at worst.[27]

Rank-in-person systems also allow an individual to be assigned, for developmental purposes, to functions outside his or her normal areas of concentration—but the tradeoff is a loss of job-related expertise. Thus, such a system is in constant tension between the

[26] Stahl, *Public Personnel Administration*, p. 63, n. 4.

[27] See, John W. Macy, Jr., *Public Service: The Human Side of Government* (New York: Harper and Row, 1977), p. 42 and ff., for a more detailed discussion of these features.

TABLE 7
Alternative Personnel System Structures

Personnel Function	Rank in Job (Civil Service)	Rank in Person (Foreign Service)
Recruitment	*Current job is key*—Does recruit have qualifications or skills needed for *this* job? Can recruit do what is needed *in this job* better than other qualified applicants? Entrants come in at any level appropriate to job requirements.	*Career* orientation—Can recruit be expected to progress, in a controlled pattern, to the senior ranks of higher career specialty, and be more likely to do so well than competition? Does recruit have potential for long-term advancement in a variety of jobs? Most entrants come in at bottom, rather than mid-career or senior levels.
Placement/ assignment	Tied to specific standards of position in question. No requirement to move from current position. Competition for placement is key to modern merit promotion system. Individual must usually initiate and agree to changes in assignment. Job level and personal rank generally must be consistent. No option to assign above or below class.	Flexible assignments which periodically change. Individual subject to "Service discipline," i.e., to accept any geographic/functional/level assignment system requires. Individuals can be assigned above or below personal class/grade, if needs of Service warrant.

Promotion	Takes place in conjunction with assignments. If selected for a job at a higher level, promotion comes automatically upon beginning duty in that job.	Separate process from assignment. Promotion occurs in competition with other members of class, with number promoted determined by "openings" at next level, in the aggregate, rather than "one-to-one" match of job seekers with positions.
Career "breadth"	Normally, little concern with later career prospects; all is keyed to job in question. The *primary* concern is the immediate job in question rather than long-term career prospects.	Intention is to prepare for senior responsibilities, so next assignment viewed in longer term (developmental), as well as in terms of who is best equipped to perform this job now.
Separation	As long as individual is meeting basic standards of performance for job in question, can retain position (only mechanism is "separation for cause" if does not meet standards of position —standards of grade level, particularly *critical elements under new* Civil Service Reform Act standards).	In order to be retained, individual must a) meet minimum standards or else be separated for cause (like GS option); b) not exceed maximum periods of time in class without promotion ("time-in-class"); c) not be identified, on a *relative basis of comparison of performance* to all other members of his/her class, or being "low ranked"— this implies "up-or-out system" (either be promoted competitively, or leave system).

TABLE 7 (cont.)

Personnel Function	Rank in Job (Civil Service)	Rank in Person (Foreign Service)
Evaluation	Employee performance evaluated only with respect to performance in current position. Only unsatisfactory rating likely to have immediate impact, if leads to separation action (rare); little impact on promotion, assignment, unless employee decides to compete for promotion/reassignment/ transfer.	Employee evaluated not only with respect to current performance, but also regarding career potential. Ratings, even if not unsatisfactory, can have major impact on retention, promotions, assignment, since they are normally used to provide a *relative* ranking of all members of competition group (class level and/or occupational specialty).

SOURCE: Prepared by the author for Bureau of Personnel, Department of State, June 1979.

NOTES: Labor-management relations and grievance regulations and procedures should provide equal due process, but likely to differ in form to meet specific circumstances of each system.

"Decoupling" of promotion and assignment in rank-in-person system needed in situations where frequent rotation of personnel (military, Foreign Service).

Most personnel systems tend to either rank-in-job or rank-in-person, but few if any "pure" systems exist in the public sector.

need for developmental assignments out of cone (to use Foreign Service terminology) and the desire to place the best-qualified individual in each job. The flexibility of the rank-in-person assignment process can be either an aid or a handicap to effective personnel management, depending upon how well the total career is managed. One of the major critiques of the current FSO system is its seeming inability to develop a sequence of assignments in advance which will give an individual officer the kinds of experience he or she needs to be prepared for senior responsibilities.[28]

In a rank-in-person system, promotions are usually decided upon by selection boards composed of members of the service and, usually, representatives of the public, which apply general guidelines (called "precepts" in the case of the Foreign Service) against supervisors' evaluations of all employees at a given level in the category in question. Since the supervisors' evaluations are weighted against standards which are general across many jobs rather than specific to one, evaluation is much more complicated in rank-in-person systems and, as is generally agreed in the Foreign Service, not candid enough (since all comments must by law be shared with the individual rated) to permit fully objective rank-ordering of individuals by selection boards.[29]

In practice, selection boards are independent of management control, once appointed. Thus, supervisors are responsible for ratings but not for promotions. This is one of the major elements inducing identification with the corps rather than with the department or other place of employment. Promotion in rank is independent of one's assignment; one can advance to a higher rank and remain at the same job or post, or vice versa. In a rank-in-job system, promotion is normally through competition for a job at the next higher level. Hence, the current or prospective

[28] Onward assignments usually have been seen as violating the principle of maximum flexibility. However, from 1978 on, State's personnel managers began to pay more attention to the importance of staging the entire career.

[29] Publication of each year's promotion list is often followed by the filing of grievances by those not promoted who feel they should have been. While the decisions of selection boards themselves are not grievable, the contents of an individual's file can be grieved if they are incomplete, inaccurate, or falsely prejudicial, and the Foreign Service Grievance Board can order the promotion made or the decision reconsidered.

superior, as the selecting officer, has direct control of both promotion and assignment. In such a system, employees are less
"independent" as a group, compared with management, except
for whatever promotion guidelines are negotiated with formal
employee representative organizations. If discipline within a rank-
in-person corps is lacking, managers of a department staffed by
that corps, given the relative independence of its employees, can
have real difficulty in carrying out the government's business
according to their own best judgment, if it does not correspond
to that of the corps.

If discipline is good, if there is a sense of the importance of
the task at hand and if a strong service ethic exists, a "rank-in-
corps" system can produce an esprit and morale hard to equal in
the more pedestrian rank-in-job approach: the Foreign Service is
(or at least was) a career and a way of life; being a government
employee in the competitive service is for most simply a job.
However, if these conditions are not met, the rank-in-person system can decline precipitiously to a state of excessive concern with
individual payoffs without any countervailing attention to the public interest. There are many who believe that the Foreign Service
has or will soon reach this state, absent remedial action.

Theoretically, most rank-in-person systems provide for self-
renewal via "up-or-out" features, whereby the least productive
performers are separated from the system. Given the closed nature
of such systems, this is essential to avoid stagnation. However,
as already noted, selection-out has become increasingly difficult
to apply.[30] The situation for rank-in-position systems is even worse
in terms of the ease of separating inadequate performers.[31] However, in the latter it is at least possible to leave people at their
first "level of incompetence,"[32] rather than promote them to higher
levels along with other members of their cohorts, as happens
frequently in rank-in-person systems. The paradox could be that
it is only possible to "grow" a true elite—in the best sense of
the term—in the nominally nonelitist rank-in-job system. The

[30] See Chap. III, notes 47 and 48.

[31] See note 5 above.

[32] See Laurence Peter and Raymond Hull, *The Peter Principle* (New York:
Bantam, 1970).

rank-in-job system, operating at optimum, seems more likely than rank-in-person to promote competence rather than defer to seniority. Stahl, one of the most vociferous critics of rank-in-person systems, may just be right in his hypothesis that "rank-in-job is the system generally more conducive to maximum performance, and rank-in-corps is more conducive to protection and in-breeding."[33]

This reversal of normal expectations arises from the qualifications required at entrance. In rank-in-person systems, and particularly in the Foreign Service, high entrance standards are for the most part maintained. This raises the expectation that all who survive the initial screening are exceptional. In contrast, rank-in-job systems are often less demanding at entry, but arguably more so for later promotions. People in the latter kind of system come to expect that exceptional performance at one level is the primary requirement for promotion to the next; those in rank-in-person systems often appear to believe that passing the initial entrance examination, or at least gaining tenure after a probationary period, should guarantee a place on the promotion escalator until the qualifications for voluntary retirement are met. In an attempt to regain an emphasis on performance, the Foreign Service Act of 1980 requires that those at the senior levels of each occupation who are not promoted after a set period of time leave the Service, unless selection boards find their performance warrants having their careers extended for another three years.[34]

The primary argument the State Department and the Foreign Service make in favor of the current rank-in-person system is that its up-or-out features, special esprit, and ability to assign individuals out of function to any location at any several grade levels are vital, if the unquestioned need for mobility between posts at home and abroad is to be accommodated. While there is some admission that on-the-job competence can suffer from a rank-in-person approach, this drawback is not held to outweigh the presumed benefits. An important question thus arises: How valid is

---

[33] Stahl, "Of Jobs and Men," p. 380.

[34] See Section 607 of the new Foreign Service Act (P.L. 96-465).

the assumption that a mobile service must be based on rank-in-person?

Those who oppose rank-in-person systems in principle argue that a rank-in-job approach can accommodate the need for mobility, if incentives and sanctions are used to further that purpose. For example, it is sometimes held that requiring service in multiple locations as a requisite for promotion would allow this kind of system to function for the Foreign Service,[35] especially if bonuses and allowances are also used to encourage members of the Service to accept demanding and undesirable assignments. Another possible adjustment which might make such a rank-in-job system feasible would be to classify a given position at a range of levels rather than only one. This would allow the assignment of an individual with the necessary competences even if he or she is not ranked at the primary level, without having to force a promotion or demotion. Whether assignments under such a system could be limited to members of the Service, however, is doubtful. Rank-in-job systems, if they are competitive, almost necessitate outside "posting" for a significant proportion of the positions to be filled, and this might be difficult to accommodate.

A final aspect of the rank-in-person/rank-in-job issue is that the latter is clearly the newer approach, and is seen by many as more democratic and less elitist. For most circumstances, in a world that is increasingly specialized, its ability to link individual competences with the requirements of a specific job seems increasingly desirable.

Thus, the conclusion is essentially that already stated with respect to closed versus open systems: use rank-in-person when rotation is essential, but otherwise employ rank-in-job in order to match job requirements and employee skills most closely.

GENERALISTS AND SPECIALISTS

Given the themes of this book, additional discussion of generalists versus specialists may appear superfluous. But for the foreign affairs community this may be the key question of per-

---

[35] Stahl, *Public Personnel Administration*, p. 65.

sonnel system design for the future. If it can be resolved, answers to most of the other problems will be much clearer.

Much of the argument over the respective roles of generalists and specialists is attitudinal: in most of modern American society, and in most parts of the federal establishment, "specialist" has been equated with holding special competences both extremely valuable and hard to obtain, and is therefore a quality worthy of esteem and even deference. In State and the Foreign Service, in contrast, "specialist" is at worst pejorative and at best an attribute worthy of only grudging acceptance, the result of an FSO attitude that this kind of knowledge is less important in foreign affairs and that obtaining it through training and experience almost inevitably produces a lack of breadth.[36] The difference in perspective was captured almost perfectly by a "specialist" in State: "From the viewpoint of science professionals, a generalist is someone who never made it. From the viewpoint of the Foreign Service, a specialist is someone who never will make it."[37]

In contrast, in most large organizations, including particularly the multinational corporations,[38] one must normally prove one's ability as a specialist before being assigned to broader responsibilities. Even among the British—originators in the West of the philosophy that an elite corps of generalists is best qualified for the public service—the idea may be in decline.[39]

The problem is also definitional: one person's generalist is another's dilettante; one's specialist is another's parochial. The vir-

[36] See note 51, Chap. II, for a sometimes lighthearted view of specialists vs. generalists from Aesop to the present; see also Wendell Berry, "Specialized into futility," *Washington Star*, September 11, 1977.

[37] Statement made at a Science Attaché Conference which the author attended, Department of State, 1976.

[38] Levine and Cordier, "Executive Manpower Systems," reviews executive development practices of some major multinational firms.

[39] See, for example, the Report of the Central Policy Review Staff, *Review of Overseas Representation* (London: HMSO, 1977) for a proposal to end the "elitist" mode of operating entirely, by combining the Foreign Service and the larger Home Service. This idea was eventually rejected, but it continues to have wide currency. See the Government's white paper, *The United Kingdom's Overseas Representation*, Cmnd. 7308, August 1978 (London: HMSO, 1978). See also note 44, Chap. I.

tue of pragmatic problem-solving so prized by Foreign Service generalists is often derided as "ad hoc-ery, the curse of the Service," by its specialists. One article, for example, suggests at least five discrete definitions of a generalist:

> The elusive generalist may be an amateur or a professional. He may be someone devoted to policy matters or someone contributing administrative support. He may be someone whose job strongly emphasizes administrative duties, or someone whose job has roughly equivalent amounts of administrative and substantive professional content, or even someone who is a professional first but has added some administrative skills later. He may be someone lodged in a specific organization's career service or someone in a flexible government-wide corps who is readily transferable. The term generalist has applied to all these ideas.[40]

The author concludes that two main ideas predominate in defining generalists: that of *mobility* (flexibility of assignment, transferability among jobs or agencies, or career progression across agency or department lines), and that of *job content* (usually at a high level, whether administrative, executive, or policy-influencing in nature).[41] Confusing the two may be a major source of the problem.

The argument here is that generalists, to fit the future foreign affairs environment, must be able to *integrate* a wide range of considerations in reporting, analyzing, and negotiating on the policy issues affecting their current duties, and they must have *enough specific knowledge* and *practical*, problem-solving *sense* to carry out a diverse range of tasks in the course of their careers. Specialists, on the other hand, must provide in-depth knowledge of increasingly complex issues, and the detailed understanding of regulations, relationships, and precedents necessary to make the system operate efficiently and legally in the morass of current constraints, regulations, and laws. They must also have a good feel how their specialty fits with all the others.

[40] Michael Cohen, "The Generalist and Organizational Mobility," *Public Administration Review* 30 (September/November 1970), 545-46.

[41] Ibid., p. 546.

The obvious point is that both clusters of skills are in desperate demand. The government cannot function effectively unless both are present in sufficient quality and quantity and, even more important, exist in a symbiotic relationship.

What is much less clear is *how* both generalist and specialist skills should be brought into the system. Two broad strategies are possible: to recruit and develop individuals with both qualities, or to produce two separate groups which can work together, providing both kinds of skills through teamwork.

Whichever strategy is adopted, it must be understood that the needs of the Foreign Service on one hand and of the Department of State and other foreign affairs agencies on the other are not synonymous; but in the past the personnel system has not reflected the differences inherent in widely different responsibilities. It cannot be argued seriously that overseas, with the range of demands which members of the Service must face, the primary emphasis can be on anything other than generalist talents; but at home, the demand for specialists is increasingly severe—as is the need for top-level integrative talent able to pull everything together.

Similarly, the system has not provided a routine way for people to move from the specialist system to the generalist one, or vice versa, according to individual talents and predilections. As long as one kind of skill is seen as being superior to the other—in contrast to the more realistic view that modern circumstances require both kinds of people—it will not be possible to solve this problem intelligently.

Thus, the challenge for the future is to provide both generalists and specialists, along with a way for them to move from one category to the other. More objectivity and less theology is required.

RULE-MAKING AND RULE-APPLICATION

Of less apparent significance than the dilemmas considered above but of great importance operationally are issues involving how rules are set, and who makes decisions under such rules: in short, how the personnel system is governed. Sometimes the issue appears as the classic public administration controversy over centralization versus decentralization. In government personnel systems, this issue is clouded because several degrees of centralization are possible: within an agency, within the foreign affairs community across agency lines, or governmentwide. And, some functions may be centralized while others are not; or primary regulation-making may be done centrally but the rules thus set may be applied by decentralized operating units, and such rule-application may or may not be subject to review or "post-audit" by the central system. In the Foreign Service, some matters can be decided by operating units (position descriptions), some by agency management (assignments), some need approval of the Board of Examiners of the Foreign Service (recruitment and hiring procedures), some require adherence to the Office of Personnel Management rules and regulations (EEO matters, classification system), some are the responsibility of a special presidential agent (salary increases), and some can be modified only through legislation (basic premises of the system, salary schedules). In addition, most of these require consultation or negotiation with employee unions.[42]

One critical problem, particularly when a personnel system such as the Foreign Service is "excepted"—that is, subject to some but not all provisions of the basic Civil Service legislation (Title 5 U.S. Code)—is that there may be ambiguity about who can do what, leading to inconsistency over time as a result of a series of ad hoc decisions.

In considering these "who ought to do what" matters, it is important to remember that the best answer to the centralization-decentralization question can differ according to what is at issue: setting the regulations, or operating under them. Table 8 may help to illustrate this point.

Because of the heightened societal pressure for due process, paralleled by the increasing importance of federal employees' unions which demand set rules and procedures,[43] a modest prediction for the future is that rule-setting will likely have to be

---

[42] John W. Macy, Jr., "Reflections on Leaving the Public Services: To Decentralize and to Delegate," *Public Administration Review* 30 (July/August 1970), 438-44.

[43] See items cited in note 4 above.

TABLE 8
Rule-setting and Rule Application

Rule Application	Rule-setting Centralized	Decentralized
Centralized	Tight system; likely to have consistency, but to be cumbersome and slow in operation. Decisions and choices may not match operational requirements. Scarce resources in well-run system may be used most economically.	The most unlikely system since rule-making precedes application; central system most unlikely to be able to make decisions, if they are not also responsible for setting the rules guiding such decisions.
Decentralized	In theory, the most efficient system, featuring common procedures with the advantage of local application to meet specific operational needs. May be resource intensive, unless central system exerts some control of priorities or limits range of discretionary actions.	The line manager's dream system, featuring maximum decentralized authority. Carried to extreme, may mean there is no central system as such, except perhaps as a service institution, providing common recruitment pool, training, new techniques, etc. May not meet overall priorities of government units the personnel system serves, and may be expensive in terms of resources.

more centralized, at least to the agency level. The critical operational issue is likely to be whether decision-making under these rules is also centralized. In the Carter Administration, particularly as a result of the Civil Service reform proposals arising out of the Federal Personnel Management Project (FPMP) in 1977 and early 1978, a trend toward splitting decision-making and rule-applying was apparent. While retaining central regulation-setting, the Civil Service Commission took a number of steps in May 1978 intended to place "more authority and accountability for taking personnel actions in the hands of responsible agency decision makers,"[44] and when the Office of Personnel Management came into existence on January 1, 1979, the trend continued, although somewhat unevenly. By 1983, however, OPM under the Reagan Administration seemed bent on recapturing tighter central control of agency personnel operations, and it withdrew a number of previous delegations to agencies, especially with respect to appointments and reductions in force.

Within State, there have been several recent swings from centralization to decentralization and back again, particularly with respect to assignments. The natural tendency has been toward fragmentation, with the various regional "clubs" seeking to control assignments in their areas, attempting to retain the services of the best officers while pushing the less talented off to others. Strong "clubs," such as the Bureau of European Affairs, normally have had considerable success in corralling a disproportionate number of the most talented officers. Periodically, this has been countered by attempts to exert more central management control, either to reduce parochialism by forcing officers to serve in more than one area or to try to use increasingly scarce resources more effectively.[45] In USIA and AID, the situation is roughly the same, with somewhat more central control. But the battle goes on.

Another question has to do more with the amount of regulation than with who regulates. It has always been true in federal personnel systems that some kinds of functions, for example the

[44] "CSC Delegates Personnel Authorities to Agencies," *CSC News* (Press Release), May 4, 1978.

[45] Because of increasingly limited resources, centralization seems more likely to prevail, but not without sustained rearguard actions by the bureaus.

retirement system, are much more rule intensive than others, such as promotion. The same can be true for one system compared with another. This has been a major force behind pressures to create independent "excepted" or "exempted" personnel systems, operating under their own legislative authority and, to a greater or lesser degree, outside the "clutches" of the Civil Service Commission (now the Office of Personnel Management).[46] The argument is that "unique circumstances make it impossible for Agency X to carry out its assigned mission unless it has a hand-tailored personnel system which Agency X controls." The goal is managerial discretion, by limiting the amount of regulation from any source.

Independent systems appear to have a limited future. Their lack of outside regulation, while it brings the cherished managerial flexibility, can also bring arbitrariness. Judicial and legislative emphasis on due process makes it likely that regulation and specificity by *someone* will be a necessity in the future. It still seems necessary to have a separate personnel system, rather than one that is part of the Civil Service, for employees of foreign affairs agencies who rotate between home and abroad (see next section); but it is almost certain to be a more regulated system than has been true of the Foreign Service in the past. The Foreign Service Act of 1980, for example, provided for considerable tightening of appointment and of tenuring procedures for non-FSO categories and for the new Senior Foreign Service (see Chapter VI), but with almost all operational authority resting with the individual agencies using the Foreign Service system. State would have preferred that more uniformity be required since as the lead agency it would have been likely to have its way, but the other agencies would not go along. It still seems likely, however, that movement in

[46] For the most complete listing of the statutorily excepted systems, and the exceptions or exemptions they have from the competitive service, see U.S. Civil Service Commission, *Statutory Exceptions to the Competitive Service*, A Report to the Committee on Post Office and Civil Service of the United States Senate, 93rd Congress, 1st session (Washington, D.C.: GPO, July 1973). Almost the only attempt to compile a complete listing, it nevertheless has some omissions, and does not deal with the very large category of administrative (versus statutory) exemptions.

138 • NO PERFECT SCHEMES

this direction will be necessary to run an efficient and equitable Foreign Service.

A SINGLE SERVICE?

Intertwined with the excepted-competitive service issue is whether it is more desirable to have a unified and independent personnel system for the entire Department of State or perhaps even for the foreign affairs community as a whole, or to have multiple systems (most likely Foreign Service and Civil Service) so as to reflect very different conditions of work (generalists and specialists; individuals serving rotational careers versus those who serve only at headquarters).

The battle between these two camps continued in State almost from passage of the Foreign Service Act of 1946 until it was replaced by the Foreign Service Act of 1980. Before 1946, the Foreign and Civil Service were so separated that FSO's had to resign to accept a departmental position for an extended period of time.[47] The major foreign affairs personnel reform studies conducted since 1946 have invariably made system structure a central theme of inquiry. Studies done by members of the Foreign Service have almost always favored a single system, while those by outsiders have tended to emphasize the advantages of separate personnel systems tailored to the special requirements of different elements of the foreign affairs community.[48]

The contest has been waged at both philosophical and pragmatic levels. Many in the Foreign Service have believed the solution rests in using the same labels and personnel system for all foreign affairs employees, or at least all professionals. The argument is usually made for an entirely separate Foreign Service independent to the maximum possible degree of outside control—rather than

[47] "Foreign Service rules required that no officer could spend more than four consecutive years in the Department between overseas assignments." Martin Weil, *A Pretty Good Club: The Founding Fathers of the U.S. Foreign Service* (New York: W.W. Norton, 1978), p. 80.

[48] For a reasonably complete bibliography of these past studies, see William I. Bacchus, "Diplomacy for the 70's: An Afterview and Appraisal," *American Political Science Review* 68 (June 1974), 736, n. 4.

for extending the Civil Service system to the entire foreign affairs community.[49] Most, however, favor not a totally unified personnel system but rather two or more related systems—perhaps one for generalists, one for specialists who serve both at home and abroad, a third for officers who serve at home exclusively, and a fourth for lower-level staff. Few are willing to follow the single system logic to the ultimate conclusion of common labels and grades for all. The inconsistency can be traced to the fact that human beings make distinctions, inevitably, between those who are in the glamour occupations of a particular organization and everyone else.[50]

There are two ways to address this problem: to expand the occupation list considered to be at the core of the organization's mission;[51] or to consider personnel systems as neutral management instruments designed to make it possible to hire, assign, evaluate, promote, discipline, protect, pay, and separate employees, and not as status symbols determining an internal pecking-order. Reality suggests that the second option is more viable. But to follow this approach would call into question the very core of the mystique which, at least in the minds of FSO's, attaches to the Foreign Service. Labels count too much and individual talents too little.

On the practical side, there is considerably more to be said for the single system approach. At State, prior to the new Foreign Service Act, it was not uncommon to find individuals in several different pay systems working side by side but subject to different rules regarding conduct, evaluation, promotion, grade structures,

---

[49] A good example was an internal commentary prepared within the Bureau of Personnel in December 1975 by Paul von Ward, a middle-grade FSO, entitled "A case for why we should not change." Ward would have gone further than most toward a truly unified system (see rest of paragraph). The Assistant Secretary for Administration in State at the time, John Thomas, was perhaps the strongest senior supporter of a single system, essentially for the reasons mentioned.

[50] For a useful discussion of this phenomenon and a helpful schematic representation, see Frederick C. Mosher, *Democracy and the Public Service* (New York: Oxford University Press, 1968), pp. 110-23.

[51] See Morton H. Halperin (with the assistance of Priscilla Clapp and Arnold Kanter), *Bureaucratic Politics and Foreign Policy* (Washington, D.C.: Brookings Institution, 1974), pp. 28-40, on the idea of "organizational essence," or the view of an organization's dominant group about what its "missions and capabilities should be."

separation, and retirement. In addition, individuals have converted from one system to another at their own advantage, without true competition or the application of any controlling standards. A system—any single system—would eliminate many of these discrepancies.

On the other hand, clarification of when each system should be used, as the Foreign Service Act of 1980 attempts, can eliminate many such problems. Many of the practical arguments leveled against a dual system are valid only in the context of the current Foreign and Civil Service systems; they are not universally true. A more stable approach to classification, position designation, and promotion procedures, all designed to accommodate the Washington situation (there is universal agreement that the Foreign Service system was designed essentially for overseas conditions, with the need for periodic time in the U.S. almost an afterthought) would make multiple systems much more manageable than they are today.

Close analysis is required before one can determine whether single or multiple systems cost more to manage. Because of the need to make frequent assignments and to evaluate virtually all individuals every year for the purpose of promotion, retention, and performance pay awards, rather than just as positions become vacant, the Foreign Service is much more expensive to manage in these respects than the Civil Service; thus, a single system devised along these lines for all of State and perhaps other agencies as well would likely be considerably more costly than the present arrangement. But as the Civil Service begins to place much more emphasis on evaluation—for example, for performance pay for the Senior Executive Service and for employees on the General Manager Schedule established by the Civil Service Reform Act (CSRA) of 1978—these differences will likely narrow. An agency using Civil Service personnel is able to borrow some services from the central system in areas such as recruitment, evaluation, and, more unevenly, approaches to personnel management. At the same time, of course, this system cannot be as well tailored to individual agency requirements, and its centralization can cause delays and rigidity. Such inflexibility was one of the major forces behind the Carter Administration's comprehensive Civil Service reform program, but the trade-off is that more fine-tuning by agencies means that less can be borrowed from the center.

Finally, some aspects of the single/multiple system dispute are only semantic. Very few actually believe that a totally undifferentiated system is workable; single-system advocates seem most concerned that an equitable "umbrella" cover the whole system. Any personnel system must be able to accommodate diverse needs. If not separate systems, there must at least be subsystems tailored to the specific requirements of individual organizations. They can either exist under a common label or be separate and independent; in principle either approach would be workable.

LABOR-MANAGEMENT RELATIONS: COPING WITH INEVITABILITY?

Evidence of changing societal norms and employee expectations in the public service is clearly demonstrated by the recent history of federal employees' unions. Should such organization be allowed? If so, should this right extend to those in occupations related to national security and foreign affairs?

It is widely accepted that there are major differences between the public and private sectors regarding the appropriate role for unions. There is less agreement about the extent to which foreign affairs officials should form yet a third category. Management usually argues that they do and should be treated differently, with more limited rights; employees usually agree they are different but assert broader rights;[52] and outsiders often downplay the differences and assert that the Foreign Service should be covered by the same laws and policy applying to all other civilian employees. Federal employees' unions are almost certainly here to stay,[53] so

[52] That is, management has usually believed that there should be either no unionization or less scope of bargaining, while employee organizations have argued that the Foreign Service requires different rules from the Civil Service, and very broad scope of bargaining and few restrictions on bargaining unit membership.

[53] Contrary to the Murphy Commission recommendations (to which the author subscribed at the time) that those serving on presidential commissions (FSO's) should be prohibited from organizing and that other members of the Foreign Service should be allowed to organize following the same rules as the Civil Service. It

the issue is how to accommodate them without rendering the system unmanageable.[54]

Government unions are old, but their current form is quite new. In 1912, federal employees gained the right to organize (as long as their unions did not authorize the use of strikes), and to petition Congress, through the Lloyd-LaFollette Act. This was the only statutory base for the organization of federal employees until 1979,[55] and it was distinctly limited compared with the National Labor Relations Act of 1935, governing the private sector.[56]

There are a number of differences between the public and private sectors, of course. One highly respected former official summarized three primary ones as follows:[57]

> First, in private enterprise authority is located clearly at the top. . . . In democratic governments, on the other hand, as in unions, ultimate authority is at the base rather than at the top of the structure. . . .
>
> The second difference that affects relationships lies in the way that management authority actually is exercised in democratic governments. While government leaders do have defined authority to act as management, the nature of their action is strongly affected by the need to weigh and balance divergent interests of major groups or among the citizens they represent. . . .
>
> This leads to the third main point of difference: Many of the working conditions of public employees that are regarded as uniquely different and perhaps less beneficial than those in

seems clear that the time has passed when "no union" is a viable alternative, except for the military, the intelligence community, and certain confidential groups of employees such as inspectors, investigators, and auditors.

[54] For a very illuminating analysis of the point that union activity has reinforced the rigidities already introduced by cumbersome Civil Service law and regulations, see James W. Fesler, *Public Administration: Theory and Practice* (Englewood Cliffs, N.J.: Prentice-Hall, Inc., 1980), pp. 113-21, which also provides an excellent short history of the union movement in the federal government.

[55] Shafritz et al, p. 196 and chapter 10, passim.

[56] Clark, "Foreign Affairs Personnel Management," Murphy Commission Appendix Volume VI, p. 214. The statutory base provided by the CSRA of 1978, effective January 1, 1979, did not notably affect the basic limitations.

[57] Macy, *Public Service*, pp. 137-38.

private business are the product of public policy. If it is a policy of any significance, the amount of pressure for change brought to bear by an employee union seldom has much to do with finding a solution.

Not until the issuance of Executive order 10988 on January 17, 1962, was there a regularized basis for conducting labor-management relations (LMR) within the Executive branch. Further developments occurred in the Nixon Administration when, after a review of federal LMR programs, Executive order 11491 was issued on January 1, 1970. It brought a number of private sector procedures into federal relationships, including adversary bargaining, and for the first time established a centralized federal mechanism for regulating LMR. This order provided for "national consultation rights" for organizations representing a "substantial number of employees."

By 1977, employees' unions no longer deemed E.O. 11491 satisfactory; what they most desired was a statutory basis for LMR in government, since a "stroke of the pen" could revoke the Executive order and abolish employees' rights to organize. Thus, the Federal Personnel Management Project (FPMP) concentrated a good part of its attention on proposals for a statutory replacement for the Executive order. The eventual outcome of this project was Title VII of the CSRA, there having been in the meantime a Byzantine series of "arrangements" by which union support for or at least acquiescence in overall Civil Service reform was the quid pro quo for Administration advocacy of a statutory base for federal government labor-management relations.[58]

Much before this, however, the State Department had become concerned with E.O. 11491, not because it provided too little but because it allowed too much. Shortly after E.O. 11491 had been issued, William B. Macomber, State's Deputy Under Secretary of State for Management, led an effort to exclude the Foreign Service from its provisions:

[58] For the range of alternatives involved, see FPMP Option Paper 4, "Federal Government Labor-Management Relations," September 20, 1977, as well as the FPMP Final Staff Report, Section 7 (Washington, D.C.: U.S. Civil Service Commission, December 20, 1977), pp. 165-80.

In letters to the Chairman of the Civil Service Commission, dated November 14 and 20, 1970, Macomber argued that E.O. 11491 applied primarily to the Civil Service and that the three foreign affairs agencies (State, USIA, and AID) required their own framework. He based his position on (1) the special conditions of employment, compensation, and benefits of the Foreign Service, (2) rank-in-the-man system, (3) the requirements of worldwide mobility under a flexible assignment system, and (4) "the more intimate relationship required between the President, Secretary of State, and the personnel who are entrusted with the execution of United States foreign policy."[59]

In particular, State objected to those features of E.O. 11491 which provided for exclusive recognition, adversary bargaining, and the settlement of disputes by outsiders, on grounds that an adversary relationship between the heads of foreign affairs agencies and FSO's could harm the conduct of foreign affairs and thus "could be detrimental to our national security."[60] The Department first proposed that agencies using the Foreign Service system be excluded from E.O. 11491 and operate instead under a memorandum from the President to agency heads, but opposition from the Federal Labor Relations Council (which believed that E.O. 11491 was entirely appropriate and that exception was not required) led the President to conclude that a separate Executive order was the best compromise. Eventually, E.O. 11636 was issued on December 17, 1971.

While 11636 followed 11491 regarding the rights of management and employees, election of exclusive representatives, unfair practices, and other aspects, it also had a number of unique features: "consultation" on proposed personnel policies vice "negotiation"; the requirement for a single, agencywide bargaining unit covering all Foreign Service employees rather than smaller units based on a community of interest; an authorization for the Secretary of State to issue regulations defining appeals procedures; and the inclusion of certain supervisors within bargaining units. It also provided an extensive structure to administer the Executive order.

[59] Clark, "Foreign Affairs Personnel Management," p. 214.
[60] Ibid., p. 215. Also source for remainder of paragraph.

AFSA became the employee representative for all three agencies in 1973 elections, although it won narrowly over AFGE in USIA. (In 1976, in a new election, the latter became the representative for USIA, a change which was to have implications for passage and implementation of the Foreign Service Act of 1980; see Chapter VI.)

By 1975, the Murphy Commission concluded that, from the viewpoint of effective personnel management, the E.O. 11636 "compromise" had not worked particularly well: "What was intended originally as continuing 'consultation' within the family of the Foreign Service is fast becoming a complex, adversary, legalistic personnel governance system where the lines between management and the 'union' are hard to find."[61] The commission argued that many problems existed: there was a lack of management direction; a central role for the Board of the Foreign Service was inappropriate when many of its members had no LMR experience; real conflicts of interest existed by virtue of members of management sometimes having a stake in both sides of the bargaining; and consultation and "rolling negotiations" acted to paralyze personnel management. Their conclusion was that it would be most desirable to "roll back the clock" by revoking E.O. 11636, covering nonofficer employees under E.O. 11491, and allowing Foreign Service officer-level employees to be represented through AFSA or other organizations as professional associations rather than as unions. There should also be, it said, a single focal point in each agency for LMR, clarification of internal policies, and streamlining of procedures.[62] By late 1982, some of these 1975 proposals which seemed sensible at the time appeared unrealistic. It is now inconceivable that termination of the right to organize, except possibly for the most senior officers, would be tolerated. The question is not whether unions, but rather how unions should be accommodated.

The Foreign Service Act of 1980 made LMR statutory for the Foreign Service, and in the process moved the foreign affairs system considerably closer to that of the Civil Service, notwithstanding the continuing differences between the Foreign and Civil

[61] Ibid., p. 216.
[62] Murphy Commission Report, pp. 190-92. See also ibid., pp. 217-18.

Service cited by Macomber in 1970. Exclusive representation, adversary bargaining, and referral of disputes and unfair labor practice charges to outsiders were all institutionalized by statute. The future is unknown, but will bear close watching.

While the past record of LMR in the foreign affairs agencies has been mixed, under the right circumstances the existence of exclusive employee representative organizations could be a positive force. If, as argued, the Foreign Service is less externally "regulated" than the competitive service, then strong and professional employee groups conceivably can help check managerial tendencies toward arbitrariness. Together with management, they can also aid in defining workable standards of employee conduct and discipline, help set realistic career expectations in a way management cannot do as well on its own, arbitrate solutions when the interests of different groups of employees conflict, provide assistance for troubled employees, and aid employees in knowing when they have a legitimate complaint or grievance about the way they have been treated, and when their troubles are of their own making.

In sum, just as there are significant differences between the private and public sectors with respect to the appropriate form of employee organization and representation, there are major differences between the general federal system and the foreign affairs community; but they are not of such magnitude as to sustain an argument for a totally different form of representation, although special circumstances do need to be accommodated. A greater explicitness of procedures, a professionalization of those handling LMR on both the union and management sides, and a greater degree of trust between management and employees would go a long way toward providing what is needed.

In recognition of these factors, the Foreign Service Act of 1980 accepted employee organization as a fundamental right, making Chapter 10 of Title I the equivalent of Title VII of the Civil Service Reform Act of 1978; for if two million civil service employees were granted statutory rights, could the rights of fewer than twenty thousand members of the Foreign Service be treated any differently? Reality suggested not.

POLITICAL CONTROL VS. PROFESSIONAL EXPERTISE

Another classic public personnel issue in the United States arises at the difficult meeting-point of partisan politics and professional administration. Political appointees and career civil servants need each other and their roles can or should be symbiotic, but tensions persist.[63]

Today, no American President can afford to leave the nation's foreign policy in the hands of officials who are not responsible to himself. To do otherwise would be to abdicate his constitutional responsibilities. So the question is not whether presidential appointees should occupy essential senior foreign affairs positions, but rather which individuals the President should appoint. The Foreign Service has almost universally contended that career officers (i.e., themselves) should be appointed to such positions. The protests at the beginning of the Carter Administration that twenty-two of the top thirty-six positions in State were filled by outsiders were typical of the latest replication of the quadrennial cycle, once again repeated at the beginning of the Reagan Administration, when AFSA issued a press release complaining that as of October 18, 1981, thirty-six of eighty-one Ambassadors selected were not members of the Career Service.[64] Both statements were based in part on a sincere belief that diplomacy requires those professionally trained if it is to be conducted successfully; in part on self-interest in retaining desirable assignments (and therefore promotions) for the Service itself; and in part on the valid contention that, through the years, a number of politically appointed Ambassadors had been less than superb choices.[65]

[63] See Heclo, *Government of Strangers*, passim., and in particular chapter 7, "Doing Better: Policies for Governing Policymakers," pp. 235-64.

[64] See Hydle's statement, cited above in note 18, for the AFSA complaint against the Carter Administration; and for that against the Reagan Administration, "Reagan faulted in choice of Envoys: Foreign Service Group Complaints," *Washington Post*, October 14, 1981, and an editorial, "Have Tux, Will Travel," *Wall Street Journal*, October 16, 1981.

[65] With respect to ambassadorial assignments, the Carter Administration attempted to ensure that anyone nominated for an ambassadorial position was in fact qualified, through creation of an Ambassadorial Appointments Commission, chaired first by former Governor Ruben Askew of Florida and subsequently by Clark Clifford, to pass on the qualifications of candidates. In the author's opinion,

Yet the assumption that the professional Foreign Service officer is always most desirable for such positions must be challenged. It is not clear, first, that the standard Foreign Service career equips officers for senior responsibilities, particularly if management and/ or policy integration and consensus-building are involved. And in the case of ambassadorial appointments, the FSO will not necessarily have any greater degree of knowledge about a specific country than the outsider or career official from another part of government, and may have less; an Edwin Reischauer is likely to know more about Japan, having spent a lifetime on work related to that country, than an FSO who may have served one tour there, or even none at all.[66] This is another way of saying that generalists do not always make the best Ambassadors; sometimes, an expert with the "right" experience may best suit a particular situation. If one believes that diplomacy is as much art as science, then the lack of diplomatic experience may not unduly handicap such individuals, if they have an acquired or intuitively have an innate sense of how to operate effectively in the environment to which they are posted.

Indeed, the juxtaposition of career officers and noncareer political appointees may lead to better policy, as Frederick C. Mosher argued in the late 1960's:

> Unless—or until—political appointees at . . . upper levels are a good deal more professionally identified with the career elites of their agencies, they will provide substantial protection against narrow professional and career domination of governmental programs. Their education, their background, and their orientation and values are significantly different from those of

---

this was a distinct improvement on previous practice, although political considerations were by no means removed from the deliberations. Attempts were made in both the House and Senate to establish this commission by statute during the consideration of the 1980 Foreign Service Act, but rejected on grounds that it was up to the President to choose his own methods for nominating qualified candidates for Senate confirmation. The Reagan Administration established a less formal review process, which appeared to be more oriented toward political loyalty, while not disregarding qualifications.

[66] Career FSO's, of course, are much more likely to have had a varied and extensive overseas experience, which is a positive factor in appointing them as Ambassadors.

the career personnel, whether civil service or career system.
. . . their experience is more varied as to employers and field
of work; their orientation is more likely to be toward that of
their political superiors than of their career subordinates. They
offer some assurance that considerations other than those of
career professionals will condition administrative decisions and
they thus contribute to a more effective and active representation
of the interests of the whole people than would a service totally
dominated by specialists.[67]

Finally, as domestic and foreign policy become increasingly
intertwined, it is necessary to be more concerned than in the past
that senior foreign affairs officials are closely attuned to domestic
politics. This calls into question whether career FSO's have an
inherent advantage in senior posts, unless that advantage is reinforced by knowledge and experience in relevant domestic areas.

For the future, the lesson is clear: it will be more important to
know who the political appointees are as individuals, rather than
who they are by affiliation or background. It will be necessary to
match individuals carefully with specific positions, and to search
more widely to find appointees. Above all, it may be dangerous
to presume that any one segment of society, or of the public
service, is inherently better suited as a group for specific responsibilities. If this argument is accepted, then it follows that the
government and its foreign affairs personnel managers will have
to be much more specific about what each position requires, and
much more sophisticated at evaluating the credentials of prospective appointees. All Ambassadorial jobs are not the same.
Hiding behind either career experience or proximity to a particular
President should not be used as a cover to avoid a better matching
of job responsibilities with individuals' attributes and experiences.

PROFESSIONAL MANAGEMENT OR MANAGEMENT BY THE PROFESSION?

A basic drive of every profession, established or emergent,
is *self-government* in deciding policies, criteria, and standards

[67] Mosher, *Democracy and the Public Service*, pp. 169-70. By "career system,"
Mosher means a rank-in-person service such as the Foreign Service.

for employment and advancement and in deciding individual
personnel matters. The underlying argument for such professional hegemony is that no one outside—no amateur—is equipped
to judge or even to understand the true content of the profession
or the ingredients of merit in its practice. The argument is
difficult to challenge, particularly in highly developed, specialized, and scientized fields with which an amateur—or a
professional in personnel administration—can have only a passing acquaintance.[68]

The tension Mosher describes above has long been present
within the foreign affairs agencies and has contributed heavily to
the difficulty of personnel management. The Foreign Service has
been unwilling either to relinquish management responsibilities
for its very complex personnel system to professional personnelists
or to make the commitment and devote the resources of its own
that would be necessary to make the system work.

This can be seen most clearly in the assignment function, which
is at the heart of the current Foreign Service system. Members
of the Foreign Service change positions, and usually posts, on a
two- to three-year cycle. This necessitates a complex process of
matching individual competences, preferences, career development needs, and circumstances with the requirements of specific
positions at specific posts. A broken assignment, for whatever
reason, can set off a chain reaction of new assignments.

These assignment decisions are made by Foreign Service members, with some acting as counselors for specific subcategories of
officers (e.g., middle-grade economic officers, or secretaries, or
junior officers) and others serving as assignment officers for particular bureaus in Washington and the overseas positions controlled by those bureaus. Counselors too, are assigned to their
positions for two or three years—which means that they assign
each individual in their pool, and assignment officers fill each job
for which they are responsible, on the average only once before
they, too, move along. Knowledge of either jobs or people—
adjudged to be critical in making assignments in other organi-

[68] Ibid., p. 124. Emphasis in original.

zations—is hardly of professional quality under such circumstances.

Similarly, the Foreign Service makes much of the rigors of its FSO recruitment process as insurance for the quality of the corps—but the deputy examiners (of the Board of Examiners of the Foreign Service) who administer the final assessment (see Chapter V), themselves FSO's, serve for only a single year, and do so with no accredited professional training. The difficulty is compounded because the Service cannot always persuade its best officers to accept these demanding assignments; so they often become dumping grounds for officers who cannot be placed elsewhere.

Personnel policy planning, the longest-range function, is also at the mercy of nonprofessional personnelists on short-term assignments. While in recent years some remarkably talented and perceptive FSO's have held the planning jobs located in various areas of the Bureau of Personnel, they usually come to them with little prior personnel experience, and only begin thoroughly to understand the complexities of the system about the time they are due to move on.

The evaluation and promotion system is consciously designed to ensure that peers—not personnel professionals—rate and rank members of the Foreign Service, and that the same individuals do not serve on annual boards more than once or twice during a career. While it may work better than elsewhere in government, this is still the Service's classic manifestation of the basic drive described above: only peers are held to be able to manage careers of other members of the Service, even if they have no experience or training in the admittedly complex function of evaluation.

The conclusion to be drawn from these admitted facts, unlike those attaching to many of the older dilemmas discussed, is clear and widely shared. If State and the Foreign Service are ever to have the personnel system required to meet their responsibilities, there will have to be more professionalism than now exists. This is not a new idea. As early as the fall of 1976, as noted in Chapter III, a survey of officer positions in the Department's Bureau of Personnel (which was approved by the then Director General and other senior officers) suggested that substantially more Bureau of Personnel (PER) positions should be filled by personnel professionals who would remain in their positions for extended periods of time.[69] The concept, which still seems appropriate, was that in central personnel functions both professional personnel competence and Foreign Service experience are needed if the system is to be managed effectively.

The mere substitution of different skills, however, will not be sufficient. And the alternative—professional personnelists as managers—itself has a serious weakness. For professional personnelists in government are almost always in the Civil Service, and have normally lacked knowledge about, and sympathy for, the peculiar circumstances of the Foreign Service. In addition, the whole field of public personnel management will become considerably more difficult and complex in the years ahead, whether for the Foreign Service or other federal systems.

This suggests that a new breed of professional personnel managers for foreign affairs must be developed: neither FS generalists nor GS personnel specialists as now trained and assigned are likely to be able to do what is needed. Attuned to foreign service "circumstances" and to sound personnel management practices, and willing to use innovative techniques, such a cadre of managers would see its career potential measured in how well the foreign affairs personnel systems—FS, GS, or whatever—are managed, and how well the "products" of these systems—the people on the job—carry out their responsibilities. Ideally, this cadre would serve all the foreign affairs agencies and would expect to cross agency lines in their own career assignments, thus providing a means of knitting together the various foreign affairs personnel systems in a way which has been much talked about in the past but never achieved.

If such a cadre can be created, the next and equally necessary requirement will be to give the personnel system they run the "clout" necessary to manage the people in the departments and agencies involved. Unless the thousands of individual decisions can be made to stick, the system will not work. Centralized,

---

[69] The author participated in this survey. See Chap. III at notes 26 and 27 for details.

professional management is essential to a successful foreign affairs personnel system.

FAMILIES AND THE FOREIGN SERVICE

Before leaving the major dilemmas and choices facing the Foreign Affairs community in the 1980's, one of a quite different order than the personnel management issues discussed earlier must be considered, because it may be the paramount factor determining whether the government can maintain competent representation abroad. The rapid emergence of family-related problems, as a major element of concern for managers, a phenomenon hardly limited to the U.S. Foreign Service or to governments alone and one which threatens to override everything else, can be attributed both to the major growth in the influence of women's rights movements in Western societies and to the changing conditions of Foreign Service life abroad. Without the first, the kind of reanalysis of the role of women in modern society, which has been extended to the Foreign Service, would not have taken place; without the latter, the problem would not have become so important in so short a time.

The distance traveled is best shown by the fact that as recently as 1972 a Foreign Service Officer was evaluated not only on *his* own performance but also on how well his wife contributed to the work of the mission abroad. In a 1972 directive, State ended the period of "two for one" hiring (that is, treating spouses as associate employees of the Department) by eliminating this type of evaluation,[70] and at about the same time rescinded its old regulation that women officers must resign upon marriage.[71] Viewed

[70] Department of State Circular Airgram A-728 of March 22, 1972; repeated for purposes of possible review as DG Notice C-36 of May 31, 1978.

[71] The regulation requiring women officers to resign upon marriage was rescinded by a Joint State/AID/USIA message (CA-3745) of August 11, 1971, also published in Washington as a State Department Notice on August 16, 1971. This policy also included other changes to improve employment opportunities for women. A State telegram (number 054807) of March 19, 1974, announced, however, that no reappointments of women forced to resign under the old policy had yet been made, due to hiring and budget restrictions, but renewed the policy and gave it

from 1982, both of these old ways of doing business seem archaic in the extreme.

There are numerous signs, however, that the early intent of straightforward replacement of an older approach with one more nearly reflecting the circumstances of modern American society was too simple-minded. If we learned that women did not view the world, particularly in an auxiliary role, in the same way as men, why should we have assumed that all women—or all men— saw things the same way?

Two benchmarks underscore this point. In 1977, The Forum of the Association of American Foreign Service Women (estab- lished the previous year to analyze the "Concerns of Foreign Service Women and Families," i.e., of both spouses and women employees) produced a comprehensive report. The areas of in- terest of the contributing study groups—Family Life, the Modern Foreign Service Wife, Orientation, Re-entry, and Women in Tran- sition (retirement, widowhood, and divorce)—provide a typical list of the range of problems, although in the past few years questions of employment, both at post during the spouse's as- signment and more dramatically in terms of interrupted careers, have come to assume ever greater importance. Along with many other recommendations, the Forum Report called for establish- ment of a Family Liaison Office, the mandate of which would be to "(1) Provide regular and dependable dissemination of infor- mation from the foreign affairs agencies to family members in Washington and abroad, and (2) Communicate the views and needs of Foreign Service families to the foreign affairs agencies, especially on policy matters and planning affecting their wel- fare."[72] "FLO" was established shortly thereafter, both in Wash- ington and at many posts abroad, but as of mid-1982 its efficacy, other than as a symbol of concern and an in-house lobbying or- ganization, was still very much subject to question.

The deeper complexities were perhaps better shown by a sym-

---

new emphasis. This, too, was announced in a subsequent Department Notice, dated March 22, 1974.

[72] "Report on the Concerns of Foreign Service Spouses and Families," Wash- ington, D.C.: The Forum of the Association of American Service Women, March 1977. The quotation is from page 6 of the report.

posium on "Diplomacy: The Role of the Wife," published by Georgetown University in 1981. Not surprisingly, it reflected a diversity of views, "six or seven," in the estimation of the symposium's editor, "four distinct approaches," in the view of a Foreign Service officer who reviewed the work.[73] Both agreed, however, that a "modernist" versus "traditionalist" dichotomy seriously underestimated the diversity of views.

This should not be unexpected: some spouses continued to want to be helpmates; some wanted nothing more than recognition for their contributions made according to traditional patterns; some wished to have their own careers, as an addition to their lives and not as a replacement for traditional functions; and some wanted nothing to do with official responsibilities.

The response of the foreign affairs agencies to these pressures has been basically supportive, albeit tentative, in part because meshing spouses' circumstances and desires with realities of service abroad is seldom easy.

First, with respect to employment, the several agencies, after some false starts, attempted to provide at least some job opportunities at embassies themselves, mostly as temporary substitutes in vacant positions, and as "FLO" coordinators, which the unkind might view as an effort to buy off the most militant spouses. Allocating such positions to Foreign Service spouses, however, created new dilemmas. For example, how can morale and esprit be maintained among career Foreign Service secretaries if they see some of the most attractive jobs given to Foreign Service wives? Similarly, how can Foreign Service nationals be kept happy if positions normally in their career ladders become the property of spouses, who, in addition, are paid on U.S. salary scales higher than those of local citizens working side by side with them?[74]

[73] Martin F. Herz, ed., *Diplomacy: The Role of the Wife: A Symposium*, Institute for the Study of Diplomacy, Edmund A. Walsh School of Foreign Service (Washington, D.C.: Georgetown University, 1981). The review is Lawrence B. Lesser, "Writers Contribute to Symposium on the Role of Wives: Four Views are Said to Predominate," *State Magazine* 233 (April 1981), 26-28. A report on a subsequent conference held about the symposium appeared as "How about a 'No Strike' clause for Foreign Service Wives? This was one of many questions at Georgetown U. symposium," *State Magazine* 235 (June 1981), 21-22.

[74] The Foreign Service Act of 1980 contained authority to pay spouses and

Efforts were also made to negotiate agreements with other governments for the reciprocal employment of embassy spouses in the local economy, but this was a slow and often complicated process.[75] Of course, while this may provide short-term employment for wives, and perhaps enhance a feeling of self-worth, it cannot address a more fundamental problem which is becoming increasingly important: how to reconcile the need to move from place to place in the Foreign Service with the career aspirations of a marriage partner. Fill-in work cannot substitute for the practice of a profession, except for those fortunate few such as artists, writers, and perhaps teachers who can carry their occupations abroad with them. Something eventually will have to give, if one spouse wishes to be a member of the Service and the other wishes to have a profession which is not compatible with frequent transfers from post to post.

As the magnitude of the employment problem became more apparent in the late 1970's and early 1980's, the foreign affairs agencies of the U.S. government began to explore additional possibilities, beyond these limited efforts. Each, however, appeared to raise as many problems as it was likely to solve.

For spouses who were career oriented, there seemed to be only two realistic possibilities short of asking one's spouse to quit the Foreign Service: either join the Service oneself, or accept long periods of separation during overseas postings. A third possibility, the creation of a special "spouse career" involving payment for traditional representational, social, and charitable activities, as well as formal recognition for such a role, did not seem, as of this writing, to be popular with the Foreign Service or easily

---

other family members on either U.S. or Foreign National Pay Scales (Section 311 of P.L. 96-465, 22 U.S.C. 3951), but pressures from spouses made it clear by mid-1981 that the only acceptable way would be compensation using U.S. government pay schedules.

[75] As of April 1983, ten such bilateral employment agreements had been negotiated with other governments (Bolivia, Canada, Colombia, Denmark, France, Jamaica, New Zealand, Norway, Sweden, United Kingdom), and others were in the process of negotiation. In addition, reciprocity agreements, providing more limited employment possibilities, existed with some twenty other countries. For a discussion of what the private sector is doing to deal with this problem, see Andree Brooks, "Job Help For Wives," *New York Times*, August 30, 1981.

NO PERFECT SCHEMES • 157

acceptable by federal personnel managers, schooled in a more legalistic tradition used to dealing only with employees, and then only in the domestic context. It should be pointed out, however, that certain Foreign Services, such as the Japanese, had paid a spouse salary or allowance for a number of years, and others such as the Canadians were considering something along the same line.[76]

With respect to more achievable alternatives, improvements are by no means easy. Take, for example, what have come to be called "tandem couples," that is, marriages where both partners are members of the Foreign Service, each wishing to continue his or her respective career while maintaining a family life as normal as possible. At first, the answer seemed simple—merely assign "tandems" to the same post but in different areas, so that one did not have a working or, especially, a supervisory relationship with the other, which would have been in violation of federal nepotism laws. Unfortunately, as the number of tandems increased, at least two kinds of assignment problems followed. First, large posts, where it is easier to find two satisfactory assignments, tend also to be in the most attractive locales. Thus arises the charge that "tandems" receive preference over the single officer, or the one whose spouse is not a federal employee. Tandem assignments are relatively easy in Paris; almost impossible in Ouagadougou. Second, if the partners are employees of two different agencies—State and USIA, for example—it becomes very difficult to coordinate the timing of two assignments. As a result, in recent years, while efforts to find placements for tandems at the same or nearby posts have continued, State has adopted a policy of requiring tandems to prioritize their desires, deciding, if necessary, whose career should receive priority if only one attractive assignment is possible at a given time. Naturally, this has caused a new wave of problems.[77]

[76] For Canada see the McDougall report, published as *Royal Commission on Conditions of Foreign Service* (Ottawa: Canadian Government Publishing Centre, 1981).

[77] The number of State Foreign Service employees who were partners in tandem couples as of April 1980 was 366, or 5.3% of State's total of 6,794 employees

The Foreign Service Act of 1980 recognized other aspects of the family problem: separation and divorce, when marriages could not stand the strain of Foreign Service life, or when the families involved had decided that a separation was the best course for a particular tour of duty. This was accomplished after intensive lobbying by women, especially the American Association of Foreign Service Women (AAFSW), and with the active support of congressional proponents of the bill, most particularly Congresswoman Pat Schroeder of Colorado (see Chapter VI for additional details).[78] The Act as passed included a number of provisions designed to deal with the new circumstances. Among them are the possibility of a Separate Maintenance Allowance for families who do not accompany a member of the Service to post, at the election of the family as well as at that of the government; additional travel allowances for children of separated parents to visit the parent with whom they do not normally reside; and, in a radical departure, the automatic division of retirement benefits between a member of the Service and a former spouse who meets the qualifying standard of having been married to the member for at least ten years of his or her time in federal service.[79] Symbolically, the latter step has major importance in ratifying the concept, advocated by the feminist movement, that a marriage should be seen as an economic partnership, with its benefits accruing by right to both parties. In a somewhat different vein, the new Act also reinforces the possibility of functional and language training for family members, if related to potential employment at the

---

available for worldwide service. This presented a significant assignment problem, as shown by the fact that 47 had been on leave without pay at some point between 1973 and 1980. Data from Bureau of Personnel Study, "Tandem Couples," sent from Douglas K. Watson via Barnes to Under Secretary Read, April 1, 1980. By December 1982 at least 532 in State were partners in tandems, a number which some argued underestimated the situation due to missing data on marital status, not required by State unless dependents were claimed. The 1982 information is from a Bureau of Personnel Study, December 1982.

[78] See, for example, the AAFSW (Association of American Foreign Service Women) testimony before the joint House subcommittees on July 24, 1979, and the exchange with members accompanying it. House hearings, pp. 296-324.

[79] These provisions are contained in sections 2307, 901(15), and 814 of P.L. 96-465, respectively.

post, and improves allowances for child care so that such training can be obtained without economic loss.[80]

As of this writing, it is much too early to know what the future will bring in the relationship between family members and the Foreign Service. It is fair to say, however, that family issues must be given a high priority if the Foreign Service is to be able to staff overseas posts with the high-caliber individuals it needs. Approaches which seem radical, when compared with more traditional personnel policies, almost certainly will be required. One possibility is that fewer individuals will be willing to serve full Foreign Service careers and that, instead, a larger number of individuals and family members will spend a part but not all of their working lives in the Service. This could, in turn, have major implications for the level of experience and expertise available, and perhaps even more for the career-based Foreign Service itself, which is the bedrock of the traditional U.S. approach to diplomacy.

CONCLUSION

Subsequent chapters will explore in further detail how well the foreign affairs personnel systems have responded to these difficult choices. In order to facilitate those discussions, particularly in Chapter VI and the conclusions in the final chapter, the arguments of this chapter are summarized in Table 9.

[80] Sections 703 and 704 of the Act.

TABLE 9
Dilemmas of Personnel System Design: Summary

Dilemma	Existing Situation	Conventional Wisdom	Prescription
1. Open vs. Closed System	Both FS (Rank in Person) and GS (Rank in Job) systems more closed than desirable, or than thought to be for GS system; closed Foreign Service system suffers from decline of discipline. GS system has "fewer peaks and fewer valleys."	FS much more closed than GS with plus of esprit and sense of mission, minus of elitism and parochialism; discipline of closed system held to be highly necessary and desirable.	"Pass through" vs. career systems a more important distinction; use "pass through" in future for larger proportion of work-force. Use closed system only where clearly needed.
2. Quality vs. Representativeness	In past, quality—at least as seen by FS—has been dominant value; future some-what uncertain, but clear trend toward more repre-sentativeness than in past.	FS has to be as high quality (in terms of general knowledge) as possible, regardless of job require-ments or effect on efforts to be more representative.	Choice between quality and representativeness not ad-missible; renewed efforts to recruit women/minorities through regular means must eventually replace special affirmative action programs.
3. Rank-in-person vs. Rank-in-job	Value of rank-in-person in building esprit and a sense of corps generally viewed as being dissipated; con-cern with need for more	Rank-in-person necessary for rotational situations and for building a sense of "corps"; this more im-portant than the need for	Avoid theological prefer-ences; use rank-in-person where objectively needed for rotational purposes; otherwise, rank-in-job.

	technical expertise, for which rank-in-person is not conducive; but also valid concerns whether rank-in-job can meet needs of rotational system and need for generalists at top. Up-or-out (selection out) feature of rank-in-person may be severely limited by societal trends.	deep specialization from rank-in-job system; up-or-out maintains quality.	
4. Generalists vs. Specialists	Generalists dominate FSO, FSIO Corps, specialists virtually everywhere else.	FS must be generalist, to cover wide range of topics and situations, and to produce senior officials with needed experience; some think "a good officer can read into any job quickly" vs. others regard this as producing "dilettantism"; specialists seen either as vital due greater technicality of issues, or as so narrow they cannot pull everything together.	Either/or argument dangerous and inappropriate; both approaches clearly needed in different parts of system. Generalists need to be more analytically integrative and have subspecialties; Specialists must avoid narrowness. Senior officials should be selected from both generalist and specialist groups, solely on basis of having job-specific experience and prerequisites.

TABLE 9 (*cont.*)

Dilemma	Existing Situation	Conventional Wisdom	Prescription
5. Rule-Setting and Rule Application	Both FS and GS are complex, mixed systems; tension in FS between central personnel system and operating bureaus and units over both aspects; tending to more centralization overall; but central system not fully capable of carrying out everything undertaken. GS system traditionally too centralized and slow in such functions as certification of potential hirees, leading to pressure to use "quicker" FS system even when inappropriate. Due process and resource scarcity portend greater pressure for centralization and less independence for subsystems.	Centralized system, run well, is more economical of resources, better able to maintain consistent standards and equity, but tends to be cumbersome and susceptible to overload and lack of understanding of operational problems and special circumstances; and vice versa for decentralized system. Too much regulation, regardless of source, inimical to needed managerial "flexibility."	Better determination of what should be centrally controlled, and what should be decentralized, for both total federal personnel system, and for headquarters vs. operating units within departments and subsystems. Ideally, make such decisions on basis of logic, rather than political/bureaucratic power considerations. More uniformity desirable, in general, in Foreign Service system, across agency lines.

6. Single vs. Multiple Personnel Systems	Immediate past featured by multiple systems and subsystems and congressional and internal pressure for simplification; unclear definition of purposes of various systems lead to misuse, inequities, managerial difficulties, grievances, unnecessary ambiguity. Preference of approach likely to be as much theological as logical. FS Act of 1980 does provide clearer rationale for when FS and GS systems should be used, and prospect of simplification.	Some believe the single system is important symbolically, while others think a single system is a fiction, dominated by core group in agency/service mission; system is and should be "way of life," vs. system should be instrumental and valued neutrally.	Treat systems as neutral management instruments; employ them on basis of differing conditions of service; resolve single system with subdivisions vs. multiple systems issue on pragmatic grounds.
7. Labor-Management Relations: Coping with Inevitability?	FS, like Civil Service, now has statutory basis for LMR, although rules differ on scope of bargaining, who can be in bargaining unit, single agency-wide bargaining units for Foreign Service. System closer to Civil Service approach than pre-1980, however.	FS, because of rotational system and Presidential commissions, blurs employee/management distinctions and requires different system of LMR; time/idea of not allowing LMR organization has passed.	Maintain existing LMR approach, i.e. all except direct management can be in unit, with possible revisions in "rolling" negotiations in the Foreign Service system, what is consultable, agency-wide bargaining units, and a more professional approach by both union and management.

TABLE 9 (cont.)

Dilemma	Existing Situation	Conventional Wisdom	Prescription
8. Political "Control" vs. Professional "Expertise"	Acceptance of need for Presidential appointment of key foreign affairs leadership, but differing opinions about whom the President should appoint; mutual suspicion and distrust at beginning of administration normally dissipates later; more insiders appointed to key positions as time passes.	Ambassadorial jobs, key Assistant Secretaryships and main policy jobs should be filled by FS as most qualified; political leadership should rely more heavily on FS guidance; FS has obligation to make case they believe is correct, but to support policy as determined by administration or leave jobs.	Less concern about percentages of FSO's appointed, more emphasis on right person for right position, whether FS, other government careerists, or outsiders; eventual use of Senior Executive Service and parallel Senior Foreign Service to bridge departments and agencies.
9. Professional Management or Management by the Profession?	Very complex FS personnel system managed by non-professionals, serving short tours of duty out of primary fields of job interest; system suffers from lack of continuity on long-range programs and from "show immediate results or don't bother" syndrome.	It would be inappropriate to turn over management of the FS system to non-FS personnel managers (except for routine work) because they do not have ability to understand what service overseas is like, or what kinds of people are needed under what circumstances.	Place responsibility for effective personnel management with professional personnel managers whose incentives for career advancement are dependent upon the system working well; staff personnel bureau with a mix of FS on short tours and continuity managers. Personnel policy

| 10. Families and the Foreign Service | Fundamental changes in attitudes of spouses toward their role, in reaction to societal change, desire for own careers, and less favorable living conditions at posts abroad. "Two for one" is dead, but replacement pattern or patterns not yet clear. | The former attitude of families, especially wives, as appendages to the employee has been dislodged, for the most part. "Replacement" concept of total volunteerism for spouses in performance of Embassy-related duties, and of the system being required to adapt to spouse career needs, even if in conflict with system needs, beginning to be seen as possible overreaction by many. | reflecting Washington/government needs in equal measure with overseas requirements.

Urgent and priority management attention must be given to family issues, if service is to be able to attract the caliber of members required, given its responsibilities. At the same time, managers must keep in mind that the possibility of accommodations of such needs is not unlimited, if mission of Foreign Service is to be fulfilled. Individual choices will be required as to whether or not a Foreign Service career, given existing circumstances, is possible for the family unit involved. |

CHAPTER FIVE

Support Systems: Data, Planning, Evaluation, Priorities

Almost all discussion about "whither the Foreign Service" or of "how staff for foreign affairs" centers on structural questions—pay plans and personnel authorities, divisions of power, system separation or integration. But this is only part of the fundamental problem: how to provide the right people at the right place at the right time in order to support fully the national interest as manifested through foreign affairs. The more pedestrian, more neglected, but equally important side of the equation has to do with the technical or administrative elements which must support any effective personnel system. In view of the extreme difficulty traditionally encountered in adopting new approaches to foreign affairs personnel management, it is also important to give careful attention to the management techniques and methods, lacking in the past, which will be essential in making *any* system work. An alternative title to this chapter might be "Tools"—the instruments necessary in the more routine operation of any personnel system. Particularly because the Foreign Service has proven to be "antitechnique," close attention is required to the question of how to make it possible to carry out whatever management strategy is chosen.

No consensus exists about which tools will be most useful in supporting foreign affairs personnel systems. In part, this depends on the kind of system being supported. A traditional foreign affairs system requires substantially less support than would be required to buttress a more finely tuned model. In this chapter, some of the tools or aids needed to improve federal personnel management are explored and evaluated.

DATA AND PLANNING: PUTTING BLOOD IN THE VEINS

At this late date, the importance of accurate and timely information in the successful management of any complex system should be unquestioned. Unfortunately, this obvious fact has only been partially recognized by those responsible for providing the people necessary to conduct the nation's foreign affairs. Both conceptually and technically, the State Department—and the rest of the foreign affairs (if not the intelligence and the uniformed military) community—were very late in emerging from the horse and buggy age. To the outsider, it may seem astounding that the Department has not given a high priority until quite recently to the development and maintenance of a data system which could provide instant, crucial information about the needs and health of its major lifelines, the personnel functions—the performance of which ultimately determine whether it is equipped to carry out its responsibilities. But such is the case.

This is not for lack of trying by some in State and elsewhere. The failure to implement suggestions for solving the data problem can be well documented. A recent example, described elsewhere in considerable detail,[1] was State's abortive Human Resources Information System (HRIS), developed largely in-house by a small group of junior officers between 1975 and 1978.

One-half of HRIS, and of any successful personnel data system, is simple in concept but usually difficult in practice: it is necessary to know enough about the requirements of jobs, and about the skills of people, to be able to match the two in a way which is both economical of scarce resources and developmental for employees. The other half—even more difficult—is to be able to take such information and to project it into the future. What was once called "manpower planning," more recently metamorphosed into Human Resources Management, has never been the strong point of any governmental personnel system, and the for-

[1] *Human Resources Information Systems for the Department of State*, Department of State Publication 8911, Department and Foreign Service Series 160 (Washington, D.C.: Department of State, September 1977), and Torrey S. Whitman and Albert C. Hyde, "HRIS: Systematically Matching the Right Person to the Right Position," *Defense Management Journal* 14 (March 1978), 28-34.

eign affairs community has been no exception.[2] No one has discovered a reliable way, within existing resource constraints, to project the dynamics of the personnel system much more than a year ahead.[3] But since officers entering the service now will not begin to reach senior levels of responsibility in most instances until after the year 2000, this is a glaring fault.

There have been a number of efforts to predict attrition and intake needs, to plan for a matching of needed skills with positions, and to devise justifiable classification levels, promotion policies, and sensible career patterns for the future; but they have without exception fallen into disuse, or have never been implemented. This because they were inaccurate or not trusted or too expensive, or because the necessary guiding assumptions about the kind of service desired in the future could not be agreed upon.[4]

The HRIS experience is instructive in showing the difficulties involved in producing the right kinds of information, in making different kinds of information interact successfully to produce usable results, and, perhaps most difficult, in making senior decision-makers believe that such a system is needed and will work. After two years of development by a departmental task force and a substantial test in five domestic bureaus and two overseas posts with results that were generally highly satisfactory, HRIS was put in limbo in 1978. Senior management at the State Department remained unconvinced of the need for such a system, and unwilling to make the initial investment in positions that would have allowed the HRIS system to become operational. This was in spite of the clear failings of the existing system, which had been readily admitted and which in large measure have been previously de-

---

[2] The problems of the Civil Service Commission in maintaining its Executive Inventory in the 1960's and 1970's, for example, were legend.

[3] By 1980, State was embarked upon another (post-HRIS) effort, more modest in concept, in order to support the various requirements of the new Foreign Service Act, most particularly the responsibility under Section 602 to maintain an orderly career progression through the ranks of the Service. Joan Clark, when she became Director General, gave new push to this effort and realigned its direction, but was under no illusion it would be easy.

[4] State experimented, pre-HRIS, with a model called PERSON, which was abandoned in the mid-1970's because it was cumbersome and because those who believed in it were transferred to other assignments.

scribed. The problem was held to be one of too much cost and too little payoff, given the size of the Foreign Service system in State.

HRIS can perhaps be used to illustrate some of what is needed. Its principle features can be seen in the following table. Prepared by Torrey Whitman, one of the developers of the HRIS system, Table 10 compares such a system with more traditional approaches, evaluating what each can accomplish with respect to the main personnel management functions. The contrast is startling, especially if one is truly concerned with paying full attention to current and future needs, rather than perpetuating the flawed but understood practice of the past.

In essence the HRIS system attempted to take account of the fact that each and every position, and individual, differs from all the rest. Normally, under traditional classification procedures, positions and individuals are forced into a relatively small number of common molds--for example, the FSO system of four cones— or all political officer positions at a given level are considered as interchangeable in required skills. It is obviously easier to match people and positions the smaller the number of categories. Even so, there was an almost total lack, until 1978, of a classification system for the Foreign Service in any of the agencies using FS authorities, even though the Department of State and the other agencies are bound by law to preserve consistency in classification standards with the basic federal system. Classification is complicated for the Foreign Service by the need for rotational personnel and by the nature of its missions and demands.

There have been numerous instances when the Office of Personnel Management or OMB or both have believed some or all of the Foreign Service to be overgraded. Such criticisms led the Department of State to begin developing a Foreign Service classification system in mid-1976, which would take several years to be fully in place. Largely because of its rank-in-person nature and generalist orientation, the Foreign Service had never been forced to develop such a system on its own initiative. The high esteem given to generalist competence carries with it an acceptance of the fact that people will serve substantial parts of their careers in areas outside their basic training and experience. This vitiates any

TABLE 10
Comparative Benefits of HRIS and Position Classification Approaches

Management Functions	HRIS	Position Classification
Resource allocation	Automated information base about positions on which to build a resource allocation system.	Manual system with inadequate breakouts for resource allocations.
	Example: Ability to define total work years devoted to science reporting, by adding up parts of positions.	Ability to identify only positions labeled as *science* jobs.
Assignments	Wider search and screening to match jobs and applicants; ability to score degree of fit as well as go—no go— qualifications.	Increased accuracy in current basis of job-person placement.
	Example: Ability to compare candidates with partial qualifications for a job requiring ARA experience, knowledge of trade promotion, and Spanish speaking.	Ability only to fit people with all 3 skills. No qualitative differentiation
Skills inventory	Multi-facet system, with automatic update, capability for review.	One-time update on skills label approach.
	Example: Shifts in emphasis of work function towards science or technology, even as parts of one position, automatically reflected	Shifts in emphasis shown only when entire position reclassified.

Position classification	Backup data for monitoring and evaluating cross-department consistency and currency. *Example:* Ability to compare automatically the job content of positions newly classified against existing patterns for the series.	Full-scale system to meet needs, but no automatic monitoring. Comparison only by classifiers' experience or memory.
Intake planning, training	Pinpoint reporting of future needs, able to encompass generalist, multi-skilled individuals filling multifaceted jobs. *Example:* Ability to project extent to which special skills (i.e., nuclear weapons expertise, petroleum, or monetary policy) need to be developed in-house or hired for—based on whether whole positions or parts of positions demand such skills.	Labeling of whole positions and people by one skill designator. No comparable planning ability.
Selection	Aggregated data on functional components of State Department work as aid to evaluation of qualifications. *Example:* Ability to tune finely the makeup of the FSO exam against the percentage of time likely spent in various skill areas.	Similar data, less specific, not automated. Ability only to pick up the four basic FSO cones as functional areas against which to test.

SOURCE: Torrey S. Whitman, Bureau of Personnel, Department of State, 1978.

felt need for accurate information about competences required for effective performance in specific positions. One effect of lack of a classification system is, however, to deprive management of a systematic means of measuring whether people are performing at the level the organization's responsibilities demand.

However, even a well-developed classification system would not accord with current realities. HRIS thus would have attempted to divide each position (job) into as many as ten "functional job components" so that

> each position can be described in terms of the aggregate work experience of the organization. Each functional job component consists of an operation, a substantive area in which the operation is performed, the percentage of work time allocated to that component, and the importance of the component relative to the overall performance of the position. . . . The chief advantage of facet analysis of job content is that it increases the manager's ability to differentiate among positions for purposes of assignment, management work audits, performance appraisal, and other personnel functions.[5]

Once all positions in the system have been analyzed in this way, it is presumably possible, though not easy, to develop a planning process based on how well the requirements of positions that need to be filled are met by existing skills of people in the system. A simplified outline of such a process might look like the diagram in Figure 1.

The way specific kinds of position and personnel information can be related to major personnel functions can perhaps be better seen through an examination of Tables 11 and 12.

This type of data collection would markedly improve the organization's self-knowledge about the current situation, but by itself would not be enough to provide the basis for effective longer-term personnel management. It would not automatically take into account dynamic situations within the system, such as evolving work requirements or a changing workforce (e.g., more handicapped individuals, more employees married to each other), which

[5] Whitman and Hyde, "HRIS," p. 30.

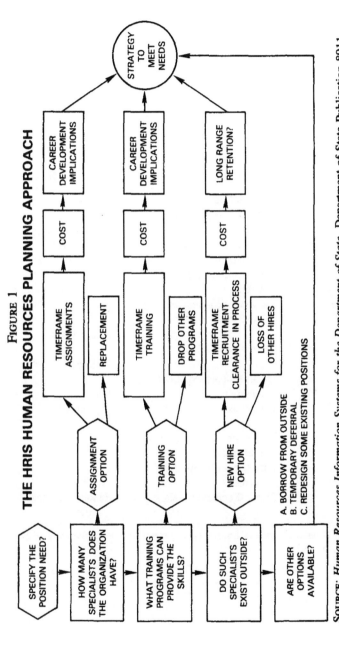

FIGURE 1

THE HRIS HUMAN RESOURCES PLANNING APPROACH

SOURCE: *Human Resources Information Systems for the Department of State*, Department of State Publication 8911, Department and Foreign Service Series 160 (Washington, D.C.: Department of State, September 1977), Figure 3, p. 14.

TABLE 11
HRIS Position Data File

Category	Data Elements	Specific Program Objective
Identification	Position title	General
	Organization location	
Level	Grade level	Classification
Occupancy period	Tour continuity	Assignments
Job content	Functional job components (by time, importance, origin)	Resource allocation
Qualifications	Language requirements	
	Education equivalents	
		Assignments
	Training equivalents	
		Training
	Organizational experience requirements	Intake
	Supervisory experience requirements	planning
	Pre-Department experience equivalents	
	Professional certification/ licenses	
Other	Physical considerations	Handicap/medical programs

SOURCE: *Human Resources Information Systems for the Department of State*, Table A, p. 28.

TABLE 12
HRIS Personnel Data File

Category	Data Elements	Specific Program Objective
Identification	Name, SSN, residence data, age, sex, race, marital status, dependents ages	General Equity monitoring Separations projections
Work field	Career fields, titles, Functional skills	Resource allocations
Organizational status	Expiration of appt., entry on duty, arrival, transfer eligibility	Assignments
Work level	Grade, promotion history	Compensation, promotion
Professional qualifications	Education, training, MLAT, languages, awards, licenses	Assignments/ training projections
Experience	Pre-Department experience, current and past assignments	Assignments
Career preferences	Assignment preferences by location and function; career and training preferences	Career planning assignments
Current position data	Location of current assignment by organization	Resource allocation
Physical qualifiers	Medical disabilities, Physical handicaps	Assignments

SOURCE: *Human Resources Information Systems for the Department of State*, Table B, p. 29.

can affect basic personnel functions such as training needs or assignment policy. Nor does such information take note of outside factors which can have a major impact on the assumptions on which the system rests, for example, significant pay increases for senior officers, which have the effect of markedly slowing retirements,[6] changes in mandatory retirement age with the same impact,[7] or a particularly tight outside job-market, which forces even the disaffected to remain with the government.[8]

Thus, what is needed, in addition to a historical data system, is a method of projecting the current situation into the future, coupled with a way of changing such projections to account for new circumstances. Operationally, this would require a formal planning process which would make explicit a question that has normally been either implicit or ignored: What are the parameters in which the foreign affairs personnel system of the future must operate? Such a planning mechanism does not now exist. The PERSON simulation model previously noted was conceptually limited, complex, expensive, and unaccepted. PERSON was in

[6] The "cap," or limit on Federal career employee salaries, was raised from $39,600 to $47,500 in early 1977, a 20% increase. A similar lifting of the cap from $50,112.50 to $58,500 occurred on January 1, 1982, and another increase come into effect at the beginning of 1983. Since retirement annuities are calculated on the basis of the highest average three years' salaries while on active duty, many senior officers in the Foreign Service and elsewhere in government, after such increases, remain on duty until they have served three years at the new limit. These episodes demonstrate the unexpected factors which can complicate longer-term planning, for the failure of these officers to retire when originally projected leads to a drastic reduction in promotions and to severe limitations on new hiring—both of which interfere with predictable advancement and lead to both morale and personnel management problems.

[7] Mandatory retirement for Foreign Service employees at age sixty was challenged in the *Bradley* v. *Vance* case and was initially overturned. The government appealed to the Supreme Court and age sixty was upheld in early 1979; those reaching sixty while the case was at issue were retained, but retired shortly thereafter. As with the raise of the salary limit, this period of uncertainty had a complicating effect on career and attrition planning in the foreign affairs agencies. In 1980, Congress raised the mandatory age to sixty-five for the Foreign Service, and there were signs it would be removed completely before much additional time passed.

[8] Since, as previously noted, FSO's typically have social science backgrounds, the drying up of college teaching opportunities in the 1970's eliminated one obvious alternative career, with the same effect as already noted.

turn successor to the MUST system of the 1960's.[9] At best, either PERSON or MUST could operate only a very few years into the future, and then only if management philosophy were assumed to be coherent and consistent, assuring that this year's policy would be next year's policy. This is a very unrealistic assumption when the Department of State is involved.

If the bias against planning could be overcome, there would still be a controversy about what kind of model would be most appropriate. The two schools of thought support what are called dynamic models on one hand, as opposed to probabilistic ones on the other. Such debates tend to the arcane, and in all likelihood are unresolvable until more is known about how accurately they predict in practice. Simply stated, the difference is that dynamic models operate on the basis of certainty once the relevant input and structural variables are known, while probabilistic models state their projections as likely outcomes admitting the more limited possibility that others may occur.[10]

It must be recognized, however, that any model is merely a simplification of reality.[11] If the simplified reality that results is not accurate, then the model will produce meaningful results only accidentally. In short, any planning, by whatever technique, must be based on assumptions that reflect the operating and managerial philosophy of those responsible for making the key decisions. If there is no such philosophy, or if it is not clearly delineated, then planning will be worthless.

Since 1976, State has been employing a so-called Interactive Manpower Model, which merely provides a set of formulas to calculate attrition, promotion, and thus intake requirements for the short-term future. This model, refined through several years' use, was quite accurate in the 1978-82 period, but it made no pretense of dealing with the longer-term future; and indeed, there

[9] See "MUST—Manpower Utilization System: New Project to Improve Personnel Management," *Department of State News Letter* 52 (August 1965), 16.

[10] A dynamic model merely gives "motion" to a static base, while a "probabilistic" one tries to deal with what is most likely, taking into account possible changes in key variables.

[11] See, for a typical discussion of models in social science, Alan C. Isaak, *Scope and Methods of Political Science: An Introduction to the Methodology of Political Inquiry* (Homewood, Ill.: Dorsey Press, 1969), pp. 142-54.

were no explicit guiding assumptions which would have permitted it to do so. A new, somewhat more sophisticated model using the same methodology was developed in 1980-81 to meet needs for new projections imposed by the Foreign Service Act of 1980, but it did not represent much of an advance in the state of the art.

The larger point deserves reiteration: without detailed and accurate information about the current situation and without the basis for projecting that situation against its "best guess" future requirements, no career personnel system can hope to confront its future intelligently. Moreover, the information produced will be worthless unless it is closely coordinated with management policy which addresses the hard issues of the time.

Until it is possible to build the kind of information and planning system proposed, the best management approach corresponds nicely with "business as usual" at State: that is, "ad hoc-ery." Ideally, the entire system would be flexible under such conditions, with no one being employed on a career basis, in order to preserve the maximum amount of flexibility to confront unplanned-for future needs. Since this is not a realistic possibility, it behooves senior officials to pay attention to the health of the Service, and not only to support but to force the development of a system which will provide them with a much more coherent idea of the directions in which the organization must move.

EVALUATION: PEOPLE, MANAGEMENT, AND METHODS

In a way the need for evaluation is an extension of the information/planning requirement suggested above: a successful organization needs information about how well its people are doing their jobs, and how well its managers are meeting system needs. The organization must also judge how well its personnel system is doing if it is to meet larger policy objectives. Here, as above, the current situation is dismal, moving slowly to mediocre.

Evaluation: People

A chronic source of irritation for all concerned, rating officers and those rated alike, has been State's Foreign Service Employee

Evaluation Report (EER) system. These reports must be completed annually, or more often if either the rating or rated officer is transferred in between. Because they are the only evaluative information legally available to selection boards, which determine promotions, selection-out, career tenure, performance pay, limited career extensions, and multiple step increases,[12] their accuracy and ability to discriminate between strong, average, and weak performers is absolutely essential for the health of the Service. If this fails, then there is no guarantee that the best will rise to the top, that the best officers will be promoted frequently enough to ensure that they are willing to remain in the Service, or that weaker performers will be encouraged or forced to leave. If these reports are not seen as producing objective and valid rankings of officers, then morale suffers and the entire personnel system is called into question by employees and managers alike.

But that is what has happened in recent years. Ironically, the passage of new legislation designed to protect the individual had made it much more difficult to rate individuals objectively.[13] Rating and reviewing officers are now required to share their evaluations with those rated, and the latter have the right to comment on and to challenge them. What was conceived as a (necessary) means of forcing superiors to be candid with subordinates has led to bland, innocuous, and almost uniformly inflated ratings, due to a desire to keep the peace for the limited duration of the current tour, even if future problems are created.

The result is that the tasks of selection boards have become more and more difficult. If everyone achieves good ratings, how can choices be made among them? Unfortunately, boards are forced to rely on very small apparent differences, which may be real but which may also be an artifact of the drafting skill or toughness of different rating officers. There is also a proclivity

---

[12] See Section 603 of the Foreign Service Act of 1980 for a listing of the kinds of records which can be included in official personnel files and therefore which can legitimately be considered by selection boards.

[13] In particular, the Privacy and Freedom of Information Acts. Together, they require that comments made about an individual's performance be available to him or her, and that there be an opportunity for their reactions to be included with the basic report.

to turn to "corridor reputation," gossip, or other highly informal (and illegal)[14] sources of information, and to award "tombstone" promotions to make sure that average officers who have been in class for a long time, but who are not clearly terrible, are not forced to leave the Service. It is also likely that proven qualities reflecting the status quo will be rewarded rather than unusual or irregular attributes, even though individuals possessing the latter may bring scarce qualities which are desperately needed in an overly static system. In short, there is wide agreement that the present system provides only limited equity (if by that term one means that rewards are commensurate with contributions) and only uncertain competence, in the sense of providing for the advancement of those individuals who best meet the needs of the system.

In circumstances where everyone has been led to believe that he or she is something special by virtue of surviving the rigorous initial selection process required to become an FSO, it may be that no rating system would be accepted unless it allowed everyone to be promoted in lockstep and frequently, except for obvious miscreants.[15]

In fairness, it must be acknowledged that strong support has recently been given to attempts to find alternative and better ways of rating, advancing, and assigning employees to keep in step with current requirements.

There have been several recent studies of alternative rating methods, such as self-rating, peer rating, or other approaches intended to force more differentiation of strengths and weaknesses of those being rated. During the developmental stages of the new Foreign Service Act, for example, considerable thought was given to including "assignability" information, on grounds that if an officer was a placement problem at the current level, selection

[14] The Civil Service Reform Act of 1978, Section 101 (5 U.S.C. 2302), Prohibited Personnel Practices, prohibits any personnel action, including those carried out by selection boards, to be taken except on the basis of official records or first-hand knowledge.

[15] This phenomenon led the author to purpose, only semi-facetiously, a thirty-six-grade promotion system, allowing everyone to be promoted every year, as the only means of turning attention from promotions to the work at hand. It was somewhat unsettling to find a number of officers willing to give the idea serious consideration.

boards should take this into account in considering whether he or she should be promoted. Such information, however, would almost certainly have to come from the central personnel system to be valid, and this proposed departure from the principle that only the supervisor can place evaluation material in an official personnel file caused considerable heartburn with AFSA and many managers. Yet without such information, evaluation likely will continue to be a never-never land.[16]

Improving evaluation will not be easy, for there are few if any good models. It may be that given current societal norms, a rating system can be acceptable to employees and useful to management only if it is directly linked to performance in or selection for a specific job, rather than being more general. The private sector clearly has its own major difficulties, and government outside the Foreign Service has been forced to confront these issues more directly due to the fundamental importance of evaluation in making the Civil Service Reform Act work. Much to their dismay those working on the Civil Service system discovered that the Foreign Service did not have a rating system which could be borrowed.[17]

The obvious difficulties with the "rating form" method of evaluation have led some to consider radically different approaches, in spite of the well-known tendencies toward the status quo of every existing personnel system anywhere. Primary among these is the assessment center, which is an attempt to simulate the conditions and demands of the next position for which an individual is under consideration, and/or to discover limitations in necessary competences and skills so that they can be corrected

[16] In its final version, the Foreign Service Act permitted assignability information to be included only for the Senior Foreign Service, but did not require it. See Section 603.

[17] The author was part of these discussions. As of late 1981, development of an effective and fair evaluation system remained of primary concern to those charged with making the Senior Executive Service work. See, for example, "Performance Appraisal and Merit Pay Under the Civil Service Reform Act of 1978," an Interim Report by the Task Group on Performance Appraisal and Merit Pay of the Panel of the National Academy of Public Administration On Civil Service Reform (Washington, D.C.: National Academy of Public Administration, May 1981), multilith.

by training or developmental assignments before they become critical weaknesses.[18]

In bureaucratese provided by the Civil Service Commission,

> The assessment center method is a comprehensive standard-ized measurement process which requires the candidates to par-ticipate in real life job situations. It involves multiple evaluation techniques, including different approaches to simulating work situations such as group discussions, in-basket exercises, sim-ulation of interviews with subordinates, oral presentations, and written exercises. The assessment center is designed to provide the candidates with an opportunity to demonstrate in a number of situations behaviors which are essential and important for success on the job.[19]

Those experienced with the use of assessment centers in the private sector and government, however, caution against putting too much reliance on the results of such exercises. They are suspect when used alone, although in combination with records of past performance they may provide useful clarification. They seem more likely to be helpful as diagnostic tools, to highlight the shortcomings of those who aspire to higher levels of respon-sibility in time to provide corrective training and assignments.[20]

In evaluation, techniques cannot substitute for understanding. However one chooses to carry it out, there must be objective standards against which to measure performance and/or potential. Thus everything comes back to the question of what are the com-petences needed if a job is to be carried out successfully, and whether the personnel system can provide people who have them.

Some way of providing the kind of information which would have been generated by the HRIS system discussed previously,

[18] State and USICA replaced the traditional oral examination for prospective new officers with a one-day assessment process in 1979, which was generally judged to provide a better indication of likely on-the-job performance. USICA at one point considered a separate assessment process, but ultimately continued to use the same one as State.

[19] Civil Service Commission Bulletin 335-20, November 10, 1975.

[20] This was the opinion of a senior Civil Service Commission official, later a key figure in the development of the Senior Executive Service, expressed at a conference held by the Bureau of Personnel at Airlie, Virginia, April 1976.

if not necessarily HRIS itself, is desperately needed to provide detailed knowledge about the substantive skills required in each job, and the kind of operations which are performed.

Even this would only be a beginning. In a rank-in-person, career-oriented personnel system, these individual job requirements must be aggregated in a way that is predictive/descriptive of the total career. An effort in 1976-77 to deal with this problem, commissioned by the Bureau of Personnel at State, produced a controversial list of seventeen key skills or job competencies required in varying degrees at different levels and in different functions for success in senior executive positions in the Foreign Service.[21] The competencies were selected on the basis of interviews with peer-identified superior officers. Intuitively the list seems right, but the question arises as to how well such broad characteristics or attributes can be evaluated, and how they can be translated into the specifics of performance.[22] A somewhat similar (in purpose if not in methodology) effort occupied most of the period

[21] McBer and Company, *Preliminary Comments on Job Competency Requirements for Various Positions in the U.S. State Department* (Boston: McBer and Company, March 3, 1977). The report was controversial in that an in-house State Department attempt to replicate or validate it showed that eight "dummy" variables made up by the Bureau of Personnel and not on the original list of seventeen were even more likely to be chosen by acknowledged successful officers as critical competencies than those identified by the McBer study. Nevertheless, the McBer study did become the basis for subsequent career development and evaluation efforts.

[22] The McBer competencies were as follows. *Leadership*: (1) presence/leadership ability/respect earned, (2) persuasive speaking/oral communication, (3) positive bias/optimistic outlook, (4) negotiating skills/developing viable alternatives, (5) social sensitivity/knowing how to approach people, (6) planning ahead/anticipation/proactive planning. *Intellectual*: (7) conceptual ability/ability to see trends, (8) logical thinking/analytical ability, (9) political judgment. *Managerial*: (10) concern for influence/appetite for power, (11) low concern for affiliation/doesn't have to be liked and isn't afraid to say "no," (12) self-control, (13) entrepreneurial drive/imagination, (14) task efficiency/concern for getting the job done. *Interpersonal*: (15) counseling skills/coaching others, (16) language ability, (17) coaching management style.

For comparison, the "dummy" variables made up for the validation study were (1) imagination, (2) persistence, (3) production under pressure, (4) substantive evaluation and perspective, (5) team player, (6) inner direction, (7) integrity, (8) self-knowledge.

when Harry Barnes was Director General (1978-81), aided by a prominent student of organizations, Michael Maccoby.[23] Its conclusions, while interesting, were vulnerable to the same critiques as the earlier efforts.

This is not the place to argue the merits of particular studies. Rather, the somewhat baffled attempts of State to deal with the problems of evaluation underscore both the positive realization that *some* better way must be found and the difficulty of doing so, given personnel managers who are not professionals in their responsibilities and given professional consultants who tend to be captives of their own methodologies.

Yet personnel evaluation is absolutely fundamental, especially when the tasks to be performed become more complex. Only with objective evaluation techniques will the system be able to achieve maximum effectiveness, while simultaneously advancing and rewarding the strongest performers and dealing with the weakest in a humane but necessary way. With the government move to "merit pay" for managers at the GS-13 level and above, and "performance awards" for those in the new Senior Executive Service (old GS-16 and above) as a result of the Civil Service Reform Act of 1978,[24] awards can be equitable only if the performances of different individuals can be objectively compared. Whatever the structure of foreign affairs personnel systems in the future, they will not succeed until the chronic inadequacies of personnel evaluation are overcome.

Evaluation: Management

It has also come to be realized that evaluation of employees alone is not sufficient to provide a healthy personnel system, for this makes the implicit assumption that the system and its management are functioning in completely satisfactory ways. For more

[23] "Management Styles in the Department of State," PER Standing Committee, Bureau of Personnel, September 1981, typescript. Barnes wrote the introduction, and Maccoby, Appendix III, "Personality and Management Style."

[24] See CSRA, Sections 407 (5 U.S.C. 5384) and 501 (5 U.S.C. 5402). The Foreign Service, too, was put into a performance pay system at the Senior Foreign Service level by the Foreign Service Reform Act of 1980 (see Chap. VI).

than a decade, the Civil Service Commission has required each agency and department of government to develop a means of evaluating its personnel management practices.[25] State ignored this requirement for years, but by 1976 the Bureau of Personnel had begun to develop a comprehensive Personnel Management Information System (PMES). Described as "an information system designed to evaluate the use of personnel in achieving mission objectives,"[26] the central component of PMES was a survey questionnaire of employee attitudes and perceptions about personnel management practices, conducted anonymously to help to ensure candid responses. It was directed both to telling the central personnel system how well it was conducting basic personnel functions and to informing line managers how well their subordinates believed they were carrying out their own personnel management responsibilities.[27] PMES, as its sponsors acknowledged, was an incomplete management information system, but it was hoped it could have a substantial diagnostic role, if supplemented by a will to take corrective action. In State's conception, PMES was to be used in tandem with the administrative and "conduct of relations" inspections carried out by the Department's Inspector General, with findings passed to the inspectors in advance of their inspection of a post or bureau. This pattern provided a logic for periodic reevaluation (since inspectors cover each office/post on two- to four-year intervals) and took "advantage of the Inspectors' presence to explore the underlying causes of indicated strengths and weaknesses,"[28]

While responses were anonymous, they could be coded to allow categories of personnel to be profiled (e.g., rank, sex, pay plan, skill area) to isolate systematic problems which impact one group more than others. If the PMES process could be refined and its

[25] Federal requirements were announced in a presidential memorandum in 1969. The lack was also noted in a generally critical Civil Service Commission inspection of the personnel function in State in January 1975.

[26] DG (Director General) Notice A-290, Department of State, March 14, 1977.

[27] Karl D. Ackerman (Acting Director General) to Read memorandum, "Personnel Management Evaluation Systems (PMES)—Employee Survey," October 28, 1977.

[28] Ibid.

questions updated, such an information system could become an instrument of considerable sophistication and one that could give senior managers, for the first time, something more than isolated examples of intuition upon which to proceed. In today's circumstances, it seems self-evident that any personnel system would work better with such information than without it. However, there are costs, too—by 1980 there were strong indications that those filling in the questionnaires were beginning to regard them as a nuisance and as being required too frequently. By the next year the Bureau of Personnel had for all practical purposes placed the PMES system in limbo, with no inclination to revive it.[29]

Of course, there are means of evaluating personnel management other than aggregating the perceptions of subordinates. The previously mentioned periodic inspections by the Inspector General are one example, especially when conducted to examine the personnel function directly rather than as just one aspect of the administration of a particular bureau or post.[30] While such inspection results are sometimes naive, in that they are carried out by generalists with limited experience with personnel operations, they can also provide a fresh outlook, and occasionally have the healthy effect of forcing management to look at radical alternatives.[31]

In addition, two other management evaluation procedures seem required: the annual budget review, both within the personnel branch and at the Department/agency level, and periodic special-purpose investigations to focus attention on and develop solutions to new problems. In State, some progress was made at the bureau level on using the budget process as a means of isolating management problems, through a device known as the Resources Review Group (RRG), run by the Bureau's Office of Management

[29] Interview with Bureau of Personnel official responsible for PMES, May 1980, and follow-up with other officials, September 1981.

[30] The most recent full personnel function inspections were conducted in 1974 and 1977, with a study of the recruitment function carried out in 1981. A full inspection would await fuller implementation of the new Foreign Service Act of 1980 than was possible by the originally scheduled date of 1981.

[31] The 1974 personnel function inspection report, although rejected by departmental managers, proposed a radically different personnel system, summarized by the title "Specialists before Generalists."

and participated in by the other major bureau offices.[32] Intended as a prioritizing mechanism at a time of constant or declining resources (in terms of positions being made available by the Department for the personnel system to fill), this group's members have taken the opportunity to identify weak areas of performance which need improvement. By the 1980 cycle, the RRG had been replaced by a less structured mechanism designed to force the same prioritizing as resources became even scarcer. There has been less success at the Department level, where the Priorities Policy Group (PPG), made up of the Under Secretary for Management, the Director General, and other senior managers, has all too often been forced back to making across-the-board percentage cuts when the total number of positions must be reduced, rather than truly prioritizing the Department's functions and cutting selectively. In 1980 there was a consensus that there had to be a better way (see next section).[33]

Special studies and investigations have been used frequently in recent years, as the author can attest from his own experience. When properly carried out and supported, they can provide a useful mechanism for forcing action which would not occur otherwise. At the same time, if they are controversial—which inherently they must be if they address major and continuing problems—they are likely to founder on the opposition of vested interests unless they have strong and sustained top-level support. This support has not usually been forthcoming, although the development and passage of the Foreign Service Act of 1980 was an obvious exception (see Chapter VI). Until the senior officers of the Department are willing to pay sustained attention to personnel

[32] The format involved individual office presentations to the Director General and other bureau leaders, with resource packages set at several levels, followed by consolidation and bureauwide choices before the next step of departmentwide budget submission preparation.

[33] Cf. Edward Joseph Perkins, "The Priorities Policy Group: A Case Study of the Insitutionalization of a Policy Linkage and Resource Allocation Mechanism in the Department of State," a dissertation presented to the Faculty of the School of Public Administration, University of Southern California, June 1978. Comments about PPG in the text are also based on frequent discussions between 1977 and 1982 with participants in the process.

management, however, such results will be the exception rather than the norm.

The larger point, of course, is that continuous attention to the quality of personnel management is critical for the success of any complex system. Without it, the personnel apparatus will inevitably fail to meet the demands placed upon it.

WHAT COMES FIRST: CAN THE SYSTEM FIT REAL PRIORITIES?

Of all the problems inherent in managing today's complicated foreign affairs personnel systems, perhaps none is more perverse than matching such systems to the real policy priorities of the day, and in none has less success been achieved. In terms of meshing the size, shape, and allocation of personnel resources with foreign policy priorities, the view of State's Inspection Corps in 1973 remains substantially correct:

> Present methods, the Team became convinced, fail to present the Department's leadership with adequate policy-oriented analysis of current resource distribution patterns or of possible alternatives. They do not provide for systematic policy inputs into resource decision-making. The incremental nature of the budgetary process, decentralized methods for allocating personnel positions, and deficiencies in information and staffing all make fully balanced consideration and decision-making on resources more difficult.[34]

The report continued by arguing that present resource management methods "are not flexible enough in bringing about prompt shifts of resources across bureau lines to meet changing inter-regional and interfunctional priorities."[35]

This report, together with the already cited personnel review conducted in 1975, led to creation in that year of the Priorities Policy Group (PPG), intended to provide a coherent and continuing mechanism for conducting the kind of policy-related review

[34] *That Priorities May Prevail: Resource Management in the Department of State*, Office of the Inspector General of the Foreign Service, November 1973, multilith. Quotation from p. i of the abstract.

[35] Ibid.

of resource allocations that was so clearly needed. Yet by 1978, the best the PPG could do, when the Department was faced with a need to reduce its total number of positions, was to suggest that each bureau cut 1.5 percent of its existing positions.[36] To those who thought zero-based budgeting—examination of programs from the ground up as a means of establishing true priorities—was the wave of the future, this was a depressing outcome.

Yet the PPG may be at least marginally better than what went before, according to a survey of knowledgeable insiders in 1976.[37] The true state of the problem can perhaps be best shown by their mixed responses: "On the question of linking resources to the broader considerations of foreign policy, the respondents clearly believed that the PPG was better than previous systems, 69 percent of those responding agreeing. Less than half of those responding agreed that the PPG was a mechanism adequate for providing an equitable distribution of resources."[38]

Better, but not nearly good enough. One must conclude that the old "policy-administration" dichotomy still lives in the Department of State. The outside observer senses that policy, even today, is regarded as the prerogative of the senior levels of the Department and the government, and that what the career service does is only incidentally related to the major concerns of the day. As a consequence, resource allocation—the determination of which positions are most important and which skills are most needed to fill them—is not seen as being particularly important as a means of enabling the Administration to carry out its stated policy priorities. Unless and until this condition is changed, yet another acronymical effort at resource allocation in the Department of State will not solve the obvious problem. As with the other "tools" discussed in this chapter, specific techniques are less important than acceptance of the notion that technique and method *are* important. One should not pretend that the translation of abstract policy notions, formulated in the here and now, to the much

[36] Barnes to Read memorandum, "PPG Activities," September 29, 1978, discusses the Director General's (and PER's) belief that improvements in the process were necessary.

[37] Perkins, "The Priorities Policy Group," p. 312.

[38] Ibid.

longer-range planning necessary to devise strong and practical personnel systems will ever be easy. But it is at least necessary to recognize that there is a connection, and that the link should be made.

If the picture within State is mixed, it is chaotic when the circumstances of the whole government are considered. OMB's efforts at developing a foreign affairs budget have to date been laughable.[39] There is as yet no attempt to develop a mechanism with the capability of ranging across the entire Executive branch in order to compare resource use with policy priorities, and there is little indication that any such program is particularly missed. But unless and until some such procedure is developed, it will only be accidental when resources allocated to personnel systems will be congruent with policy priorities.

INTEGRATED PROCESSES

Although the title of this section may sound like one more example of the claptrap of the new management lingo, it is intended to convey what may be the most important notion of personnel management for the future: complex as they are, personnel systems must be viewed as *systems*, in the sense that changes in

[39] The Murphy Commission and virtually every other recent study has recommended this, with the thrust being that the Department of State should play an active role in evaluating the various departmental and agency budget proposals in terms of how resources requested would contribute to attainment of the nation's foreign policy objectives. In part because OMB apparently does not desire competition in the integrator role, and in part because of State reluctance and lack of capability to carry out this responsibility, the idea has never been tried seriously. See Murphy Commission Report, pp. 151-59, and Arnold Nachmanoff, "Budgeting, Programming, and Foreign Policy," in Appendix T to Murphy Commission Report, "Budgeting and Foreign Affairs Coordination," Appendix Volume VI, pp. 439-52. In 1980, reflecting President Carter's apparent displeasure with the foreign affairs area of the budget process in 1979, OMB attempted to impose a system under which State would be responsible for prioritizing some but not all of the budget items relating to foreign affairs, while OMB would reserve the right to overturn this ranking. State, not surprisingly, viewed this as a "no-win" situation and protested strongly. This system was never implemented.

one area can have a strong influence in others.[40] Typically, this
has not been the perspective taken in federal, or foreign affairs,
personnel management. Perhaps because of the division of labor
inherent in bureaucracy, initiatives and reforms in one area tend
to take place with little concern for their obvious ramifications in
others. As an example, the Department of State in 1975 agreed
to a desirable five-year, mid-level outside or lateral entry program.
Designed to increase the representativeness of the FSO corps, this
special program was expected to bring in twenty minority-group
members and/or women per year, but almost no attention was
paid to the impact these new people would have. Specifically, in
a system as small as the FSO corps, twenty new middle-grade
officers per year could reduce the total number of promotion
possibilities by as many as eighty or a hundred per year, highly
significant if one considers that for 1979 the total number of FSO
promotions was 527.[41] In addition, no adjustments were made at
first in junior officer recruitment to compensate for additional
intake at the middle levels.[42] As argued earlier,[43] lateral entry is
essential if the Foreign Service is to be enriched with new perspectives, exceptional talents, and greater representativeness. But
it must be part of a coherent management strategy which adjusts
other recruitment accordingly. Otherwise, newcomers are perceived as denying opportunities to those already in the system,
and internal tensions take away the advantages of system renewal.

In this example, affirmative action recruitment was decided
upon without reference to the assignment potential of those recruited. As a result, many of those initially selected for the program were immediate assignment "problems," because there were

[40] For the classic works on systems and politics, see Charles E. Merriam,
Systematic Politics (Chicago: University of Chicago Press, 1945; new printing
Phoenix Books, 1966), and David Easton, *A Systems Analysis of Political Life*
(New York: Wiley, 1965).

[41] 1979 Promotion List, reprinted as "Special Supplement," *Department of
State News Letter* 215 (August-September 1979). This number of 527 was itself
significantly higher than in immediately prior years.

[42] When the program was revived in 1979 through strong pressure from Secretary
of State Vance (see Chap. IV), better meshing of recruitment at all levels did
occur.

[43] See Chap. IV, section on "Open vs. Closed Systems."

no jobs immediately available for which they were qualified.[44] If the "integrated processes" idea had prevailed, this anomaly would not have resulted: the mid-level program would have been designed from the beginning with a clear idea of what the new recruits would be doing, once they had joined the system.

The larger point is clear: a career personnel system requires sustained attention to the system as a totality, rather than as a series of unrelated parts.

A similar problem exists in the complicated matrix of issues involving provision and maintenance of skills. To decide which skills are needed at what levels, and further to determine whether individuals who already possess such skills should be hired from outside the system, or alternatively whether in-service training and developmental assignments should be used to provide them, would be a demanding task under the best of circumstances. It becomes almost impossible in the absence of a coherent professional development plan closely related to organizational missions. But to date, the foreign affairs community has succumbed to two kinds of fallacious reasoning: that specialists with professional qualifications can maintain them over a sustained period of time without any action by the system, and that generalists properly selected can "read into" any job in a relatively short period of time, without the necessity of additional training or experience. Neither proposition is true, but there is no way of correcting their defects in practice unless the whole personnel system is viewed as an entity, and unless the capability exists to monitor what the various parts of that system are undertaking, and to relate them to some overall design.[45]

[44] Several discussions with both recruitment and assignment officers, as well as Deputy Assistant Secretary for Personnel, 1976-1978. See also Chap. IV.

[45] As of the initial writing of this section (August 1980), there was some hope, if severe budgetary constraints could be overcome, that a much more effective approach to the skills problem might emerge, through joint efforts of Barnes and Read to construct a sensible career development program and through an innovative and almost complete redesign of FSI's training programs, featuring a much closer relationship of training to service needs. This program was the brainchild of one of the Foreign Service's brightest and most rapidly rising young officers, Ambassador Paul Boeker, who became the Director of FSI in early 1980. Two years later, when this section was revised, however, there was more cause for skepticism.

The reasons State has major difficulties in following the integrated process approach should now be obvious: the longer view is virtually impossible to sustain if individual managers change jobs every two or three years. But there is no other answer: an integrated system requires comprehensive management with a long-range view.

CONCLUSION

Personnel systems do not live by grand designs alone. Day in and day out, routine hirings, assignments, evaluations, and disciplinary actions must take place. The essential question of this chapter is whether technique and approach should be applied problem by problem, in a reactive fashion, or whether coherent and consistent principles should govern day-to-day operations.

Today, every available approach which can assist coherent management must be used. Honest differences may exist about which techniques are appropriate, but there can be no doubt that modern management must be applied. Without planning *and* execution, there can be no personnel *system*.

Although substantial resources for additional training had survived the rigors of the extraordinary Reagan-Stockman budget revisions of 1981, State's new management, while continuing to support strongly the need for such programs, had made no firm choices about what the specifics of the complete program should be, and whether it should be required of all officers seeking to reach senior level. Unless the system can make clear choices and hold to them, such programs will not work.

CHAPTER SIX

The Foreign Service Act of 1980: Moving from Diagnosis to Action

Many were aware, from at least the mid-1970's, of the malaise surrounding the Foreign Service personnel system which has been described earlier. In this chapter, the focus turns to two closely related efforts to deal with some of these problems. One was a clear failure, but the other provided the statutory basis for the most comprehensive reform of the Foreign Service since passage of the Foreign Service Act of 1946.

At the outset, it must be noted that many of the most important and pressing difficulties discussed earlier are not easily susceptible to legislative remedy; rather, they can be overcome only through application of a coherent, long-range management strategy, a responsive and enlightened approach to administration, the willingness of the Foreign Service itself to accept necessary change, and a fair amount of luck. The Foreign Service statutes of 1946 and 1980 did and do provide much authority and latitude, available to be used wisely—or wasted. A brief excursion from complaint and diagnosis to the real world of attempting to design and run better personnel systems for foreign affairs may provide some insight into both the possibilities and the limitations involved.

Reform in government is sometimes naively viewed as neat and straightforward, following, almost by rote, the logical steps of identifying problems, gathering information, planning, consulting, making final decisions, and eventually implementing reforms. Such efforts, however, are almost always diffuse, and final outcomes are often not those intended. Nevertheless, sometimes reform works, perhaps in spite of the efforts of reformers, but certainly only with a considerable dose of good fortune. Since the two most recent attempts at Foreign Service personnel reform dealt with virtually the same issues, were not widely separated in time, and had radically different outcomes, comparison is instructive. It is not often that the opportunity exists to examine truly comparable episodes, and when one appears, it is worth making the most of it.

STRUCTURE I (SPRING 1975–DECEMBER 1977)

In early 1975, Ambassador Carol Laise was selected to be the next Director General of the Foreign Service. Because the Senate delayed in confirming her predecessor in his new assignment, she had the opportunity, unusual in State, of spending several months "reading in" to her new responsibilities. Through a wide-ranging consultative process, she was exposed in detail to the Department's major personnel problems.

Soon after becoming Director General (DG), she directed the preparation of the comprehensive problem statement and detailed recommendations previously mentioned. This memorandum, prepared in May 1975,[1] was submitted to Secretary of State Kissinger and apparently received his support, in a speech given in late June to a new Foreign Service officer class.[2] It included recommendations on the issue with which this book has been heavily concerned: the proper structure for the personnel system or systems of the Department of State and the Foreign Service. The subissues were mostly those previously discussed: a single or dual system, rank-in-person versus rank-in-job status, specialists versus generalists, and open versus closed access. By normal logic, this study should have begun a successful reform effort. In fact, after a convoluted and sometimes agonizing process lasting the entire two and a half years of Laise's tour as DG, the effort died in December 1977, and was judged by all involved to have failed.

Why this happened is best understood by looking at the episode more closely. From the outset, believers in the Laise "dual system" (GS and FS) plan were limited to the senior officials of the

[1] Laise to Kissinger, "The Professional Service of the Department of State," May 17, 1975. (See Chap. III, note 31.)

[2] Henry A. Kissinger, June 27, 1975, distributed in Department of State Press Release No. 349, June 27, 1975. (See Chap. III, note 32.)

Bureau of Personnel, and some but by no means all of their immediate staff. The Deputy Under Secretary of State for Management (M), Lawrence S. Eagleburger, was open-minded but not inclined to be an advocate in view of substantial opposition to the plan, which was diametrically opposed to the Department's policy for at least the preceding decade. Secretary Kissinger, although critical of the Foreign Service in many areas, was essentially unengaged in the issue.

The project languished during the summer of 1975, but in September a study of the advantages and disadvantages of the proposed dual-system approach was begun. Shortly thereafter, the author joined the DG's staff as a consultant, assigned to organize an October conference of insiders and outside experts to consider the subject, and then to play a role in the study itself.

When the review started, disputes quickly broke out within the Bureau of Personnel. The draft was strongly attacked by some as an "advocacy document," since it concluded that a dual system was the only sensible one for the Department to follow. But after several revisions, Laise approved it in late December, and submitted it to M in early January 1976.

In retrospect, a choice was then made which almost guaranteed that the project would lose momentum. In early February, Eagleburger approved the dual-system plan "in principle," but requested additional in-house consultation. A staff-level working group drawn from throughout the Department was formed, which proved to be heavily stacked against the plan. Many managers, and therefore their representatives on the task force, were strongly opposed to it because they felt that a unified Foreign Service system provided much greater flexibility for management, better equity for all employees, and independence from the interference of the Civil Service Commission. After a number of contentious sessions in March 1976, the group prepared a paper which showed agreement on a number of peripheral points but none at all on the fundamental issue. Laise then disbanded the working group and decided to proceed in other ways.

Eagleburger had also asked that Personnel work with other bureaus to determine which positions in Washington should be filled by Foreign Service personnel and which by civil servants, assuming that a dual system would be used. But in the absence of a firm decision to use such a system, the negotiations were only partly successful, since many who were consulted hoped that a unified approach would be followed and thus argued that virtually all positions in their organizations should be designated for Foreign Service incumbency. This effort took almost six months, and even then designation of some 500 positions (of about 4,000) was still contested; in September these disputes had to be referred to M for a decision.

By then, the 1976 presidential election was imminent. Once it was known that Carter would succeed Ford, Eagleburger was disinclined to make the final decision. Instead, shortly before leaving office he submitted a required report to the Congress which endorsed the single-system approach but deferred a final choice to the new administration.[3]

Thus in the spring of 1977 the issue had to be taken up again, but with some new twists. A number of Carter appointees to the State Department, including Richard Moose, the new M, took up their duties with an inherent suspicion both of holdovers from the past Administration (into which category Laise as DG clearly fit) and of the career service in general. This suspicion was augmented by the well-known "not invented here" syndrome. In translation, this meant "If it wasn't our idea, it's no good."

Several formal review meetings on the plan, held in March and April and attended by a number of individuals at the Assistant Secretary level, proved inconclusive, partly because of continuing opposition to the dual-system idea, partly because of the skeptical atmosphere, and perhaps also because Moose was thinking beyond his current assignment. In May he was named Assistant Secretary of State for African Affairs, which brought the review to an end until a new Deputy Under Secretary of State for Management could be recruited and brought on board.

By August a new M—Ben H. Read—had assumed his position, and it was obvious that the end of the Laise era in Personnel was at hand. The "structure" issue was taken up again and pursued

[3] "Meeting Future Foreign Affairs Personnel Needs," Report submitted to the Speaker of the House and the President of the Senate by Deputy Under Secretary of State for Management Lawrence S. Eagleburger, January 12, 1977.

vigorously by Read, who had prior experience in State in the 1960's as Executive Secretary and had served subsequently as a foundation executive. Much of the opposition to the dual-system plan persisted, and Read's own inclinations were unknown. By October another factor further clouded the picture. The Carter Administration had by that time made it clear that it would attempt to reform the Federal Service governmentwide, through a major legislative effort to pass a new Civil Service Reform Act.[4] But in the fall of 1977 it was very uncertain whether such a bill could pass, and if so what changes it would make in the Civil Service system, or the extent to which the Foreign Service would be affected.

Although he tended to share the Laise-Eagleburger view that a single system on the Foreign Service model was unobtainable and unrealistic, Read had become convinced that reform of State's personnel system should be deferred until the outcome of the Civil Service reform effort was known. In the interim, he decided that departmental efforts should concentrate on administrative reforms compatible with a dual system. After consulting with Senator Pell and with Representative Dante B. Fascell, Chairman of the House International Operations Subcommittee, Read obtained the concurrence of Secretary of State Vance. The Foreign Service and the Department were notified of this choice on January 12, 1978.[5]

On December 31, Laise retired, having reached the mandatory retirement age of sixty. She was replaced by Harry G. Barnes, Jr., most recently Ambassador to Romania. Like his predecessor, he was to show a willingness to entertain nontraditional solutions to personnel problems. Also, and of major importance, he was

[4] During the summer of 1977, the previously cited Federal Personnel Management Project (FPMP), of which the author was a staff member on detail from State, was assembled at the out-of-the-way federal office building at Buzzard's Point in Washington to develop the plan (thus the sardonic designation as the "Buzzard's Point Expeditionary Force"). Eventually, this led to introduction and passage, after substantial modification, of the Civil Service Reform Act, which became law on October 13, 1978.

[5] DG Notice No. A-314, January 12, 1978. The thrust of this notice, reflecting Read's discussions with the Members of Congress, was earlier conveyed to the new Director General, Harry G. Barnes, Jr., on January 9, 1978.

to develop a close and reinforcing relationship with Read. Thus, "Structure I" came to an end, with little to show for the efforts made except two and one half years of frustration.

STRUCTURE II (OCTOBER 1978–OCTOBER 1980)

Read's decision to defer action was met with relief both by those who wished to have business as usual and by advocates of the dual system, who were worn down from the long effort and not unhappy with a respite from bureaucratic infighting. For them, the non-decision was at least better than a negative one. More generally, there was an assumption that Read had decided that the political costs of choosing *either* a dual *or* a single system would have been so high (in the Department if a dual system were chosen, and with the Congress, OMB, and the Civil Service Commission in the event of a unified system being chosen, since all had raised serious questions about this approach) that they were not worth bearing at that moment.

An alternative reading of Read's thinking, given credence by developments in early 1978, held that the "lack of will/political cost" interpretation missed the point. Specifically, regulations were issued which stated that in the future employees who would work only in Washington would either be hired in the Civil Service system or remain in that system, rather than be hired in the Foreign Service or allowed to convert to the Foreign Service system. Thus the hypothesis emerged that he had decided to make a de facto rather than de jure decision: the dual system would be used, and the new regulations would implement that choice, without announcing a formal decision. Read confirmed this interpretation to the author much later, in September 1980.

All this speculation became moot, however, in October 1978. Immediately upon passage of the Civil Service Reform Act (CSRA), Read called the first of an intensive series of meetings to discuss possible changes in the Foreign Service personnel system, including a resolution of the "structure" issue. Unlike previous meetings on the subject, this was a small informal grouping (to become known as the "PER group") of Read, Barnes, and a few staffers.[6] The operating mode was to prove to be, in distinct contrast to "Structure I," collegial and consensual rather than confrontational.

Read began the first meeting by saying that now that the CSRA had become law, it was time to consider what State should do; and he stated his initial assumptions. The first of these, which in effect made the structure decision which had been the cause of so much controversy, was that for the foreseeable future it would be necessary to have a dual personnel system, using the Foreign Service authority for those who would work overseas as well as at home and the Civil Service system for those who would be employed only in the United States. One or two of those present made a mild protest, but Read was very firm in his conviction that there had to be a separate domestic service, and that political realities required that it be in the Civil Service system. New flexibilities in Civil Service personnel regulations and substantial delegations of additional authority to operating departments such as State made the argument for a separate domestic system much less compelling. Added to this was the close escape of the Foreign Service from being included, willy-nilly, in the CSRA legislation. Only the cooperation of Scotty Campbell, Chairman of the Civil Service Commission, Senator Claiborne Pell, and Congressman Jim Leach of Iowa, a former FSO, kept senior levels of the Foreign Service out of the new Senior Executive Service, which would have been unworkable. In Read's opinion, if State were to avoid a renewed threat of having the Foreign Service folded into the Civil Service, it had to decide to accept the Civil Service system for domestic employees.

Although there was some grumbling about the dual-system approach, it was never seriously challenged throughout the subse-

[6] Including two of Read's assistants, William Galloway and Dwight Mason, one of Barnes's deputies, Robert Gershenson, and the author. Soon thereafter, it was enlarged to include the Assistant Secretary for Administration, John Thomas, Joan Clark, Director of Management Operations, James Michel, Deputy Legal Adviser, Gene Malmborg, Assistant Legal Adviser for Management, and Tony Kern, and Bob Hull, both of Personnel. Fairly early in the process, Thomas retired and Clark became Ambassador to Malta, but the others remained with the project to the end.

quent two-year process; instead, almost all later attention was devoted to changes in the Foreign Service system. Read's political assessment that the Department would accept the Civil Service system for domestic employees was sustained.

A second fundamental premise, more recent in origin but perhaps overriding in Read's thinking, was the result of a dangerous imbalance in the senior officer population in the Foreign Service, caused by much lower attrition than anticipated. A number of factors were responsible: mandatory retirement at age sixty was in abeyance, owing to a court suit on grounds of age discrimination; a 20 percent executive pay raise in January 1977 meant that many officers who otherwise would have retired stayed on to earn a higher retirement credit; selection-out for substandard performance had all but ended at the senior levels; and in 1976 time-in-class limits for senior officers at the class 1 and 2 levels (Career Ministers being subject neither to time-in-class limits nor to separation for substandard performance) had been extended significantly.

The last two realities meant there was virtually no quality control at the senior and most responsible levels of the Foreign Service, which Read knew was a point of concern to Secretary Vance, just as he knew, from personnel contact, that it had been of concern to Presidents Kennedy and Johnson. Each had concluded that there was too much deadwood at the top, and no way to prune it. If all this were not enough, there had been a reduction in State's personnel ceiling, meaning that the extra senior officers had to be accommodated within a lower limit of allowable senior positions. The result was near chaos. At the worst point, as many as 130 senior officers were unassignable, and thus reduced to "walking the halls" or to make-work special projects.

Read thus resolved that a new senior system must be created, which would provide for better control of the senior population, a better match of skills with available jobs, and an emphasis on performance for rewards, retention, advancement, and assignments. Thus was born the "Senior Foreign Service."

Proceeding from these two basic decisions, and many subsidiary ones on less visible problems, the review quickly gathered momentum. Through free-form discussions, followed by staff efforts to capture on paper what had been agreed to, then more discussions and redrafting, a structure "package" began to evolve. It was much more comprehensive than "Structure I": rather than being limited to the question of a unified versus a dual system, it went to the very heart of the Foreign Service system itself. It called for creation of a separate senior cadre, paralleling the newly enacted Senior Executive Service in some respects but tailored to specific Foreign Service needs; for combination of many Foreign Service categories and the two existing pay scales[7] into only two categories (for generalists and specialists) sharing a common pay system;[8] for extension of the highly endorsed but at that time only marginally effective concept of "selection-out for substandard performance" to the entire Foreign Service, including communicators and secretaries formerly exempted along with Career Ministers (the seniormost FSO's); and for a more sophisticated and realistic relationship to the Civil Service personnel system used by most of the rest of the federal government. As planning progressed, the decision was reached to produce an entirely new foreign service act, rather than to seek limited amendments to the existing 1946 legislation. In addition to the changes suggested, this comprehensive approach would have the advantage of codifying and rationalizing the confusing accretion of more than three decades of amendments to the 1946 Act, further provisions in annual authorization and appropriation acts, and additional law which had accumulated through the years. Almost unprecedented for such a usually staid establishment as the Department of State,

[7] One pay scale for officers and a separate one for staff corps members. Both were identical at some points but not at others, and both were linked to the GS schedule at three points. Different intervals were required in the two systems before step increases could be awarded, and different numbers of steps existed for each. Two distinct pay schemes covering those in identical circumstances were chaotic and unfair, and the source of major problems when individuals converted from one plan to another.

[8] The new categories, as discussed in Chapter III, were FSO for generalists, and a follow-on specialist category replacing the existing FSR, FSRU, and FSS groups and designated as "FP" in State. A single nine-class Foreign Service (FS) pay schedule was to be shared by the two categories, identical at every grade and step in pay. Above this new schedule there was a separate Senior Foreign Service schedule, similar to and linked to that for the Senior Executive Service.

all of the push was for serious reform rather than for cosmetic improvement.

Between the time the basic plan emerged in November 1978 and the introduction of the formal legislative proposal in Congress in June 1979, there was an intense, rough-and-tumble period of consultation. First, in a two-hour meeting in early November 1978, Secretary Vance and his immediate subordinates were briefed and brought on board. A session the next day with Scotty Campbell, Chairman of the Civil Service Commission, gained his support and offer of help. Heads of the other foreign affairs agencies proved to be less enthusiastic but hardly in a position to oppose the plan outright (a posture which they generally maintained throughout the whole congressional process). Next came briefings of the American Foreign Service Association (the Foreign Service union in State and AID), OMB, and critical members of Congress and their staffs. Over the next six months, there were many difficult negotiations with the other agencies, OMB, and the Office of Personnel Management (which replaced the Civil Service Commission on January 1, 1979), AFSA, and subgroups within the Foreign Service such as senior officers and secretaries. Out of all this, a draft bill was laboriously pieced together, cleared through OMB, and sent to the Hill just before the initial hearing on June 21, 1979, at which Secretary Vance was the lead witness.

Provisions of the Proposed Foreign Service Act

The bill's contents, modified in many details but not in basic thrust from the original plan, were summarized by the Department upon its introduction as follows:

—It simplifies and consolidates in one place legislation concerning the administration of the Foreign Service. This was a primary purpose of the Foreign Service Act of 1946, and, now that 33 years have passed with numerous amendments and the passage of numerous other new laws affecting the Service, codification is needed again.

—The proposed Bill, which is the product of three years of work and which complements the 1978 Civil Service Reform

Act, starts with a Congressional Finding that it is in the national interest to have a Foreign Service and that it must be representative of the American people, aware of the principles of American history and knowledgeable of other cultures and languages.

—There is a new statement of objectives stressing career and merit principles and improved efficiency and economy.

The Bill also:

—Establishes a more rigorous process for selection into the senior ranks, using existing, independent Boards for promotions, retention and selection out.

—Mandates the establishment of the Senior Foreign Service, comparable to the General and Flag Officer ranks of the armed forces and the Senior Executive Service of the Civil Service, based on standards of excellence and controlled as to size and advancement by performance standards.

—Offers the possibility of significantly higher levels of compensation for outstanding performance.

—Provides new and added emphasis to the career principle by limiting the number of non-career appointments to the top levels and by requiring that all persons appointed to career status pass through a tenuring process.

—Makes a clear distinction between personnel obligated to serve abroad and those who serve only at home and limits Foreign Service benefits to those who serve abroad; and converts those serving domestically to the Civil Service while preserving their pay and benefits.

—Places employee-management relations on a statutory basis.

—Reduces Foreign Service personnel categories from more than a dozen to two and provides a single pay schedule for them.

—Makes no significant change in Foreign Service retirement benefits or conditions.

—Is intended to promote maximum compatibility among the Foreign affairs agencies.[9]

[9] Quoted from the Executive Summary of the bill, drafted by the PER group to accompany its submission to the Congress.

CONGRESSIONAL MODIFICATIONS

The proposed Act took sixteen months to emerge from Congress, becoming the Foreign Service Act of 1980 rather than 1979 along the way. It was signed into law by President Carter on October 17, 1980, with most provisions (except changes in pay and raising the mandatory retirement age from sixty to sixty-five, which came into operation immediately) effective on February 15, 1981.[10]

During this period of congressional activity, the House International Operations and Civil Service Subcommittees, sitting jointly

[10] The legislative history of the Foreign Service Act of 1980 is contained in the following documents:

(a) The initial administration bill: H.R. 4674, introduced June 28, 1979; and S. 1450, introduced in the Senate July 9, 1979. The two were identical.

(b) House hearings: Subcommittee on International Operations of the Committee on Foreign Affairs and Subcommittee on Civil Service of the Committee on Post Office and Civil Service, *Hearings on H.R. 4674, The Foreign Service Act*, 96th Congress, 1st Session (Washington, D.C.: GPO, 1980).

(c) Senate hearings: Senate Foreign Relations Committee, *Hearings on S. 1450, The Foreign Service Act of 1979*, 96th Congress, 1st Session (Washington, D.C.: GPO, 1980).

(d) House reports: No. 96-996, Pt. 1 (Committee on Foreign Affairs), No. 96-996, Pt. 2 (Committee on Post Office and Civil Service), both May 15, 1980; No. 96-1432 (Committee on Conference), September 28, 1980. The latter contains the final text of the bill, and the manager's report of reconciliation of differences between the bills passed by the House and Senate. This conference report is also printed in 126 *Congressional Record*, September 29, 1980, H9955-H9991. All the above relate to H.R. 6790, the final House bill.

(e) Senate report: No. 96-913 (Committee on Foreign Relations) to accompany S. 3058 (the final Senate version), August 22, 1980.

(f) House floor consideration: 126 *Congressional Record*, September 8, 1980, H8487-H8524, H8643-H8662 (the latter is continued in the *Record* for September 9, 1980).

(g) Senate floor consideration: 126 *Congressional Record*, September 10, 1980, S12361, S12363-S12369, S12380-S12382; September 11, 1980, S12444-S12450; September 15, 1981, S12498-S12554.

(h) Agreement to conference report: Senate, 126 *Congressional Record*, September 30, 1980, S13866-S13871; House, 126 *Congressional Record*, October 1, 1980, H10233-H10238.

(i) President's statement on signing P.L. 96-465: 16 *Weekly Compilation of Presidential Documents*, No. 43, 2332-2333, October 17, 1980.

in an unusual procedure, held fourteen witness hearings and several more markup sessions to draft a final bill. The Senate Foreign Relations Committee, less interested in detail, held three hearings in addition to markup. There were also innumerable working sessions between State staffers and their Hill counterparts, between Members of Congress and Read and his close associates, among the several agencies and between the latter and union representatives. In a variety of ways, many affected interests—senior officers wanting security and junior ones intent on faster advancement, women, minorities, divorced spouses of members of the Service, advocates of a totally independent Foreign Service and those who preferred a Foreign Service completely a part of the Civil Service, academic observers, those who wanted to defer any action until a new Administration might be elected, and especially the unions—had weighed in heavily, and often effectively. On two or three occasions, the bill almost died from opposition, lack of interest, no sense of urgency in Congress, or simply running out of time.

Nevertheless, the plan developed by Read and his staff emerged essentially intact, although there were modifications in some important details, a few near misses with potentially damaging amendments, and some notable additions not originally a part of the plan. A brief review of these changes is necessary in order to evaluate, in the final chapter, how well the new Act is likely to meet the needs for change presented earlier.

Modifications in tone or detail, but not in basic thrust, were most numerous. The chapter of the bill dealing with labor-management relations, to take a major example, was originally designed to do little more than to transform Executive order 11636 into statutory authority, with some changes in third-party mediation and arbitration mechanisms. But pressures by the unions for greater rights, and by the Post Office and Civil Service Committee staff for closer conformity with Civil Service procedures enacted in the Civil Service Reform Act of 1978, led to some weakening of reserved management rights and to third-party mechanisms tied closely to the Federal Labor Relations Authority. These changes would bear close watching as the new system came into being, but did not at first impression appear to be unworkable.

A second group of changes were designed to monitor and perhaps inhibit management's ability to operate some of the new provisions of the Act, especially those relating to basing retention and rewards in the Senior Foreign Service on performance, and, in a related way, to provide greater protections for the career service against politicization or, more generally, undue competition from outsiders. Senator Pell, in particular, was concerned, as were some in AFSA, that the new mechanism for "Limited Career Extensions (LCE's)"—which provided that after a much shorter time than the existing time-in-class allowed,[11] retention for each class including Career Ministers was to be based on selection board review coupled with management decisions about the number to be retained[12]—could be used by an unscrupulous Administration to purge the senior ranks, and either to bring in outsiders or to promote a more docile group to senior levels. What resulted was a series of amendments and some restrictive legislative history. Thus, LCE's had to be granted in strict "rank-order" as determined by selection boards; individuals not renewed could be extended for only one year by management, and only under unusual circumstances; and career candidates for the SFS would be required to serve at least four years before being granted career tenure. Further, an unusual reporting provision was added, requiring management to report to the Congress, after sharing relevant data with the appropriate union at "each stage," on five-year projections of attrition, retention, promotion, and recruitment into the Service.[13] The clear message of all this was that however

[11] Formerly, senior officers had been allowed up to twenty-two years of combined time in classes two and one (with no more than ten years at class two) before being separated for expiration of time-in-class. There was no limit at the highest class of Career Minister. Under the new system, the TIC limits were set at seven years at the Counselor class (equivalent to the former class two), five years at the Minister-Counselor class (equal to the former class one), and four years at Career Minister. One or more renewals of three years, based on Service needs and individual performance were also possible—hence the name "Limited Career Extension."

[12] The LCE provisions are contained in Section 607(b) of the Act.

[13] Sections 2402(a)(3) and 2402(b)(2) of the Act. The first of these reports, due on February 1, 1982, was not submitted to the Congress until almost four months later, owing to major disputes in State and in USICA centering on management

much management might wish to have flexible instruments to control quality, skills, and size of the workforce, it would not be able to operate in isolation. The unions and the Congress would have their say.

In a third area, outside pressures forced revisions in the section of the Act providing a statutory base for the Department of State's Inspector General (IG). State had had an Inspector General since 1946, operating on the philosophy that useful management information could be provided by having senior members of the Service review the totality of an embassy's performance (including Washington support) and make recommendations for improvements. In 1978, the inspector idea was discovered by the House Government Operations Committee, chaired by Representative Jack Brooks of Texas, leading to passage of the "Inspector General Act of 1978." It created independent Inspectors General in most agencies except State and Defense, but with a primary focus on "waste, fraud, and mismanagement," soon to become "WIF-FIM." After much pulling and hauling, made more difficult by House staffers who thought that only one organizational and procedural approach, their own, could accomplish what they felt was needed, the IG provisions in the Foreign Service Act preserved a modicum of the older IG role in State, but came close to bestowing as much independence as the IG Act.[14] As foreseen by State sponsors of the new Foreign Service Act, by 1982 this latitude had led to a series of conflicts within the Department, given the appointment of an IG who gloried in his independence and who was less concerned than his predecessors with the original elements of his role, designed to improve management. This was one more example of the old maxim that it is impossible to legislate good sense, and conversely that poor operations can overcome sound legislation.

In the "near miss" category of amendments were a complete substitute bill introduced by Senator Jesse Helms of North Car-

desires to protect their prerogatives in staffing, and union wishes to obtain more information and eventually a share of control. Preparation of the 1983 report was almost as difficult.

[14] The Inspector General provisions are in Section 209. The Inspector General Act of 1978 is P.L. 95-452, 92 Stat. 1101 (1978).

olina which would have drastically reduced the size of the Foreign Service and required it to operate on principles much closer to those of the Civil Service,[15] and an effort inspired by AFSA and supported by Congressman Jim Leach of Iowa which would have imposed much greater uniformity on the several agencies in operating the Senior Foreign Service but which would have likely eliminated support for the entire effort by all agencies other than State. A third example involved the Foreign Service's statutory grievance procedure, enacted in 1975, largely in response to the sad case of Charles Thomas.[16] Not content with the remedies provided at that time, his widow, who had been hired in the meantime by State, continued to press Senator Birch Bayh for modifications in the 1975 statute which would have made virtually any action—including selection board decisions on promotion, retention, or selection-out—grievable, thus limiting considerably the ability to manage the Service. The Bayh bill had been defeated in conference twice previously, after having been passed by the Senate. As part of his efforts, Helms had picked up the Bayh proposal and reintroduced it in the context of attempting to modify the Foreign Service bill. Eventually, by a vote of forty-five to thirty-six, it was defeated.

Several items in the category of additions were also important. Primary among these was a substantial reduction in the pay dis-

[15] The Helms bill had several incarnations: first, as S. 2986, which was introduced and printed in the *Congressional Record* on July 29, 1980; as an updated version, in the form of Amendment No. 2290 to the Committee (administration) bill, S. 3058, which was printed in the *Record* on September 11, 1980, pp. S12249-50; and a substitute for Amendment No. 2290, unprinted Amendment No. 1573 which made minor technical corrections to 2290 and which was printed in the *Record* on September 15, 1980, pp. S12499-S12501.

[16] Thomas had failed to be promoted in the late 1960's and was separated from the Service for expiration of his allowed time-in-class. Subsequently, he was a suicide. While he had received severance pay (but not an immediate annuity, as he would have if he had held the next higher rank), a special bill giving him a posthumous promotion had become law, and his widow had been hired by the State Department. She continued her campaign, pressing for basic changes in the grievance system to make it even more favorable to employees, notwithstanding that the existing system had been enacted in 1975 largely in response to the Thomas case and was widely held to be more favorable to employees than others in the federal government.

crepancies between the Foreign Service and the Civil Service, especially at the middle levels. The story of this episode is much too complicated to relate here, but in effect congressional advocates of higher pay for the Foreign Service held the Foreign Service Act hostage until an agreement could be reached with OMB to establish an acceptable pay schedule by Executive order. Otherwise, congressional proponents of the new Act were resolute about legislating a schedule they found suitable. Under the agreement which was finally obtained, the new statute established the grade structure and number of steps for each grade in the Foreign Service schedule, but dollar amounts for each grade and step were set by Executive order, thus following the pattern used in other federal pay systems.[17]

A second group of new provisions dealt with improvements in allowances and benefits, sometimes for the Foreign Service alone but often for all federal employees serving abroad. These included the possibility of drawing advance pay upon transfer to a post abroad in order to meet extraordinary expenses, a special incentive differential in addition to the existing post or hardship differential for hard-to-staff posts, danger pay for particularly hazardous posts, some special per diem authorities, extensions of the circumstances when family members could be paid a per diem while on temporary duty with a member of the Service, and some technical modifications. Taken together, these amendments corrected a number of irritants and real or preceived inequities in the allowance structure, but seemed unlikely to have a fundamental impact in solving some of the overseas staffing problems facing the Foreign Service.[18]

Perhaps the most interesting additions, threatening to some, were highly innovative provisions designed to force recognition

[17] The pay issue had an historical component, in that as early as 1974 the Civil Service Commission had been willing to improve pay levels for middle-grade FSO's if the Department of State would in turn agree to downgradings of the staff corps (largely secretaries and communicators), an outcome State's personnel managers refused to accept. Thus, there had been no changes in linkage between the Civil Service and Foreign Service pay systems in the interim.

[18] See Sections 901-905 and 2301-2313 of the Act for these modifications in allowances and benefits.

of the changing role of families in the Foreign Service, and especially to improve the lot of spouses and former spouses. The most important of these was a direct recognition of the contributions which spouses have often made to the careers of members of the Foreign Service, an acknowledgment in the form of a vested right to a pro rata share of retirement annuities and survivor benefits, once a couple has been married for ten years while one spouse has been in government service, even if the couple subsequently divorces. The theory behind this set of amendments, the special project of Representative Pat Schroeder, Chair of the Civil Service Subcommittee, and of the Association of American Foreign Service Women, was that Foreign Service spouses, because they accompany their husbands (or rarely wives) overseas on assignment, have had to sacrifice their own careers and therefore have lost the chance to provide for their own retirement if they should have happened at that point no longer to be married. These provisions were fiercely resisted by many, especially veterans' groups, but were included after a compromise on the bill in conference, the major aspect of which was that the benefit-sharing would apply on an automatic basis only in the case of divorces taking place after the effective date of the Act.[19]

Other changes relevant to families included authority for a separate maintenance allowance (SMA) at the request of a member of the Service when he or she has deemed there would be special hardships in bringing the family to post (previously, SMA was available only at the convenience of the government), additional training for family members and grants for child care during training, emphasis by statute on employing family members abroad when possible to do so without cutting into permanent positions reserved for career members of the Service, provision of medical care after divorce for continuing conditions which began while a spouse was married to a member of the Service, and the ability to be paid directly, instead of only through one's spouse, for representational expenses incurred in furthering the interests of

[19] The spouse and former spouse annuity provisions may be found primarily in sections 814, 825, and 2403(e) of the Act.

the U.S. government. While they did not gain all that was desired, Schroeder and AAFSW did force the Congress—and the Department of State and other foreign affairs agencies—into making a direct response to some of the problems of families and spouses discussed in Chapter IV.

There were still other new provisions, but most of the rest were individual items advanced by one Member of Congress and accepted by other interested parties. Among them were a Pell amendment requiring a formal professional development program for all members of the Foreign Service; a Simon amendment requiring that two "model foreign language competence posts" be established as an experiment, where everyone assigned would be required to know the local language at some level; and some additional protections of salary for members of the Foreign Service who would be required to convert to the Civil Service because they were not available or needed for service abroad. Less helpful to those charged with managing the Foreign Service were a number of required reports to the Congress in various areas—reports about the general implementation of the Act, the new attrition and promotion mechanisms, affirmative action, career development—all of which would require substantial amounts of staff time and in some cases move congressional oversight very close to interference in the day-to-day management of the Foreign Service.

A detailed summary of the provisions of the new Act is contained in the Appendix.

IMPLEMENTATION

An earlier version of this chapter included a section called "Implementation is Not Fun," in contrast to the excitement of guiding a major piece of legislation through the vagaries of the congressional process. Perhaps this is why so many sensible reform efforts ultimately fail, as time runs out and the enthusiasm of proponents runs down. A major change in a federal personnel system such as that mandated by the Foreign Service Act of 1980, for example, cannot be fully in place for several years, even if implementation takes place smoothly and more or less in accordance with what the Congress and the designers of the new system had in mind.

Nevertheless, after several rocky periods, by spring 1983, more than two years after the effective date of the Act, the project was still essentially on track. Although the new M, Richard T. Kennedy, and the new DG, Joan M. Clark, who had assumed their duties at the change of Administrations almost simultaneously with the effective date of the Act, were not its parents and therefore could not be expected to be committed to it quite the same way as their predecessors, they undertook, with some occasional grumbling, to bring it to life. Kennedy in particular had reservations about some provisions. But the intent of Congress was honored.

The initial task was to convert individuals to new personnel categories where required by the Act: to the Senior Foreign Service; to the new specialist category, replacing the Foreign Service Reserve and the Foreign Service Staff Corps; to the new pay schedule for this group and for middle-grade and junior FSO's; to the Civil Service/Senior Executive Service for Foreign Service domestic employees; and, for members of the Foreign Agricultural Service, from a hybrid Civil Service system to the appropriate Foreign Service category. During the first part of the allowed three-year period for conversions, there was substantial progress, but also a number of problems. The conversion of individuals clearly available for service overseas to the new Foreign Service categories was largely uneventful, although AFSA and one senior officer successfully brought suit, winning the point that those who did not choose to convert to the Senior Foreign Service, and who were therefore required by the Act to leave the Foreign Service by February 15, 1984, were being forced to leave involuntarily and should therefore receive an immediate annuity, even if they did not have the twenty years of service and fifty years of age normally required to be eligible for retirement.[20]

Converting domestic employees from the Foreign Service to the Civil Service, even with the extensive retention of rights pro-

[20] The case was *Meresman et al.* v. *Haig*, U.S. District Court for the District of Columbia, Civil Action No. 81-918, decided June 8, 1981.

vided by the Act, proved to be more difficult. In USIA, where both management and the employee representative organization, the American Federation of Government Employees, clearly preferred moving to the Civil Service by attrition rather than by a conversion program, regulations to govern the conversion process were not even close to being implemented by mid-1983. Apparently, there was some hope that before conversion was legally required, a way could be found to avoid it. In State, the large majority of those initially identified as being in the domestic category (some 330 of 470) accepted domestic status, but most deferred conversion until 1984, since there were some financial advantages in remaining in the Foreign Service as long as possible, owing to the fact that step increases were possible annually for most paid on the Foreign Service Schedule, while in many cases they were possible only every second or third year under the General Schedule.

A number of others, slightly more than one hundred, appealed the finding of domestic status to a special committee formed for the purpose of deciding such cases. It determined that some thirty of these should in fact be in the Foreign Service, while about seventy had been correctly identified as being in the domestic category. The majority accepted these findings, but some filed grievances contesting what they regarded as adverse decisions on their proper status, as was provided for in State's conversion regulations. Generally, those who grieved were successful, either by winning their grievances before the Foreign Service Grievance Board or by accepting settlements offered by management based on guidance that the Grievance Board would find in the individual's favor if required to make a formal decision. Apparently, in spite of the Act's protection of the financial rights, tenure, and status of those who converted to the Civil Service, membership in the Foreign Service was held to be more important, viewed as an individual right, than whether or not the individual could be used effectively in a Foreign Service career involving substantial service abroad. Nevertheless, in spite of such problems, which were transitional in nature and limited in their impact, successful completion of the conversion process went a fair way toward simplifying the Foreign Service system, which had been a point of congressional interest and of management difficulty for at least the previous decade.

Even more difficult was the complicated and lengthy process of revising almost all personnel regulations issued by the several agencies. Most changes required negotiations with employee representative organizations, and many, reflecting the common statutory base which had come into being, needed to apply jointly to all five of the primary foreign affairs agencies. This produced a five-agency/three-union (Agriculture and Commerce not being organized) negotiating format which was at best unwieldy and at worst highly contentious, because of suspicions among both the agencies and the unions as well as the normal union-management differences. Moreover, the new Administration's senior managers in the foreign affairs agencies were notably more protective of reserved management rights than their predecessors had been, which naturally led to more disputes with the unions and to a number of issues being referred to the third-party mechanisms brought into existence by the new Act.

Nevertheless, the process of negotiating new regulations generally held together, and at the end of the first two years of the new Act a number of important new regulations were in place, particularly those bringing the new Senior Foreign Service to life and those making new benefits and allowances effective, about which the unions were naturally most concerned.

New institutional arrangements were also required, especially the previously mentioned third-party mechanisms in the labor-managment area, a reconstituted Board of Examiners for the Foreign Service, and a revised Board of the Foreign Service, with a different set of responsibilities. In some cases Executive orders were required to do this, but nevertheless all the required new organizational units were in operation by the summer of 1982. Gradually, too, new operating procedures and new approaches to managing the Service were developed and brought into being.

In short, while progress was slower than desirable, it was taking place, and there seemed a reasonable chance that the policies required by the new Act would be initiated, and would survive. Whether or not such policies could meet the problems and diffi-

culties which have been the primary subject of this book is the
subject of the final chapter.

WHY A NEW ACT WAS POSSIBLE

The problem of implementing change in government has received considerable recent attention, as a growing number of failed
efforts demonstrate that the execution of reform plans *after* they
are adopted may be most difficult of all.[21]

A rational plan which will meet real problems is helpful, but
alone is no guarantee of success. The logic of running dual Civil
and Foreign Service personnel systems was as compelling in 1975
and 1976, when no progress was made, as it was during the
successful "Structure II" period just two years later—in fact, it
was the identical logic.

Not only is a sensible plan not a sufficient condition for success,
but there is considerable evidence that it is not even a necessary
one. Two reform plans placed into effect during this same period
in the Carter Administration, one a reorganization of foreign aid
and the other of trade promotion, were deeply flawed both or-
ganizationally and in their ability to confront the problems they
were designed to correct. They were nevertheless adopted and
implemented. Why was this so?

Although a single case is a risky basis for pushing general
conclusions, there seem to be three characteristics which successful government reform efforts share; there is a client who
wants change; it is possible to overcome or to co-opt opposition
(which there will always be if the issues at hand are of any
importance); and the proponents of reform are lucky in their tim-

---

[21] Implementation, formerly a wasteland 10954$$$37 terms of study and anal-
ysis, has recently received substantial attention. For example, see Jeffrey L.
Pressman adn Aaron Wildavsky, *Implementation* 2nd ed. (Berkeley, Calif.: Uni-
versity of California Press, 1979), and Eugene Bardach, *The Implementation
Game: What Happens After a Bill Becomes Law* (Cambridge, Mass.: The MIT
Press, 1977). Wildavsky notes, in his preface to the second edition explaining the
addition of a substantial listing of works, that "the bibliography (replacing the
appendix saying there was 'no there there') can only be suggestive rather than
comprehensive." More work does not necessarily mean progress, but raises the
probability there will be some.

ing, in the individuals involved both for and against the proposed change, in outside but related developments, and in the attention their efforts draw.

The need for a client seems indisputable. There must be someone influential who wants the plan to succeed and, ideally, a wide spectrum of supporters for it. Further, the client must be willing to devote time, energy, and political capital to seeing the proposal through. Perhaps the classic case of this was the Brownlow Committee in the 1930's, whose efforts from the very beginning had the direct and positive support of President Franklin D. Roosevelt.[22] In contrast, the Murphy Commission, whose research efforts and conclusions are often cited, mostly positively, in this book, was a political orphan which lost any clients it may have had early in the game.[23] As a result its conclusions, at least as commission recommendations, were never seriously considered for adoption.

In the case of the Foreign Service Act, there was indifference in the White House, but a strong and committed client at State. This was Under Secretary for Management Ben Read. He had four major assets: close and supportive relationships with Secretaries of State Vance and Muskie; good working associations with the small number of Senators and Members of Congress who cared about the issue; a competent group of subordinates who were able to devise a reasonable plan and sell it where needed;

[21] The Committee report was published as U.S. President's Committee on Administrative Management, *Report with Special Studies* (Washington, D.C.: GPO, 1937).

[23] The Murphy Commission originated in the Senate Foreign Relations Committee in 1971, with a political purpose of causing potential embarrassment to President Nixon and National Security Adviser Kissinger. When the Administration declined to appoint its members of the Commission, its birth was deferred for a year. Finally, the tables turned and the Commission began to function with an eight-to-four Republican majority in 1973, and an implicit determination not to cause problems for the Administration. By the time it issued its report, in mid-1975, Gerald Ford was President, Henry Kissinger was Secretary of State, and the next election was only sixteen months away. Because of timing and the several political transformations involved, its report, while probably largely right in its recommendations, received almost no serious attention, if measured by real attempts to use its findings as the basis for organizational, personnel, or operational change.

and although it was a long time in coming, the eventual support of the American Foreign Service Association, whose approval was needed to encourage the Congress to move.

Even so, passage was a near thing. Read and the "PER Group" were able to marshal enough support from the two Secretaries of State at critical points, but stretched their resources to the limit in doing so. In the face of more determined or effective opposition, the outcome might have been quite different. The secret was that Read and the few congressional members who cared, with the exception of Senator Jesse Helms, all shared the perspective that a new Act was desirable, although there were substantial differences among them on many specific issues.

It was possible to co-opt initial opposition, especially from AFSA, through the combination of the election in 1979 of new officers and board members who were reform oriented, a management willingness to modify the plan to meet the union's strongest concerns, and "sweetening the pot" by provision of a substantial Foreign Service pay increase and authority for additional allowances and benefits. The lukewarm support of the other foreign affairs agencies, and outright opposition of USICA's union, the American Federation of Government Employees, could be shunted aside because Read and his staff and the key Members of Congress, especially Pell and Fascell and their staffs, were close enough and trusting enough to override objections.

Finally, considerable luck was involved. A lack of attention, and therefore of serious opposition, was foremost. The friendly personal relationships between State and Congress were another element of luck. And passage of the Civil Service Reform Act of 1978, together with the prevailing political mood which made it possible, made it clear that State and the foreign affairs agencies had no prospect of developing a domestic personnel system which did not use Civil Service authorities. Thus at one stroke the fundamental issue of "Structure I" was resolved. There had to be a dual system to account for very different conditions of service overseas and service only at home, and the domestic system had to be Civil Service. In addition, it became obvious early in the process that political necessity required that needed changes at the senior levels of the Service parallel those made by the CSRA, at least with respect to trying additional compensation to performance rather than to seniority. Thus a prior reform effort helped to set the ground rules which would apply, and in turn diverted debate over the Senior Foreign Service idea into a more restricted context. The Civil Service Reform Act had already taken some of the steps, such as instituting performance pay, which would have been most controversial had they been proposed only for the Foreign Service. Sometimes, catching up is much easier than breaking new ground.

Implicit in all this is that quite limited attention was paid to the proposed reform, and most of those who were most vocal and involved were supporters of change, in one way or another. Since one of the constants which proponents of reform must face is the preference of most of the people most of the time for a known situation rather than an unknown new one, even if the new approach is potentially better, this was fundamentally important. Supporters of the status quo never really got their act together and were not able to present their case effectively, in the face of determined if narrow support for change.

Aside from this, there was also good luck in timing. If the new Act had failed to become law, it would have been because of the adjournment of the ninety-sixth Congress, not because of opposition. The ability of Secretary of State Muskie, as a respected and recently departed Senator, to call in enough chips to ensure that the Senate Foreign Relations Committee would have a quorum to vote out the bill made the difference. Once this happened, the "sunk costs" of the other participants, together with their influence, made sure that the bill would come up for final passage. And once brought to the floor in both houses, passage was certain.

Similarly, once the bill had passed into law, respect for legal processes by all concerned helped limit attempts to thwart the Act's implementation. This of course did not mean that there were not major disagreements about what the Congress had intended and what the new law required, and even some lost lawsuits, but it did mean that the issue became not whether to implement the new Act, but rather how to do it.

It should be clear, in conclusion, that the Foreign Service Ac of 1980 does not provide a guaranteed blueprint for developmen and implementation of other reforms. It seems entirely possible that reform in government is so situation-specific that only obvious, general guidelines can be developed. Individual cases may show the broad requirements for successful reform, but they do not provide a detailed plan for obtaining such outcomes.[24]

[24] For a detailed treatment of legislative activity connected with Foreign Service Act, see William I. Bacchus, *Inside the Legislative Process: The Passage of the Foreign Service Act of 1980* (Boulder, Colo.: Westview Press, forthcoming).

CHAPTER SEVEN

What Remains to Be Done?

The Foreign Service Act of 1980 represents, on balance, both a successful reform in government and, in the author's opinion, a substantial contribution to providing the foreign affairs personnel systems needed in the future. At the same time, even if it is completely implemented according to what was intended, it is only a part of what will be required. This final chapter has one primary purpose: to weigh the new personnel systems now evolving as a consequence of the new Act, together with other recent improvement efforts, against the needs and problems described in the earlier chapters of this book, in order to suggest areas which still require serious attention.

Further Needs

It may be that the new Foreign Service Act will prove to be a successful first step toward providing the necessary competences described in Chapter I and argued to be dangerously absent in Chapter II, but by itself it is no solution to the problems discussed there. It does provide the necessary means, if used sensibly, to facilitate rather than impede acquisition and development of the additional specialist, diplomatic, and policy development and integration skills so obviously needed. By providing for both generalists and specialists in the Foreign Service, available for rotational service at home and abroad, by reestablishing the basis for a strong headquarters cadre in the Civil Service, and by requiring a coherent career development and training program for all, the Act allows, but does not force, a constructive policy to be developed.

As of late 1982, however, this had not happened. The old generalist versus specialist arguments continued, together with primary emphasis on managerial skills and lesser concern for the substantive competence levels of FSO's. There was little evidence that lessons of the past had been learned. A 1980 initiative to require more structure in the FSO career by establishing "senior threshold" requirements which would have to be met before an officer could be considered for promotion to the SFS, so that the necessary competences would be present when an officer reached senior levels, faltered in 1981. Considerable opposition emerged in the Service, and while supporting the idea of improved skills and better career development, the new leadership of the Bureau of Personnel and in M questioned whether a mandatory set of requirements was capable of being fulfilled in practice, under the existing assignment system. Instead they initially opted to make the list one of desirable experiences, with no requirement that they be met before one could be considered for promotion. Even this effort subsequently lapsed, leaving no additional specific requirements for advancement to senior ranks.

A second source of skepticism is the considerable difficulty encountered, during the period after the Senior Executive Service was created in July 1979, in convincing the bureaus of the Department of State to create even a small number of SES positions, to provide continuity in management of the headquarters Civil Service cadre. Later, after the passage of the Foreign Service Act made it clear that there could no longer be a domestic Foreign Service category, this attitude eased somewhat, but acceptance of the need for a system jointly managed by senior officers in the Foreign Service and the Civil Service was still grudging (this was not helped, after the Reagan Administration took office, by OPM's extreme unwillingness to provide additional SES positions). Until this attitude is broken, progress will be very difficult.

SOURCES OF WEAKNESSES

A brief reprise of the sources of current weaknesses, as presented in Chapter III, may help clarify the problem. The first difficulty presented there was the primary one of role ambiguity: What should the Foreign Service in the field, State's headquarters staff, and more generally the Department of State as a whole be doing, in relation to the other parts of the government? Naturally, a consensus about what each unit in the government apparatus should do would aid greatly in designing and operating a personnel system to staff it. One senses, however, in reviewing the tired litany of Rusk vs. McNamara vs. Rostow, Kissinger vs. Rogers, Kissinger vs. Haig, Brzezinski vs. Vance, and Haig vs. Weinberger vs. Allen/Clark, that this desired state has not been reached.

It seems likely it never can be, in terms of formal organization and delegation of authority from the President. Both the strengths and the weaknesses of the American political system derive from its complexity and ambiguity, allowing bureaucratic entrepreneurs to seek their own places by targeting their contributions on the tasks at hand at a particular moment. This does not make life easy for career foreign affairs officials, who are expected to serve each administration with their full talents, or for those charged with managing the personnel system which supplies them, but it does suggest a course of action which, while not easy, is most likely to work. Simply put, since role is a relational concept, implying interactions,[1] the best way for any given set of foreign affairs officials—Foreign Service, foreign affairs community at large, intelligence analysts, or those serving in the Department of State as a collectivity—to make their mark is to be useful to other actors in the play. If you have something they want, they will come beating on your door.

Arguably, the Foreign Service has caused itself immense difficulty with too much concern about its role (which it has often confused with the not at all identical role of the Department of State as a whole), and not nearly enough attention to getting the job done. The new Foreign Service Act addresses this problem only peripherally, but in requiring a headquarters cadre in the Civil Service it may at least emphasize the difference between State's role and that of the Foreign Service. After countless discussions with members of the Foreign Service over the last decade, however, the author is skeptical that the lesson of utility being superior to natural right as the basis of influence has been fully

---

[1] For a review of role theory in essentially the same context, see the discussion and sources cited in Bacchus, *The Country Director*, Chap. III, pp. 76-80.

learned. Even those who admit the validity of the argument intellectually tend to lapse back emotionally into a desire that the Foreign Service be approached with deference. There seems no surer way to guarantee that it will be scorned and become irrelevant than to have this attitude persist much longer. "What have you done for me lately?" is the operating premise in Washington generally, and should be remembered by the Foreign Service.

The picture is brighter with respect to the twin problems of complexity and fragmentation, but much still remains to be done. Paradoxically, the creation of distinct personnel systems for those available for service anywhere in the world on one hand and those serving only in the United States on the other, while superficially adding to the fragmentation, has the potential of reducing complexity markedly. In the process of sorting out numerous "hybrid" groupings of employees, those who were neither truly Foreign Service nor Civil Service were being consolidated into one main category on the other. If the lesson that the single system is fatally flawed has been learned after thirty-four years from 1946 to 1980, then much progress is possible, since future efforts can then be devoted to making each system work rather than to trying to combine the two, with losses of effectiveness on both sides.

More modest gains were made in the slow process of creating a true "Foreign Service of the United States" by the enactment of a common statutory base for the Foreign Service components in various agencies, and by the admittedly largely hortatory requirement that personnel processes and procedures should be consolidated whenever feasible.[2] The first demonstrable result of this requirement was the development, mostly at State insistence, of joint implementing regulations for the new Act shared among agencies to a much greater extent than previously. This goal largely

[2] Section 203 of the Act requires that "The Service shall be administered to the extent practicable in a manner that will assure maximum compatibility among the agencies authorized by law to utilize the Foreign Service personnel system" (22 U.S.C. 3923). Section 204 calls for uniformity of personnel policies and procedures, and consolidation of personnel functions among the several agencies, as needed (22 U.S.C. 3925). An effort to require greater statutory uniformity was, however, defeated during House committee consideration of the bill, primarily because of the reservations of agencies other than State, which feared they would be dominated by the latter.

caused the considerable difficulties encountered in negotiating those regulations, but eventually resulted in a revised system which at least at the beginning would be operated much more in common than the one it replaced. At the same time, no centralized authority—no Foreign Service equivalent of the Office of Personnel Management—was created to manage and enforce the "Foreign Service umbrella" across agency lines. The only broad-gauged interagency mechanism created by the statute, the Board of the Foreign Service, was purely advisory, and its utility would ultimately be determined by the willingness of personnel managers in State and the other agencies to acquiesce in its recommendations. The Board of Examiners for the Foreign Service (BEX), also statutory, did have explicit powers to force uniformity and maintenance of standards in hiring, but since the Act clearly left operating powers with the heads of the agencies using the system, it was unclear how much BEX's theoretical powers would mean. The generally cooperative spirit shown by the agencies during initial stages of implementing the Act was, however, a positive early sign.

The quality of management of the Foreign Affairs system, unfortunately, was not the beneficiary of comparable improvements. The Director General gained no new authority, and nothing in the Act required or allowed the DG to assume the role of overseeing the system at large, or required that he or she have operational personnel expertise (although recent DG's have in fact had considerable personnel experience) or remain in the position for any extended period of time in order to provide managerial continuity. The same was true for Personnel Directors of other agencies using the system. When Harry Barnes completed his tour as Director General in February 1981, he had served slightly over three years in the position—the longest incumbency since the modern Foreign Service and the DG position were created by the Act of 1946. Moreover, nothing required that a personnel management system staffed by personnel professionals be created, although recent DG's had endorsed the idea in principle and attempted some modest steps in that direction.

The potential for truly effective personnel management, always available to State and the other Foreign Affairs agencies at least since passage of the 1946 Act by virtue of the flexibility and freedom provided, has never been fully exploited. There is depressingly little reason to believe it will be now.

Much the same is true with respect to the creativity needed to turn a statutory personnel system to the specific demands of an evolving situation. The Foreign Affairs agencies simply have not been very good at adapting personnel systems—Foreign or Civil Service—to new demands and responsibilities. Nothing in the new Act prevents such adaptation, but there is little that forces it to take place. The opposite danger, of making every decision on a case-specific basis, is equally present. This is largely a question of managerial will and sustained attention to development and operation of a consistent system, one in which the rules do not change every few years, or worse, case by case.

Sponsors of the new Foreign Service Act often heard this last kind of criticism—the charge of changing the rules before the old ones had a chance to work—and there was a certain measure of correctness in the assertion that the previous system, the unified approach, had been badly bungled in operation and never given a fair opportunity tò succeed. But even if true, the time for that system had passed. The new law addresses many of the dilemmas of system design, and if given continued attention and nurturing it could result in a responsive, flexible, and at the same time coherent and consistent system. But that outcome is not guaranteed.

The final source of current weaknesses discussed in Chapter III was the negative effect of elitism and of public perceptions on morale and on employee-management relations. The highly visible tribulations of service abroad seem for the moment to have provided a counterweight to the effete stereotype which has long dogged the Foreign Service, as a comparison of the kinds of articles cited in the Introduction with those discussed in the final section of Chapter III will show.[3]

---

[3] Although the persistence of the older kind of critique was taken note of by Congressman Dante B. Fascell, a primary sponsor of the new Foreign Service Act and strong advocate of the Department and the Foreign Service, during House floor debate on the Department of State's Fiscal Year 1982 and 1983 Authorization bill, on September 17, 1981, Fascell argued the contrary point forcefully. See the *Congressional Record*, September 17, 1981, pp. H6333-H6334, for Fascell's remarks.

Given this turn for the better, however unhappy the reasons for
it may be, the Foreign Service has the opportunity, if its members
and managers will seize it, to establish a more mature relationship
with the American public and to take a better-understood and
more effective place in the totality of the American foreign policy
apparatus. Finding and accepting a viable role will have much to
do with this, and in this endeavor there are some new assets.
Expansion of the Foreign Service system under the new Act to
include some elements of Commerce and Agriculture brings with
it the possibility of more clout, with major domestic departments
for the first time co-opted into supporting the Foreign Service in
the future, and makes it more difficult for the Service to ignore
nonmembers and retreat into isolation. Paradox though it may be,
this expansion may actually create some breathing room which
will make it easier for the Foreign Service to demonstrate its
undoubted quality, and thus to be seen as an elite based on merit
and performance rather than as one attempting to assert its right
to be deferred to simply because of title or place.

DILEMMAS AND THE LONG SEARCH FOR PERFECTION

Chapter IV presented the difficult choices faced in designing
or reforming government personnel systems in today's world.
Without attempting to repeat the conclusions there, a few comments on the situation since passage of the new Foreign Service
Act are pertinent.

With respect to opening all federal systems to outsiders, there
are limited signs of progress, but also some negative features.
The problem, of course, is how to make more opportunities available for "in-and-outers" who do not seek career status, while
avoiding opening the prospect of political abuse. A system that
is open to bring in new competences to match specific needs is
almost invariably also open to political operatives, providing opportunities to bring in supporters whose loyalty is secure, whether
or not their abilities are. Thus congressional sponsors of Civil
Service reform in 1978 and of Foreign Service modernization in
1980 attempted to avoid politicization at the top by limiting the
proportion of the senior cadres in the SES and SFS who could be
noncareer, while recognizing the necessity for a new Adminis-

tration to be able to control enough positions to bring into government those individuals needed to carry out its policies.[4]

In another area signs were initially hopeful, with the Carter Administration's push for increasing part-time federal employment, accompanied by a new accounting system which would count position incumbency in terms of "full-time equivalents" (FTE's), thus making it more desirable to hire part-timers, since they would not, contrary to the former system, count as occupying a full position.[5] While this proposal was intended largely to ease affirmative action problems, it would provide a greater degree of openness, although the jobs thus made available were not likely to be the most influential ones. However, as of late 1982, it was unclear whether the Reagan Administration would continue to push this program with the same fervor. For its part, the new Foreign Service Act, while providing the necessary statutory authority both for outside hiring at all levels and for part-time employment, did not make greater openness a major point of emphasis. As with many of the dilemmas discussed in Chapter IV, finding a way to improvement is much more a question of policy than of statutory authority.

With respect to the dilemma of quality versus representativeness, recent developments in recruitment and the terms of the new Foreign Service Act presented, in different ways, positive signs by 1982, although some countertrends began to surface during the first year of the Reagan Administration. On the one hand, the numbers of minorities and women taken into the Foreign Service, as a result of both special programs and regular recruitment, have increased considerably, as the comparison presented in Tables 5 and 6 clearly indicates. To reinforce these tendencies, largely out of suspicion that the Executive branch would not of its own accord

[4] The Civil Service Reform Act of 1978 provided that no more than 10% of the members of the Senior Executive Service governmentwide, and no more than 25% in any one agency, could be noncareer (i.e., political) in status (Section 402, P.L. 95-454, 5 U.S.C. 3134). Similarly, the Foreign Service Act of 1980 provided that 5% of the members of the Senior Foreign Service, governmentwide, could be noncareer (Section 305, 22 U.S.C. 3945).

[5] See OMB Circular No. A-64 of July 30, 1980, "Position Management Systems and Employment Ceilings," for discussion of the "Full Time Equivalent Position" approach.

maintain an ongoing equal employment program, congressional advocates of representativeness forced a number of affirmative action requirements upon the Foreign Service during consideration of the new Act, including a formal, statutory affirmative action program (section 105), substantial female and minority representation on selection boards (section 602(b)), and explicit adherence to prohibited personnel practices and merit principles already applicable from sections of the Civil Service Reform Act (also section 105).

Psychologically, it seems to the author that an important threshold has been crossed, at least in State. The grudging acceptance of the need for representativeness and therefore of some affirmative action programs during the mid-1970's had given way by the early 1980's to a more sophisticated general understanding that the Service must be representative, that substantial progress had been made, and that the most desirable outcome, when possible, would be the abandonment of special programs as proportional numbers of women and minorities entered the Service through the standard processes. There were still holdouts on both ends of the spectrum. On one hand, some clearly preferred the old Foreign Service, while others would have been unhappy with any degree of progress because it would have deprived them of the opportunity to flagellate the Department and the Service, but there seemed some reason for hope that an emerging consensus in the middle could drive the advocates of the two extreme positions out of action, given enough time. Whether this spirit will survive a clear de-emphasis on affirmative action by the Reagan Administration as a whole (although State's new managers reaffirmed their commitment early on) must await a later assessment.

With respect to rank-in-job versus rank-in-person personnel systems, it was argued in Chapter IV that the latter should be used only when the former could not meet the needs of the organizations involved. If one accepts this philosophy, the new Foreign Service Act was clearly an important breakthrough, since it limited the Foreign Service rank-in-person system to the circumstances where it had to be used, that is, to individuals having rotational careers with frequent movement from one job and location to another. If there is no backsliding during implementation of the Act, it is possible that this longstanding point of contention will recede into ancient history.

Unfortunately, the resolution of what may be the most important of all these dilemmas, in terms of meeting job requirements in the foreign affairs area—that of generalists versus specialists— seems no closer than earlier. This is primarily a State problem, since the other foreign affairs agencies are limited to specific although very important functions, which almost inevitably forces an emphasis on specialist competence. The management of State, however, continues to emphasize the qualities required by senior officers as Ambassadors and Deputy Chiefs of Mission, while giving relatively less importance to the qualifications and training required to ensure that the more technical and specialized jobs at the mid-levels are carried out with the necessary skill and subtlety.

Unless State decides that its proper role overseas is to become a "super General Services Administration," responsible for up- keep and maintenance but deferring to other agencies on all or most significant policy issues, this is not tolerable. The new For- eign Service Act is essentially unengaged in this particular con- troversy: while it contains the necessary personnel authorities to provide the government with both generalists and specialists, it does not mandate rules for deciding the relative attention given to each category or, except in general terms, how each category should be recruited, trained, and employed. This is left to system managers.

The Act does provide that both specialist and generalist officers may become members of the Senior Foreign Service, but unless concentrated attention is given to matching people and respon- sibilities, the result is unlikely to meet demands.

At the risk of appearing to be nagging, the specialist-generalist problem (which in turn depends on coming to terms with the question of the right role for the Foreign Service and the De- partment of State) must be solved definitively if it is going to be possible to develop appropriate personnel systems. Who does what, when, how is still the basic personnel question.

Moving to the issues of rule-making and rule-application, the Foreign Service Act of 1980 provides considerable change from prior practice. It mandates that there be "maximum compatibility," in administration among agencies authorized to utilize the Foreign Service system. It also calls for uniform and consolidated administration. Rule-making thus was intended to be much more unified than previously. The first two years of implementation of the new Act showed that this was possible, but difficult. Even with initial agreement among the five agencies who were primary users of the Foreign Service system that all regulations should be uniform among them unless there were compelling reasons, the road has been hard. The causes are many: prior interagency disputes and suspicions, admittedly diverse circumstances, and quite different relationships between agencies and their employees.

In terms of rule-application, it still is too early to tell whether a workable balance between central authority and delegation to the operational level will result. As the Foreign Service system is structured, this is essentially an agency decision, and wide variations are likely. With respect to the Civil Service system, there were signs that the pattern of decentralization following passage of the CSRA in 1978 was being reversed by 1982, under the new OPM Director Don Devine. The "cop mentality" had once again reasserted itself. Compliance with general regulations was apparently seen as being more important than allowing individual agencies sufficient authority to solve their own problems. What is frustrating here is that choices concerning whether or not to delegate authority do not seem to be taking account of the facts of the particular situation. Political and bureaucratic factors seem to weigh much more heavily than operational logic.

For the single versus multiple system issue, the answer is much the same as that for rank-in-person versus rank-in-job: for the foreseeable future, at least, there will be dual Foreign Service and Civil Service systems. The new Foreign Service Act admits of no other outcome, given its required differentiation between those who serve rotational careers and those who spend their entire working lives in the United States. The concern here is more one of sensible implementation in specific cases than of challenging the governmentwide philosophy which for the moment seems to have been adopted.

It seems too early, however, to make firm predictions about the outcome of the next dilemma, that of the appropriate form of labor-management relations in the foreign affairs elements of government.

From the viewpoint of 1977, when the first draft of the LMR section of Chapter IV was written, it seemed inevitable that the employees of the federal government and the Foreign Service in particular would not only continue to exercise their right to organize but would likely expand areas which were negotiable, and perhaps also increase the range of federal employees who could become members of bargaining units. Both the CSRA in 1978 and the Foreign Service Act in 1980 seemed to reaffirm this conclusion. There were those who felt that ultimately this would make it almost impossible for the government to run a coherent personnel policy, but it was striking how much time was spent during the passage of these statutes in trying to convince federal employees' unions to go along, and how little in attempting to constrain their rights to organize and represent federal employees, or in attempting to make stronger rules on the level of employee conduct or performance required for retention.

By 1982, with the 1981 strike and subsequent firing of air traffic controllers who were members of PATCO, their union; with rising labor difficulties in the Post Office; with labor union membership declining throughout the country; and with an Administration markedly less supportive than its predecessors of the idea of sharing personnel responsibilities with employees, it seemed necessary at least to add a question mark after the phrase "Coping with Inevitability?" For example, in 1982 some senior managers in State, AID, and USIA gave serious thought to seeking legislation which would prelude all members of the Senior Foreign Service from being represented by a union. It takes a strange scenario indeed to conclude that at some point federal employees will no longer be organized, but it no longer seems quite as improbable as it seemed a few years ago.

The beginning of the Reagan Administration brought the usual attention to the uneasy relationship between career professionals in government and political appointees. Tension was exacerbated in this instance because it was the first transition after passage of the CSRA and the Foreign Service Act, with their limits on the number of noncareer officials who could be brought on board at the senior levels. Coupled with a political personnel process replete with internal difficulties and subsequent delays, which meant that presidentially appointed positions such as Ambassadors were very slow in being filled, this episode showed that those problems were no closer to permanent solution. At the same time the new political leadership, following the normal pattern at first suspected the holdovers from the last Administration, but eventually recognized the important contributions they were making to the government, totally apart from partisan considerations.

The outcome was acceptable, at least in the Foreign Affairs agencies, but the sad fact is that this process must be endured every four or eight years. There is no indication that the new Foreign Service Act or any other recent developments have in any way moved the government toward a system where individual credentials, experience, and expertise count more than affiliation. Career officials continue to think, by and large, that only senior leadership chosen from among their ranks will have the expertise necessary; politicos tend to the view that anyone who served a previous Administration must by definition be unacceptable to those who have won the most recent election. Somehow this problem is usually overcome, but only at the cost of losing some extremely talented individuals, advancing some others who should not be in positions of major responsibility, and enduring a great deal of confusion. There should be a way to do better.

No recent developments regarding the proper locus of management authority for foreign affairs personnel systems have occurred warranting deviation from the prescription offered in Chapter IV: if a professional Foreign Service is desired, it must have professional personnel management. There was some cautious movement in this direction in State as of late 1982, but more as a result of individual staffing decisions than of a conscious overall policy. What has been done is somewhat encouraging but not nearly enough, if all the difficult problems discussed earlier are to have a reasonable chance of permanent solution. One of the most important messages of this study is that unless much more attention is given to what personnel systems can do, and who makes sure that they do them, the current difficulties will inevitably continue.

The final dilemma, that of how to meld concerns of families and spouses with effective operation of the Foreign Service, provides at once the most difficult problem and the best chance for innovative personnel management, and both for the same reason: as a new condition, there are no past guidelines and few precedents either to suggest new policy or to restrict its implementation. It is perhaps too early to go further than the conclusions suggested in Chapter IV, but not too early to know that the problem must be faced.

The ultimate point, at the risk of undue repetition, is that there is no conceivable foreign affairs personnel system which can be equally successful in meeting all problems or in solving all the dilemmas presented here. The dual Foreign Service and Civil Service systems mandated by the Foreign Service Act of 1980, together with accompanying developments, in the opinion of the admittedly biased author, have the potential if intelligently employed of permitting acceptable compromises among some very hard choices. But continued attention is clearly required.

The conclusions presented in Chapter V, concerning the importance of developing usable information and data, methods of evaluation, and systems of resource allocation to support whatever personnel system is employed, must be reemphasized. The stakes are too high and the problems too great to attempt to operate with anything less than the best backup systems possible. Whether State and the other foreign affairs agencies have the will or even the capability of doing this is open to serious question.

If anything, Chapter VI underemphasizes the difficulty of making personnel system changes. Nevertheless, this example does show that constructive change is not impossible, and that the effort is worth making. While it is much too early to judge the worth of the final outcome, something potentially useful has happened. If allowed to survive, the new system just may set the stage for developing a foreign affairs personnel system which can come closer than systems of the past to meeting overall requirements.

In the uncertain world of designing and establishing effective foreign affairs personnel systems, drawing overall conclusions to a study such as this is a high-risk enterprise. Most of what the author believes must be taken into account has been previously stated, usually more than once. But one argument must be reiterated. The foreign affairs community must address frontally the need to provide the right kinds of competences in both its Washington and overseas arms—competences argued here to consist of necessary specialist expertise, well-developed diplomatic talent, and above all the ability to develop policy and to integrate U.S. government activities across a staggeringly large range of activities—and then it must develop a personnel system which can produce individuals, routinely, who have these skills. One final paradox is that such a system must simultaneously be more individualized, seeking out those people who have the talents and attributes needed, and more systematic, developing programs for recruitment, assignment, training, evaluation, and advancement which can produce a suitable pool of individuals to meet the demands placed upon them. Whether this is possible is likely to be the most fundamental question of foreign affairs personnel management in the next decades.

Summary Analysis of H.R. 6790—Foreign Service Act of 1980

INTRODUCTION

The last comprehensive revision of Foreign Service legislation was contained in the Foreign Service Act of 1946. While many of the 1946 Act's provisions remain valid, H.R. 6790 has a number of additional purposes:

—To provide a clear distinction between Foreign Service and Civil Service employment, and to eliminate the anomalous "domestic" Foreign Service personnel category;

—To simplify and rationalize the various categories of Foreign Service personnel and to establish a single Foreign Service salary schedule;

—To make more uniform the statutory terms and conditions of Foreign Service employment;

—To establish a Senior Foreign Service (SFS) with rigorous entry, promotion and retention standards based on performance, and with performance pay for outstanding service;

—To provide a statutory basis for labor-management relations in the Foreign Service;

—To improve interagency coordination in the interest of maximum compatibility among agencies employing Foreign Service personnel, and compatibility between the Foreign Service and the Civil Service; and

—To consolidate the various laws relating to Foreign Service personnel which have been enacted outside the framework of the existing Foreign Service Act.

PROVISIONS OF THE ACT

The Act is divided into two titles. Title I, made up of eleven chapters, is a permanent body of law concerning the Foreign Service personnel system. Title II, made up of four additional chapters, contains transitional and technical provisions, and amendments to and repeals of other laws. The Act's provisions are summarized below.

TITLE I—THE FOREIGN SERVICE OF THE UNITED STATES

Chapter 1—General Provisions

Chapter 1 contains a statement of findings and objectives, definitions, a description of Foreign Service personnel categories and functions, and a statement of the rights and protections of Foreign Service personnel. The statement of objectives reaffirms the principles of merit and impartiality set out in the 1946 Act, and refers as well to the current objectives. The definitions are primarily adapted from the 1946 Act.

The description of Foreign Service personnel categories omits the previous distinction between "Reserve officers" and "Staff officers and employees." The bill seeks to avoid distinctions which imply preferential status to one category or another, and refers to Foreign Service personnel throughout as "members of the Service" rather than as "officers" and "employees." The description of functions of the Service includes reference to the Vienna Conventions on Diplomatic and Consular Relations, which are codifications of modern international practice. It also contains a new reference to the role of the Service in providing guidance in the field of foreign relations.

A final section in the chapter emphasizes employee rights, drawing together and emphasizing current law with respect to the applicability of merit principles, protection against discrimination and reprisals for members of the Service, and equal employment opportunity.

Chapter 2—Management of the Service

Chapter 2 begins by identifying the officers who have primary responsibility for the management of the Service. Chief among these is the Secretary of State, who is responsible for administration of the Service under the direction of the President. It notes that there are certain functions that only the Secretary of State may perform, which are expressly vested in the Secretary of State by the Act, e.g., issuance of government-wide regulations, administration of the Foreign Service Retirement and Disability System, and designation of posts as diplomatic or consular in nature.

The Act also authorizes the Director of the International Communication Agency, the Director of the United States International Development Cooperation Agency and, in more limited fashion, the Secretaries of Agriculture and Commerce (and other agency heads when authorized by law) to utilize the provisions of the Act for their Foreign Service personnel. Chapter 2 incorporates existing law on the authority and responsibilities of chiefs of diplomatic missions with respect to government agencies and personnel, which has not previously been a part of the Foreign Service Act.

Chapter 2 requires that the Foreign Service be administered so as to assure maximum compatibility among agencies authorized by law to utilize the Foreign Service personnel system. It encourages among such agencies the development of uniform policies and procedures and consolidation of personnel functions. It continues the existing statutory directive for compatibility between the Foreign Service and other Federal government personnel systems.

This chapter also provides a statutory basis for two officers who will have significant roles in the administration of the Foreign Service. These are the Director General and the Inspector General, both of whom are to be appointed by the President, by and with the advice and consent of the Senate. The Director General is to assist the Secretary generally in the management of the Service, including interagency coordination. The Inspector General will inspect the operations of posts abroad and offices and bureaus in the Department of State, as well as carrying out functions assigned to Inspectors General in most other departments under the Inspector General Act of 1978.

Chapter 2 also provides that the President will establish an interagency Board of the Foreign Service to advise the Secretary on matters relating to the Service, including matters concerning interagency compatibility. The Board will be chaired by a career member of the Senior Foreign Service, and will include one or more senior representatives of concerned federal agencies.

Finally, this chapter provides for a Board of Examiners for the Foreign Service to develop and supervise examinations to be given candidates for appointment in the Service. The Board is required to review examinations periodically for possible bias and to report its findings annually to the Secretary of State. It will have at least five members from outside the government chosen for expertise and knowledge in the fields of testing or equal employment opportunity.

Chapter 3—Appointments

Chapter 3 provides the authority for appointments in the Foreign Service, and describes the types of appointments which can be made. Appointment as a chief of mission, ambassador-at-large, minister, career member of the Senior Foreign Service (SFS) or Foreign Service officer (FSO) may be made only by the President, by and with the advice and consent of the Senate. Other appointments in the Service may be made by the Secretary; these include limited SFS appointments, FSO candidates, and appointments (limited and career) of all other American and foreign national personnel.

This chapter is intended to strengthen the career nature of the Foreign Service. In particular, it limits non-career membership in the Senior Foreign Service to not more than five percent, and retains the present maximum of five years on limited appointments to the Service.

Chapter 3 strengthens previous expressions of Congressional policy on the desirability of appointing career Foreign Service personnel as chiefs of mission. It also requires additional reporting to Congress on the qualifications of prospective ambassadors, on steps taken to gain needed language competence, and on designations of individuals to serve with the personal rank of ambassador.

All candidates for career appointments must first serve under limited appointments (as is now the case for Foreign Service officers and Reserve officers). The duration of these probationary periods will vary, but may not exceed five years. For Senior Foreign Service, they will be at least four years. Records of performance by career candidates will be reviewed by boards composed primarily of career personnel before career appointments are granted. Retired members of the Service may be recalled and former career members may be reemployed without undergoing this process.

Chapter 4—Compensation

Chapter 4 governs the basic salaries of Foreign Service personnel, as well as additional compensation based on performance or conditions of service. Chiefs of mission will continue to receive salaries at one of the annual rates specified for levels II through V of the Executive Salary Schedule. However, career SFS personnel who are appointed as chiefs of mission may elect to continue to receive their normal Foreign Service salary and continue to compete for performance pay.

The President will establish a salary range for the SFS comparable to the salaries established by the President for the SES under the Civil Service Reform Act. Below this level, a single nine-class Foreign Service salary schedule for American personnel will supersede the two overlapping schedules that now exist for Foreign Service officers and Reserve officers on the one hand and staff officers and employees on the other. Linkages to the General Schedule will be set by the President. Within-class salary increases, if performance is satisfactory, will be annual for steps 2-10 and every two years for steps 11-14. Provisions are included for use of multiple step increases for outstanding performance, and for withholding them for mediocre performance. Foreign national employees and consular agents will be paid on the basis of locally prevailing compensation practices.

Members of the SFS will be appointed to a salary class, and their promotions will be effected by reappointment to a higher class. Foreign Service officers below the senior threshold, however, will be assigned to an appropriate salary class by the Secretary, and their promotions will be effected without interruption in their Presidential appointments. This change will permit all Foreign Service personnel of comparable rank who are promoted to have their salaries adjusted at the same time under a single procedure.

Chapter 4 establishes a performance pay plan for the SFS similar to that provided by the Civil Service Reform Act for the SES. Recommendations concerning awards of performance pay will be made to the Secretary by selection boards. Additional awards for especially meritorious or distinguished service may be made by the President, as is the case for the SES.

The bill retains the prohibition on premium pay for FSOs, but has new provisions which permit compensatory time off, and which require a report to Congress if any limitation is contemplated on the special differential in lieu of overtime, in terms of numbers eligible or amounts paid.

Chapter 5—Classification of Positions and Assignments

Chapter 5 continues the existing authority of the Secretary to classify Foreign Service positions in the Department and at posts abroad, and to assign Foreign Service personnel to those positions. A new subsection requires that members of the Service not be assigned to a post in a particular geographic region solely on the basis of race, ethnicity, or religion.

This chapter also facilitates interchange with the Civil Service by authorizing the assignment of non–Foreign Service personnel to Foreign Service positions for specified tours of duty and the assignment of Foreign Service personnel to Civil Service positions. A new feature of the bill is a limitation of four years on the assignment of members of the Foreign Service to non–Foreign Service positions.

Chapter 5 retains the existing eight-year limitation on the assignment of Foreign Service personnel to duty within the United States, but allows for shorter periods to be set for specific groups by regulation. In addition, it requires that all career Foreign Service personnel accept the obligation to serve abroad as a condition of employment.

At the same time, the bill recognizes the need for periodic service by Foreign Service personnel within the United States. It directs the Secretary to seek to assign all career personnel in the Service to duty within the United States at least once during each fifteen years of service.

Chapter 6—Promotion and Retention

Chapter 6 retains the basic concepts of promotion and retention in the Foreign Service based upon demonstrated merit.

This chapter extends the Selection Board process (now applicable by statute only to Foreign Service officers) to all American personnel. Selection Boards, which must include public members, women and members of minority groups, will rank the members of each class on a comparative basis for purposes of promotion, award of performance pay, retention in the senior ranks, and separation of members whose performance falls below the standard of their class.

Chapter 6 also specifically provides a rigorous threshold for entry into the Senior Foreign Service and authorizes the Secretary to prescribe the period during which members of the Service may be considered for entry into the SFS. Promotions into the SFS must be based upon long-term projections of personnel flows and needs designed to provide more predictable recruitment, advancement and career development. A report to Congress on steps taken to insure this predictable flow is required annually.

This chapter continues the authority for retirement based on expiration of time-in-class and extends that authority to all members of the Service who receive salaries comparable to those of Foreign Service officers and who are in occupational categories designated by the Secretary. It eliminates the exemption of those in the top rank from the time-in-class limitations, while providing that those members whose maximum time-in-class expires after they have attained the highest class for their respective personnel categories may continue to serve under renewable limited extensions of their career appointments. At the same time, it provides protection against politicization by statements of Congressional purpose, that time in each senior class before the extension mechanism comes into play shall not be less than 3 years. The grant and any renewal of such an extension would be in accordance with Selection Board recommendations.

Chapter 6 continues the Secretary's authority to separate a member of the Service for cause, after a hearing. The bill provides that such a hearing will be conducted by the Foreign Service Grievance Board, which will assure appropriate due process protections. This hearing would be in lieu of any other administrative procedure.

This chapter also directs the establishment of a Foreign Service awards system to supplement the Governmentwide incentive awards program and to recognize exceptional service to the nation by members of the Foreign Service.

Chapter 7—Foreign Service Institute, Career Development, Training and Orientation

Chapter 7 continues the authority of the Secretary to maintain the Foreign Service Institute and to provide training and counseling. This chapter makes only minimal changes from existing law, but adds a strong new section requiring systematic career development programs for members of the Service. Primarily, it vests authority for the operation of the Institute in the Secretary of State, consolidates in a single chapter various existing authorities for training, career development and counseling, and makes explicit reference to training for family members of Foreign Service personnel.

Chapter 8—Foreign Service Retirement and Disability System

Chapter 8 continues the Foreign Service Retirement and Disability System as it has existed under Title VIII of the 1946 Act, and incorporates voluntary and mandatory retirement features now in Title VI of that Act, except that the mandatory retirement age becomes 65 on the date of enactment. Those reaching age 60 on or after October 1, 1980 will be covered by this new provision. Changes have been made primarily in style and terminology, and to maintain existing conformity of the Foreign Service [with the Civil Service] System. Recent statutory changes to the latter system have been incorporated into the bill in accordance with existing law authorizing such conforming changes.

New provisions have been added to protect the interests of former spouses. Specifically, the Act provides for an automatic pro rata division of retirement annuities and retirement benefits for qualifying former spouses (those married for 10 years or more while the employee was in the Service), unless a court orders a different division within one year of the divorce. This provision will apply only in the case of those who become former spouses after the effective date of the Act. In a related provision, an individual who, prior to the effective date, has a former spouse, may elect to provide a survivor benefit for that former spouse (Sec. 2109). Finally, a spousal agreement may be entered into by affected parties with respect to their respective rights under chapter 8. Such an agreement will be given the same effect as a court order, so the parties may adjust their respective rights without the necessity of obtaining such an order.

Chapter 9—Travel, Leave and Other Benefits

Chapter 9 continues the Secretary's authority to pay travel and related expenses, and to provide for home leave and health care for Foreign Service personnel and their families. The following new discretionary authorities have been added:

—Authority to pay relocation allowances to members of the Foreign Service on domestic transfers.
—Authority to grant an additional R&R trip in extraordinary circumstances.
—Authority to authorize travel for a child when a parent is medically evacuated and the child is unable to remain at post alone.

—Authority to provide one round-trip per year between post abroad and nearest port of entry in the U.S. for children of divorced members of the Service to visit the parent with whom they do not normally reside.

—Authority to authorize travel for family to accompany members on extended travel orders, whether or not such travel is in connection with a reassignment.

—Provision for payment of representation allowance to family members when authorized, as well as to employees.

Chapter 10—Labor-Management Relations

Chapter 10 draws from the existing system in the Foreign Service established by Executive order 11636 as well as Title VII of the Civil Service Reform Act which governs Labor-Management relations in the Civil Service. This chapter authorizes collective bargaining on conditions of employment in the Foreign Service, subject to certain excluded areas of management rights comparable to those matters excluded from bargaining under Title VII. This chapter continues the present arrangement of a single agencywide bargaining unit, and the inclusion of many employees who perform supervisory functions.

Chapter 10 establishes a Foreign Service Labor Relations Board, as an entity under the Federal Labor Relations Authority, to manage this new statutory program. The Board would be chaired by the Chairman of the Federal Labor Relations Authority and would have two public members appointed from nominees approved by the agencies and the exclusive representatives. In addition to the Board, Chapter 10 would retain the disputes panel as constituted under E.O. 11636. However, a major difference is the authority of the panel to make final and binding decisions on negotiation impasses. This chapter also introduces a new, independent third party, the General Counsel of the Federal Labor Relations Authority. The General Counsel would investigate alleged unfair labor practices and would file and prosecute such complaints. The chapter also provides for appeals to the Foreign Service Grievance Board, under negotiated procedures, in disputes arising out of the implementation of collective bargaining agreements.

Chapter 11—Grievances

Chapter 11 follows the major features of the 1946 Act for the resolution of grievances by individuals within the Foreign Service, including appeals from internal agency procedures to the independent Foreign Service Grievance Board. The Board has broad authority to establish its own procedures (which must include a hearing in any case involving separation or other disciplinary action), compel the production of evidence and the attendance of witnesses, and direct remedial action by the Department.

The chapter provides that every grievant has a right to representation of his or her own choice, both at the agency level and before the Grievance Board. The exclusive employee representative, however, is allowed to appear at all grievance proceedings involving members of the bargaining unit.

Also added is the authority of the Grievance Board to direct payment of reasonable attorney fees as may be required by Section 7701(g) of Title 5, United States Code. Deleted from chapter 11 is the authority of the Secretary to reject a recommendation of the Grievance Board on grounds that the recommendation would substantially impair the efficiency of the Service.

TITLE II—TRANSITION, AMENDMENTS TO OTHER LAWS, AND MISCELLANEOUS PROVISIONS

Chapter 1—Transition

Chapter 1 governs the transition of all Foreign Service personnel to the new categories and salary schedules established by Title I of the bill. For pay purposes, all FSO, FSR, FSRU and FSS personnel will be paid as if converted to the new pay schedules, effective the first day of the first pay period beginning after October 1, 1980. It provides that on the effective date of the Act (February 15, 1981) personnel who are already obligated to worldwide availability will convert automatically to the Foreign Service schedule or have the option to join the Senior Foreign Service, depending on their current rank. Personnel not so committed will convert only after they have undertaken an obligation to serve abroad and the Department has certified that there is a need for their services in the Foreign Service. Those "domestic" personnel who are not converted to one of the new Foreign Service categories will be converted into the Civil Service without loss of salary or grade, within 3 years, or otherwise leave the Foreign Service.

This chapter provides that all conversions will be without loss of salary or grade (including protection from downgrading as long as not voluntarily leaving one's current position), and that persons covered by the Foreign Service Retirement and Disability System may elect to continue to participate in that system.

The Act's provisions for conversion of "domestic" Foreign Service personnel to Civil Service status will be deferred with respect to the International Communication Agency (ICA), until July 1, 1981, in view of a pre-existing agreement with the labor organization representing the employees who would otherwise be affected on the effective date.

Chapter 2—Amendments Relating to Foreign Affairs Agencies

Chapter 2 contains amendments to statutes concerning the Foreign Affairs agencies required by Title I of the bill. These include the relocation of provisions in the 1946 Act which deal with subjects other than Foreign Service personnel, such as the State Department's authority to accept gifts. This chapter also contains conforming amendments to the authority of other agency heads to utilize the Foreign Service personnel system. In addition, it modifies the basic authority of the Department to allow payment of additional subsistence expenses of security officers on authorized protective missions, and members of the Foreign Service and Department generally when required to spend extraordinary amounts of time in travel status. This chapter also contains necessary conforming amendments to other laws relating to Foreign Service personnel, e.g., the Peace Corps Act and the Arms Control and Disarmament Act. The Peace Corps will continue to be authorized to use Foreign Service personnel authorities for its headquarters staff. A new provision requires the Secretary to designate at least two Foreign Service posts as model foreign language competence posts.

Chapter 3—Amendments to Title 5, United States Code

This chapter contains a number of amendments to laws applicable to the Government as a whole as they relate to the Foreign Service. These changes include explicit reemployment rights for employees of any agency who accept limited appointment in the Foreign Service, provision of a statutory salary base for Ambassadors at Large, authority to pay advance pay upon any departure from an overseas post when the Secretary determines this to be in the national interest (rather than as currently, only when an evacuation is ordered), authority to pay a separate maintenance allowance at the request of a member of the Service, rather than, as presently, only for the convenience of the government. This chapter also extends to the Foreign Service provisions of existing law regarding attorney's fees in unfair labor practice and grievance cases, and conforms accumulation of SFS annual leave with the exemption for SES personnel.

For posts where a special incentive for service is determined to be necessary due to especially adverse conditions, the post differential could be as high as 40% of base pay, rather than the current 25% ceiling. A separate new allowance authority would allow a danger pay allowance of up to 25% of base pay, at posts where civil insurrection, civil war, terrorism, or wartime conditions threaten physical harm or imminent danger. However, the increased post differential and danger pay could not be paid simultaneously.

*Chapter 4—Saving Provisions, Congressional Oversight
and Effective Date*

Chapter 4 provides that actions taken under the authority of the Foreign Service Act of 1946 or any other law repealed, modified, or affected by the new Act shall continue in full force unless modified or revoked by current authority. It requires annual reports on steps taken to insure maximum compatibility among agencies employing the Foreign Service personnel system, on conversion of individuals under the Act, concerning the upper and lower limits planned by each agency for recruitment, advancement and

retention of members of the Service, for each of the five suc-
ceeding years, and the number, names and grades of members of
the Service assigned more than one grade higher or lower than
personal rank. Finally, it provides that the effective date of the
new Act will be February 15, 1981, with certain limited exceptions. These exceptions include: mandatory retirement age is raised
to 65 on date of enactment; pay under the new FS schedules
begins with the first pay period beginning after October 1, 1980;
the five per cent limitation on non-career SFS members for Commerce is deferred until October 1, 1985, with a maximum of ten
non-career SFS members in Commerce in the interim; and personnel actions (e.g., awards of performance pay for SFS) may
take place on basis of the current evaluation cycle, as if the Act
had been in effect at the beginning of that cycle.

SOURCE: Department of State Notice, October 7, 1980.

spouses (*cont.*)
211; career aspirations of, 156-57;
employment of, 155; training for,
158-59. *See also* Foreign Service
Act of 1980, family issues in; family issues
staffing, mismatches in Foreign Service, 41-43, 91
Stahl, O. Glenn, 123, 129
State, Department of: functional bureaus of, 19; possible informal submission of, to Murphy Commission, 26-27; possible roles of, 32-
33, 74-75, 230
Stein, Harold, study of Foreign Service Act of 1946 by, 4n, 70n
studies of Foreign Service, major,
12n, 50-52, 70n, 76n, 77n, 87
style, of Washington officials, 38
Szanton, Peter L., 12n, 46, 53, 56-57

"tandem couples," 98; problems of,
157. *See also* assignments, Foreign
Service; family issues
Thomas, Charles, 209
Thomas, John, 139n, 200n
time-in-class (TIC) limitations, 95-97.
See also "up-or-out"
training, resources for, 99-100
Treasury, Department of the, 27
turnover, managerial, 193
"two for one" hiring, in Foreign
Service, 153

Under Secretary for Management, in
State, 84-85
unions: in government, history, 142-
46; possible contributions of, 146.
See also labor-management relations
United States, changed role in international affairs, 15

United States government agencies,
representation abroad, 19, 28
United States Information Agency
(USIA), xvi, 5, 136, 214, 218,
232. *See also* United States International Communication Agency
United States International Communication Agency (USICA), 55, 62,
74n; changes of name from and to
United States Information Agency,
82. *See also* United States Information Agency
"up-or-out," 95-97, 99, 111-12; in
Foreign Service Act of 1980, 202
"us against them" mentality, in
State, 102; possible solutions to,
102-3

Vaky, Viron P., 61, 73, 75
Vance, Cyrus R., 90n, 101, 198,
201, 203, 217; attitudes of, about
affirmative action, 116, 119n; letter
to, by FSO's, 118

Ward, Paul von, 139n
War Department, 27
Washington officials, style, 38
"waste, fraud, and mismanagement"
(WIFFIM), 208
Whitbeck, Phillip M., study on science officers by, 52
Whitman, Torrey, 169
wives, 1972 directive on (State), 153-
54. *See also* family issues;
spouses, Foreign Service
working conditions abroad, compared
with Washington, 38
workload, shifts to consular area, 93
Wriston Committee, 5, 71, 76

LIBRARY OF CONGRESS CATALOGING IN PUBLICATION DATA

Bacchus, William I., 1940–
  Staffing for foreign affairs.

  Includes index.
  1. United States. Foreign Service—Personnel management.   2
United States—Foreign relations administration.   I. Title.
JX1706.Z5B3   1983   353.0089   83-42546
ISBN 0-691-07660-X